LAYERS

A MEMOIR

PÉNÉLOPE BAGIEU

TRANSLATED BY MONTANA KANE

First Second
New York

First Second

Published by First Second
First Second is an imprint of Roaring Brook Press,
a division of Holtzbrinck Publishing Holdings Limited Partnership
120 Broadway, New York, NY 10271
firstsecondbooks.com

Library of Congress Cataloging-in-Publication Data is available.

Our books may be purchased in bulk for promotional, educational, or business use. Please
contact your local bookseller or the Macmillan Corporate and Premium Sales Department at
(800) 221-7945 ext. 5442 or by email at MacmillanSpecialMarkets@macmillan.com.

First English edition, 2023
Translated by Montana Kane
English edition edited by Mark Siegel and Michael Moccio, with help from Robyn Chapman
Interior book design and cover design by Molly Johanson
Jacket design by Casper Manning
Production editing by Kat Kopit and Helen Seachrist

Originally published in French under the title *Les Strates* © 2021 by Gallimard

Drawn and colored with an Apple Pencil using Procreate custom inking brushes. Lettered
digitally with the Soliloquous font by Comiccraft.

Content warning: The following scene contains depictions of sexual assault that may be
upsetting to some readers: pp. 43–49.

Printed in the United States of America

ISBN 978-1-250-87373-6 (hardcover)
10 9 8 7 6 5 4 3 2 1

Don't miss your next favorite book from First Second! For the latest updates go
to firstsecondnewsletter.com and sign up for our enewsletter.

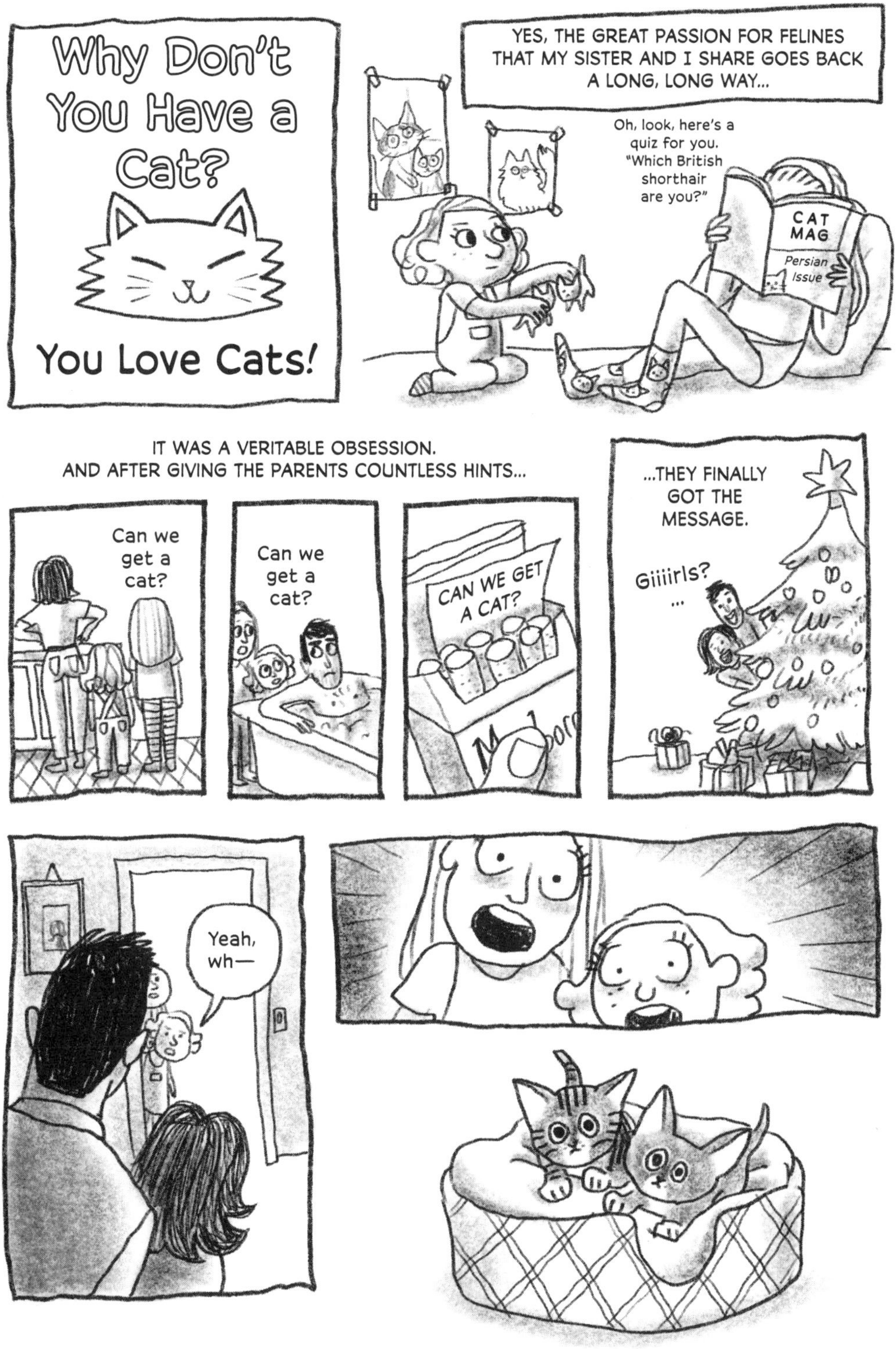
Why Don't You Have a Cat?
You Love Cats!
YES, THE GREAT PASSION FOR FELINES THAT MY SISTER AND I SHARE GOES BACK A LONG, LONG WAY...
Oh, look, here's a quiz for you. "Which British shorthair are you?"
CAT MAG
Persian Issue
IT WAS A VERITABLE OBSESSION. AND AFTER GIVING THE PARENTS COUNTLESS HINTS...
Can we get a cat?
Can we get a cat?
CAN WE GET A CAT?
...THEY FINALLY GOT THE MESSAGE.
Giiiirls?
...
Yeah, wh—

Oh my GOD!!

You're the best parents in the world!!!

Thank you thank you thank you.

Look, there are two of them. Two sisters. This way, you each pick one.

I WAS SIX AND A HALF, AND I REMEMBER IMMEDIATELY RECOGNIZING...

...MY CHILD. FLESH OF MY FLESH. IT WAS OBVIOUS.

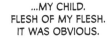

I'm your mommy.

Since she's gray...

...I'll call her Smokey.

Reminder: 6.5 y.o.

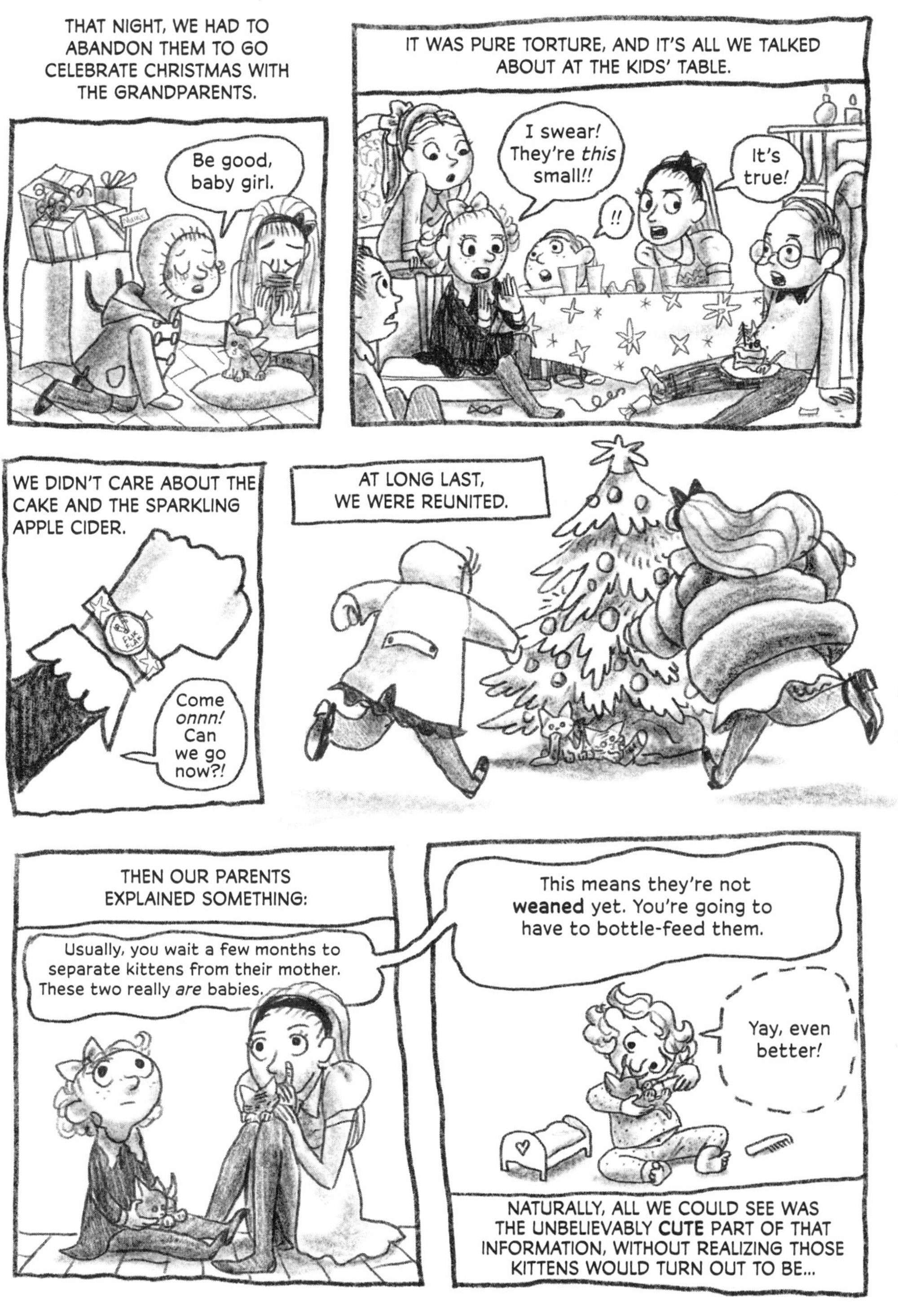
THAT NIGHT, WE HAD TO ABANDON THEM TO GO CELEBRATE CHRISTMAS WITH THE GRANDPARENTS.
Be good, baby girl.
IT WAS PURE TORTURE, AND IT'S ALL WE TALKED ABOUT AT THE KIDS' TABLE.
I swear! They're *this* small!!
!!
It's true!
WE DIDN'T CARE ABOUT THE CAKE AND THE SPARKLING APPLE CIDER.
FLIK FLAK
Come *onnn!* Can we go now?!
AT LONG LAST, WE WERE REUNITED.
THEN OUR PARENTS EXPLAINED SOMETHING:
Usually, you wait a few months to separate kittens from their mother. These two really *are* babies.
This means they're not **weaned** yet. You're going to have to bottle-feed them.
Yay, even better!
NATURALLY, ALL WE COULD SEE WAS THE UNBELIEVABLY **CUTE** PART OF THAT INFORMATION, WITHOUT REALIZING THOSE KITTENS WOULD TURN OUT TO BE...

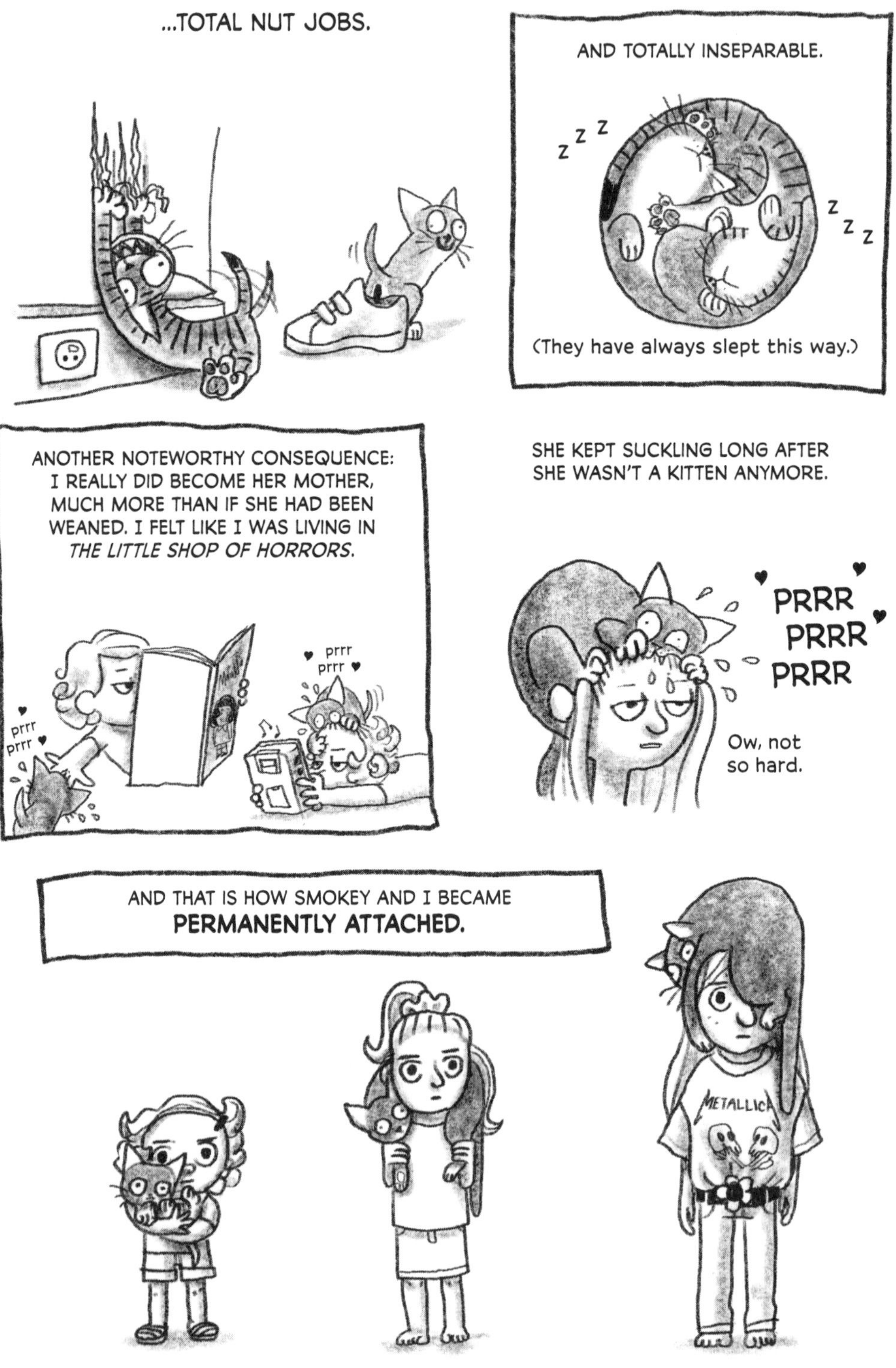
...TOTAL NUT JOBS.
AND TOTALLY INSEPARABLE.
Z Z Z
Z Z Z
(They have always slept this way.)
ANOTHER NOTEWORTHY CONSEQUENCE: I REALLY DID BECOME HER MOTHER, MUCH MORE THAN IF SHE HAD BEEN WEANED. I FELT LIKE I WAS LIVING IN *THE LITTLE SHOP OF HORRORS*.
prrr prrr
prrr prrr
SHE KEPT SUCKLING LONG AFTER SHE WASN'T A KITTEN ANYMORE.
PRRR PRRR PRRR
Ow, not so hard.
AND THAT IS HOW SMOKEY AND I BECAME **PERMANENTLY ATTACHED.**
METALLICA

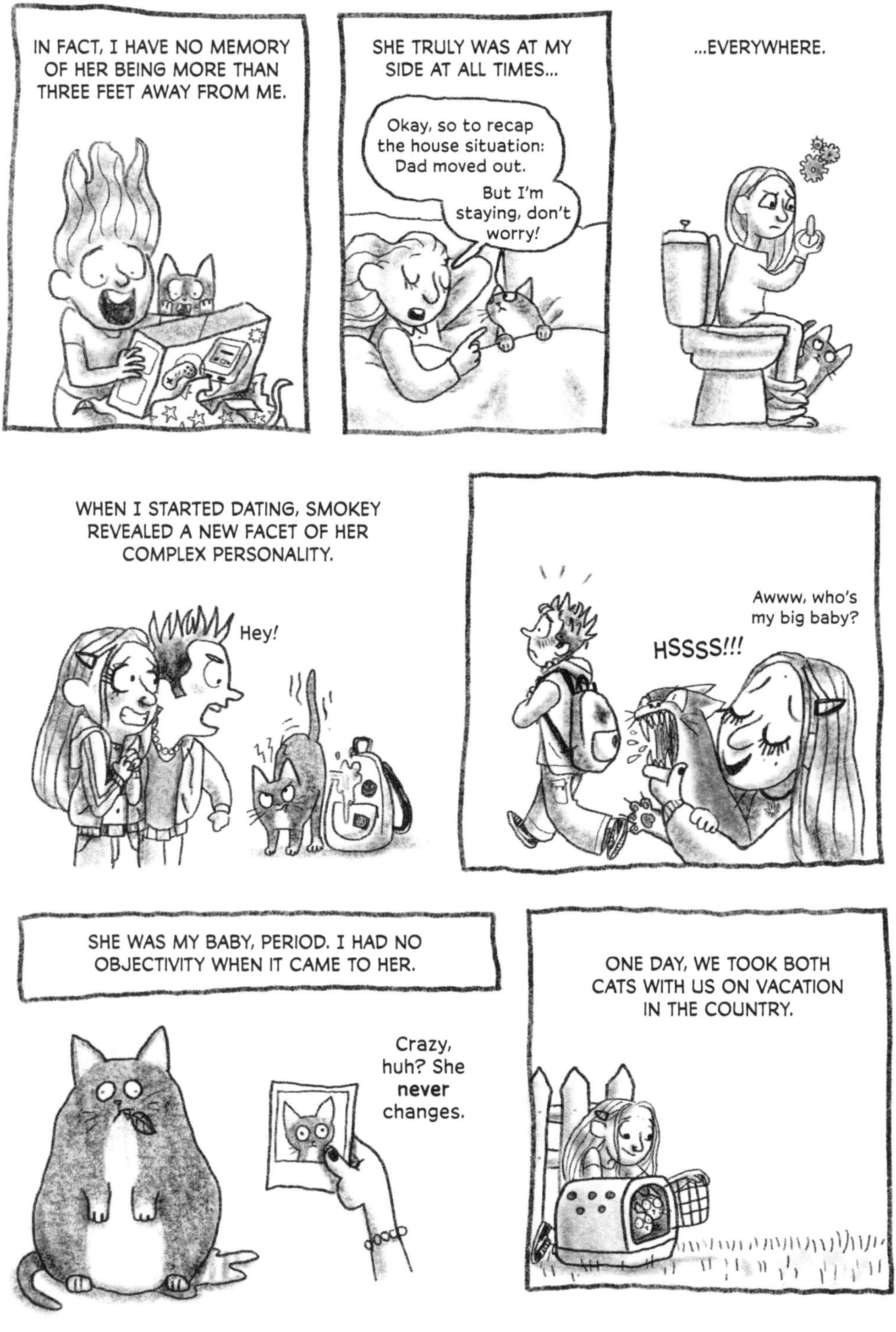
IN FACT, I HAVE NO MEMORY OF HER BEING MORE THAN THREE FEET AWAY FROM ME.
SHE TRULY WAS AT MY SIDE AT ALL TIMES...
Okay, so to recap the house situation: Dad moved out.
But I'm staying, don't worry!
...EVERYWHERE.
WHEN I STARTED DATING, SMOKEY REVEALED A NEW FACET OF HER COMPLEX PERSONALITY.
Hey!
Awww, who's my big baby?
HSSSS!!!
SHE WAS MY BABY, PERIOD. I HAD NO OBJECTIVITY WHEN IT CAME TO HER.
Crazy, huh? She **never** changes.
ONE DAY, WE TOOK BOTH CATS WITH US ON VACATION IN THE COUNTRY.

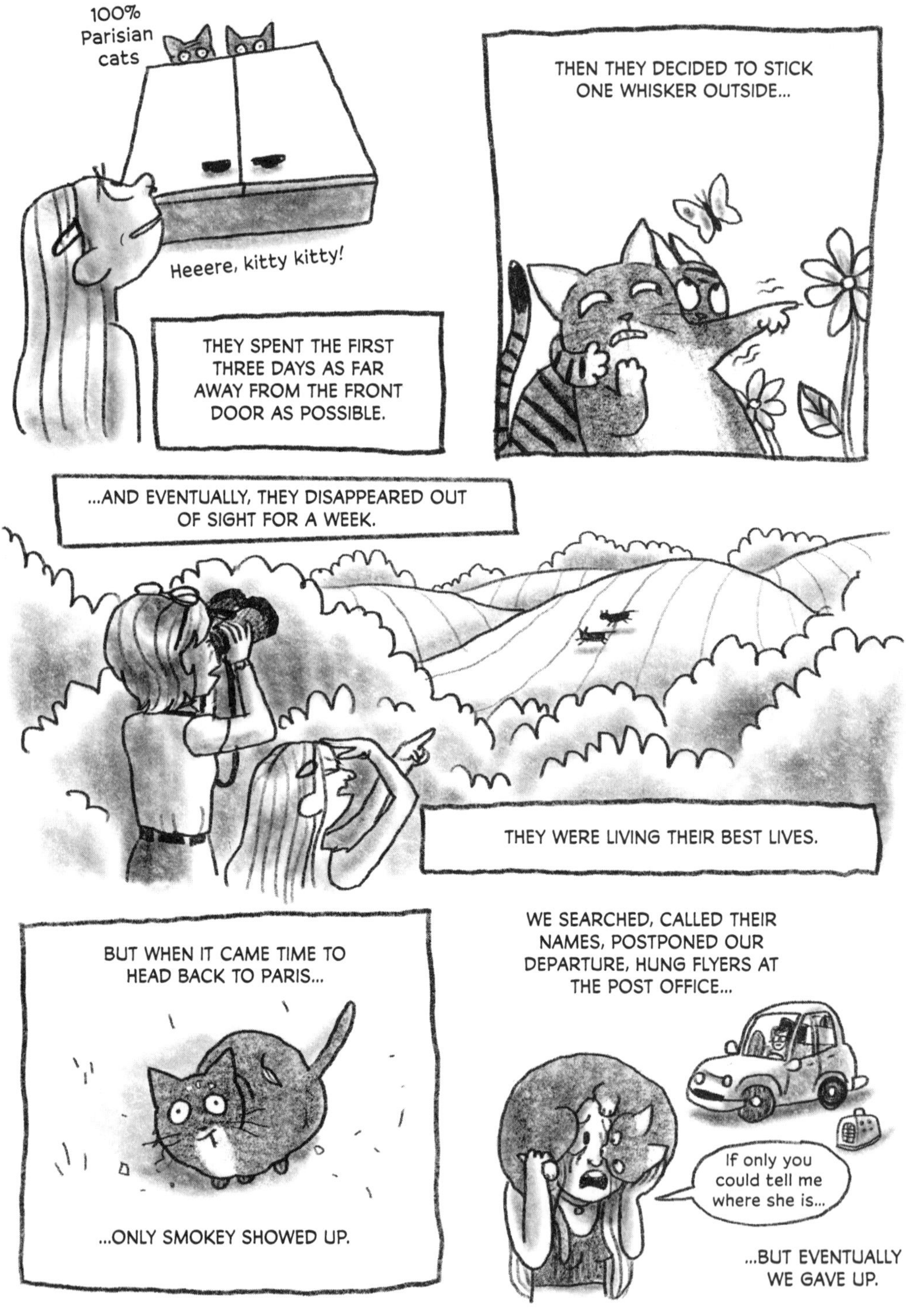
100% Parisian cats
Heeere, kitty kitty!
THEY SPENT THE FIRST THREE DAYS AS FAR AWAY FROM THE FRONT DOOR AS POSSIBLE.
THEN THEY DECIDED TO STICK ONE WHISKER OUTSIDE...
...AND EVENTUALLY, THEY DISAPPEARED OUT OF SIGHT FOR A WEEK.
THEY WERE LIVING THEIR BEST LIVES.
BUT WHEN IT CAME TIME TO HEAD BACK TO PARIS...
...ONLY SMOKEY SHOWED UP.
WE SEARCHED, CALLED THEIR NAMES, POSTPONED OUR DEPARTURE, HUNG FLYERS AT THE POST OFFICE...
If only you could tell me where she is...
...BUT EVENTUALLY WE GAVE UP.

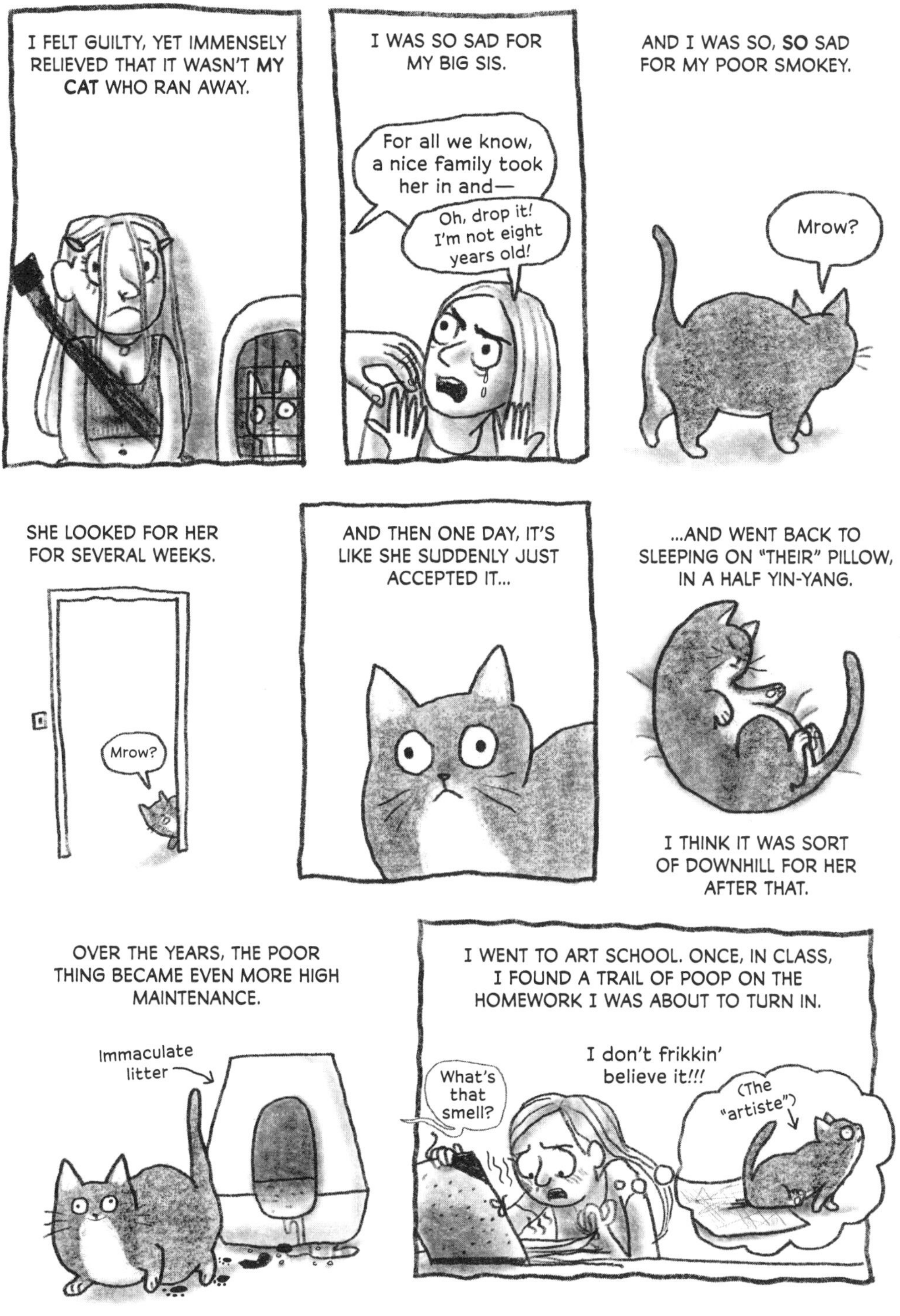
I FELT GUILTY, YET IMMENSELY RELIEVED THAT IT WASN'T **MY CAT** WHO RAN AWAY.
I WAS SO SAD FOR MY BIG SIS.
For all we know, a nice family took her in and—
Oh, drop it! I'm not eight years old!
AND I WAS SO, **SO** SAD FOR MY POOR SMOKEY.
Mrow?
SHE LOOKED FOR HER FOR SEVERAL WEEKS.
Mrow?
AND THEN ONE DAY, IT'S LIKE SHE SUDDENLY JUST ACCEPTED IT...
...AND WENT BACK TO SLEEPING ON "THEIR" PILLOW, IN A HALF YIN-YANG.
I THINK IT WAS SORT OF DOWNHILL FOR HER AFTER THAT.
OVER THE YEARS, THE POOR THING BECAME EVEN MORE HIGH MAINTENANCE.
Immaculate litter
I WENT TO ART SCHOOL. ONCE, IN CLASS, I FOUND A TRAIL OF POOP ON THE HOMEWORK I WAS ABOUT TO TURN IN.
What's that smell?
I don't frikkin' believe it!!!
(The "artiste")

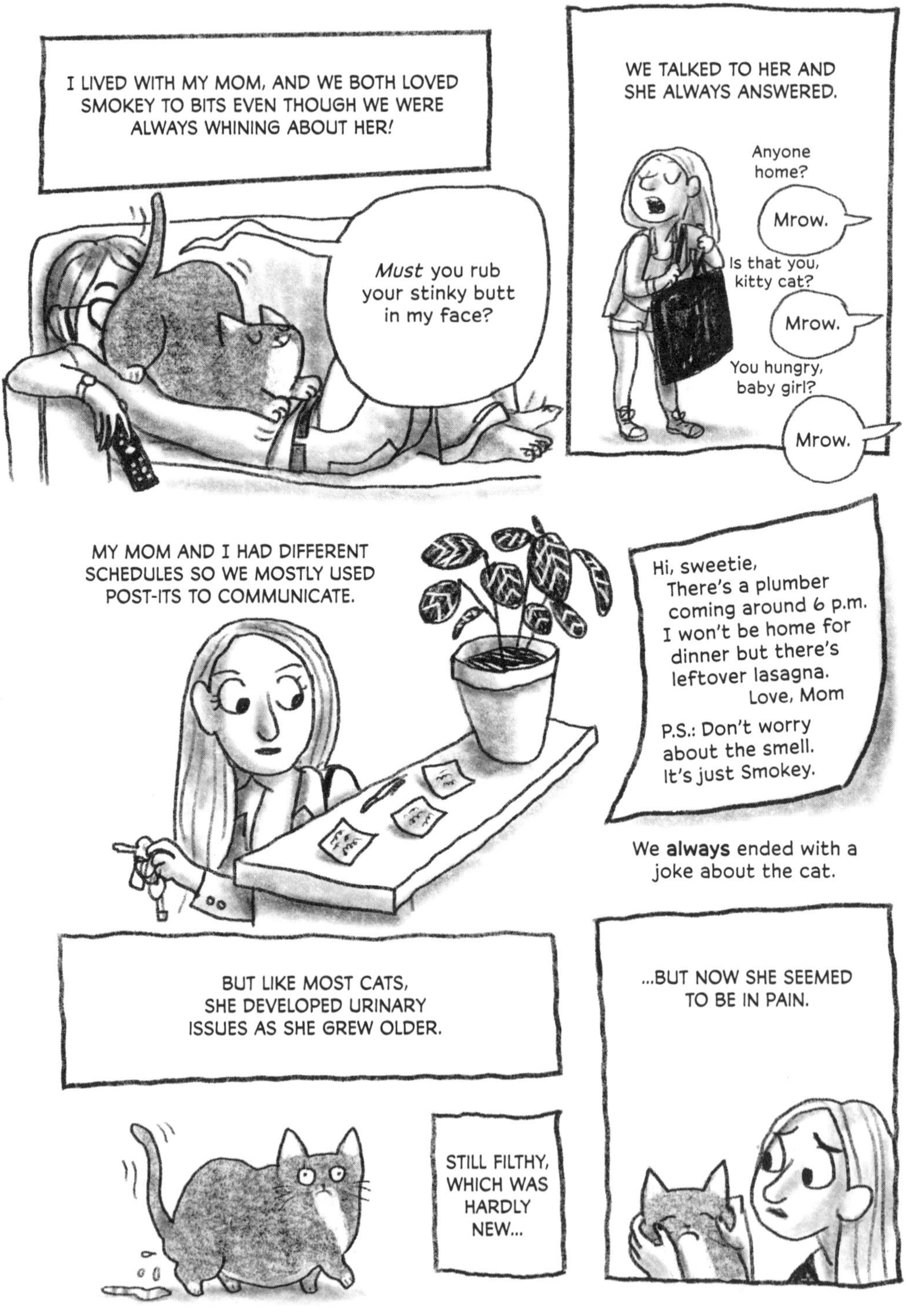
I LIVED WITH MY MOM, AND WE BOTH LOVED SMOKEY TO BITS EVEN THOUGH WE WERE ALWAYS WHINING ABOUT HER!
Must you rub your stinky butt in my face?
WE TALKED TO HER AND SHE ALWAYS ANSWERED.
Anyone home?
Mrow.
Is that you, kitty cat?
Mrow.
You hungry, baby girl?
Mrow.
MY MOM AND I HAD DIFFERENT SCHEDULES SO WE MOSTLY USED POST-ITS TO COMMUNICATE.
Hi, sweetie, There's a plumber coming around 6 p.m. I won't be home for dinner but there's leftover lasagna. Love, Mom
P.S.: Don't worry about the smell. It's just Smokey.
We **always** ended with a joke about the cat.
BUT LIKE MOST CATS, SHE DEVELOPED URINARY ISSUES AS SHE GREW OLDER.
STILL FILTHY, WHICH WAS HARDLY NEW...
...BUT NOW SHE SEEMED TO BE IN PAIN.

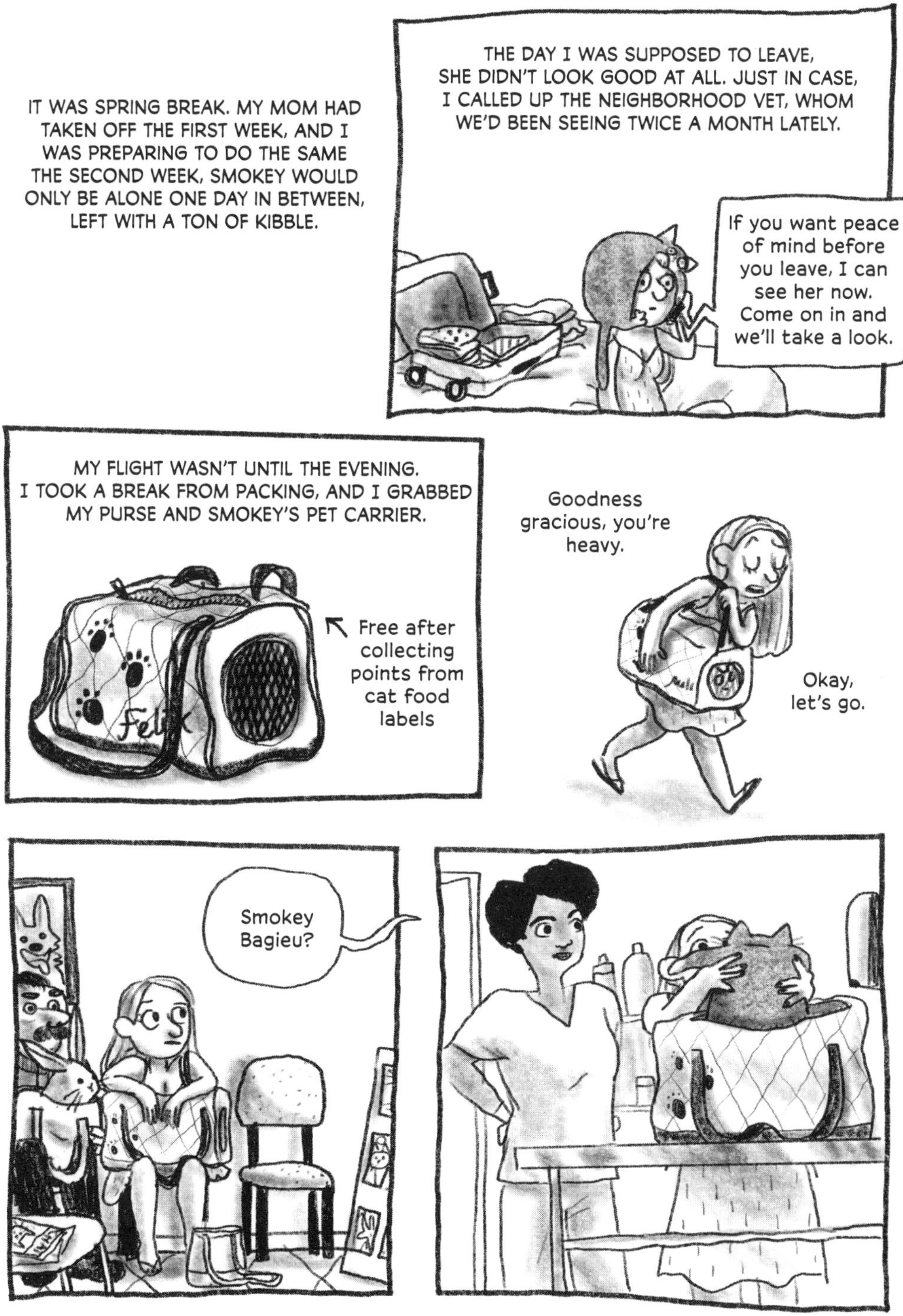
IT WAS SPRING BREAK. MY MOM HAD TAKEN OFF THE FIRST WEEK, AND I WAS PREPARING TO DO THE SAME THE SECOND WEEK. SMOKEY WOULD ONLY BE ALONE ONE DAY IN BETWEEN, LEFT WITH A TON OF KIBBLE.
THE DAY I WAS SUPPOSED TO LEAVE, SHE DIDN'T LOOK GOOD AT ALL. JUST IN CASE, I CALLED UP THE NEIGHBORHOOD VET, WHOM WE'D BEEN SEEING TWICE A MONTH LATELY.
If you want peace of mind before you leave, I can see her now. Come on in and we'll take a look.
MY FLIGHT WASN'T UNTIL THE EVENING. I TOOK A BREAK FROM PACKING, AND I GRABBED MY PURSE AND SMOKEY'S PET CARRIER.
Felix
Free after collecting points from cat food labels
Goodness gracious, you're heavy.
Okay, let's go.
Smokey Bagieu?

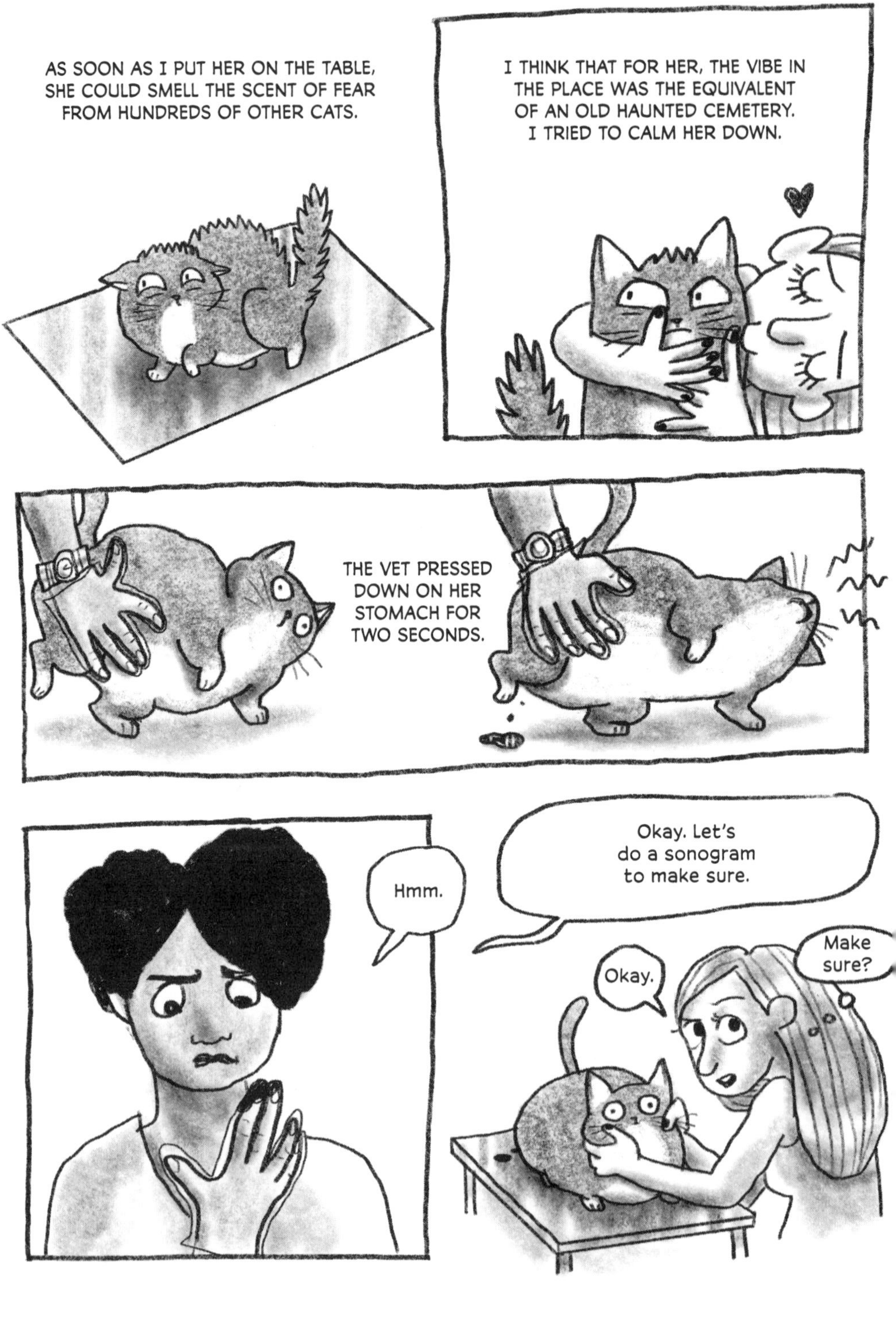
AS SOON AS I PUT HER ON THE TABLE, SHE COULD SMELL THE SCENT OF FEAR FROM HUNDREDS OF OTHER CATS.
I THINK THAT FOR HER, THE VIBE IN THE PLACE WAS THE EQUIVALENT OF AN OLD HAUNTED CEMETERY. I TRIED TO CALM HER DOWN.
THE VET PRESSED DOWN ON HER STOMACH FOR TWO SECONDS.
Hmm.
Okay. Let's do a sonogram to make sure.
Okay.
Make sure?

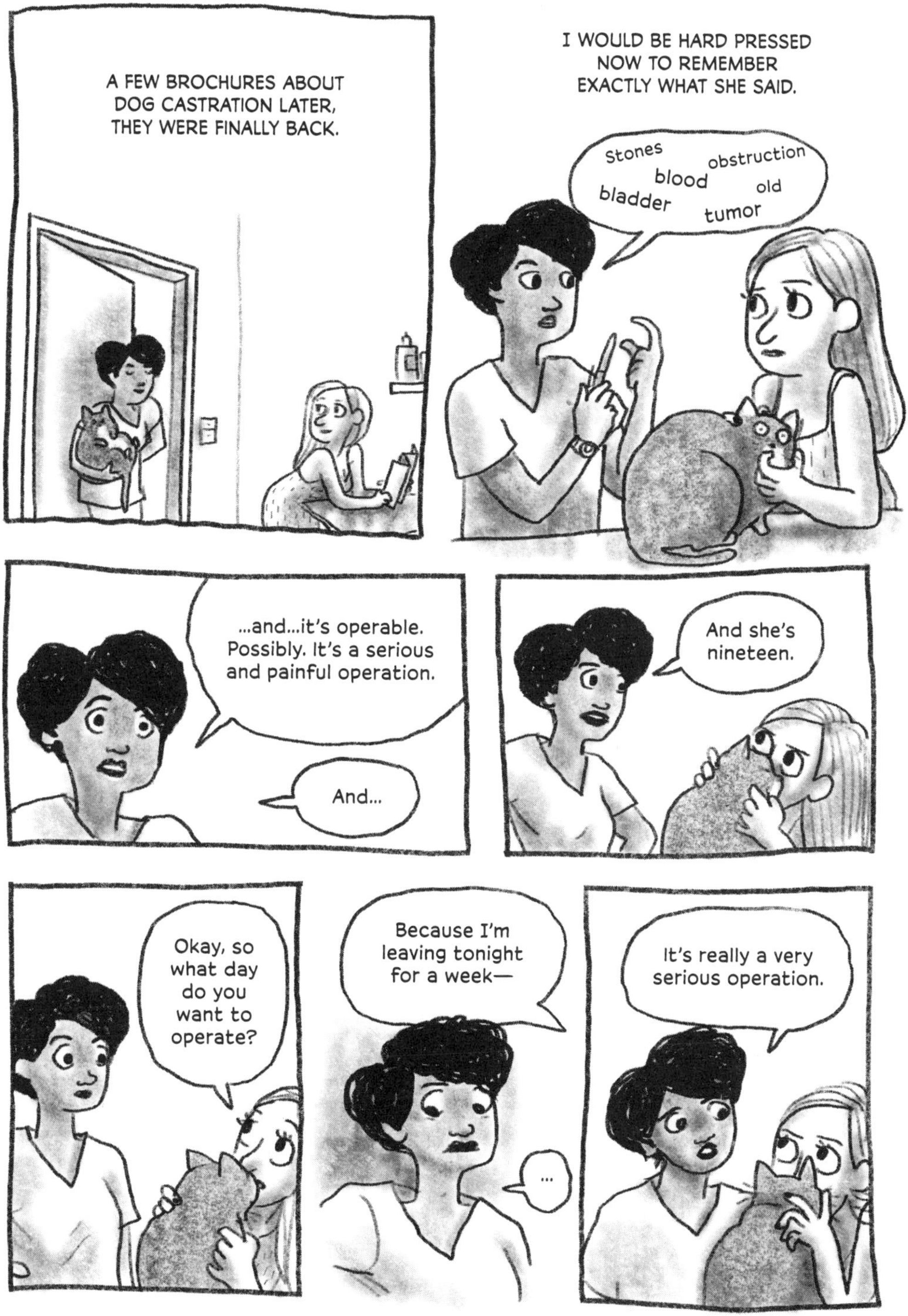
A FEW BROCHURES ABOUT DOG CASTRATION LATER, THEY WERE FINALLY BACK.
I WOULD BE HARD PRESSED NOW TO REMEMBER EXACTLY WHAT SHE SAID.
Stones blood obstruction bladder old tumor
...and...it's operable. Possibly. It's a serious and painful operation.
And...
And she's nineteen.
Okay, so what day do you want to operate?
Because I'm leaving tonight for a week—
...
It's really a very serious operation.

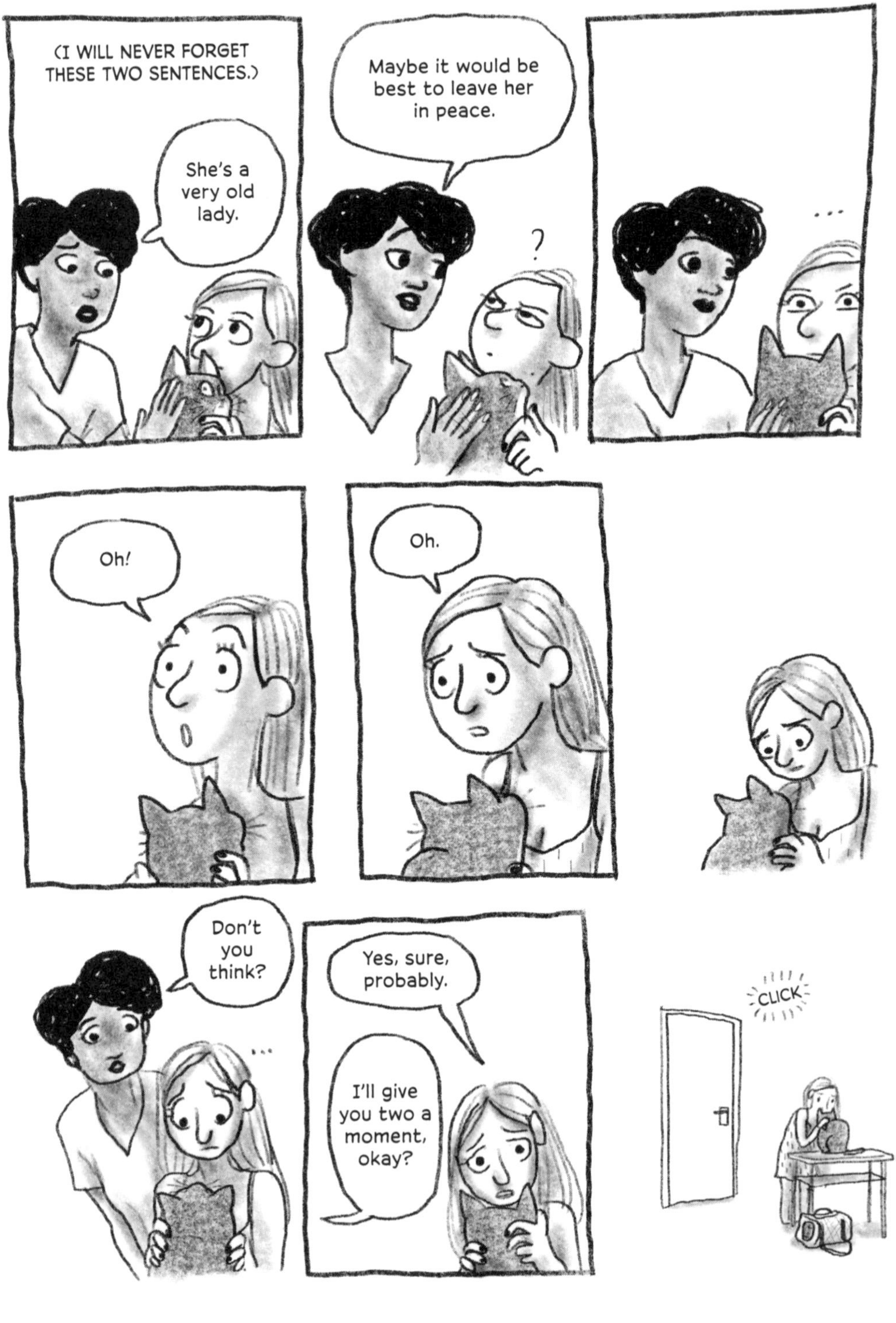
(I WILL NEVER FORGET THESE TWO SENTENCES.)
She's a very old lady.
Maybe it would be best to leave her in peace.
?
...
Oh!
Oh.
Don't you think?
...
Yes, sure, probably.
I'll give you two a moment, okay?
CLICK

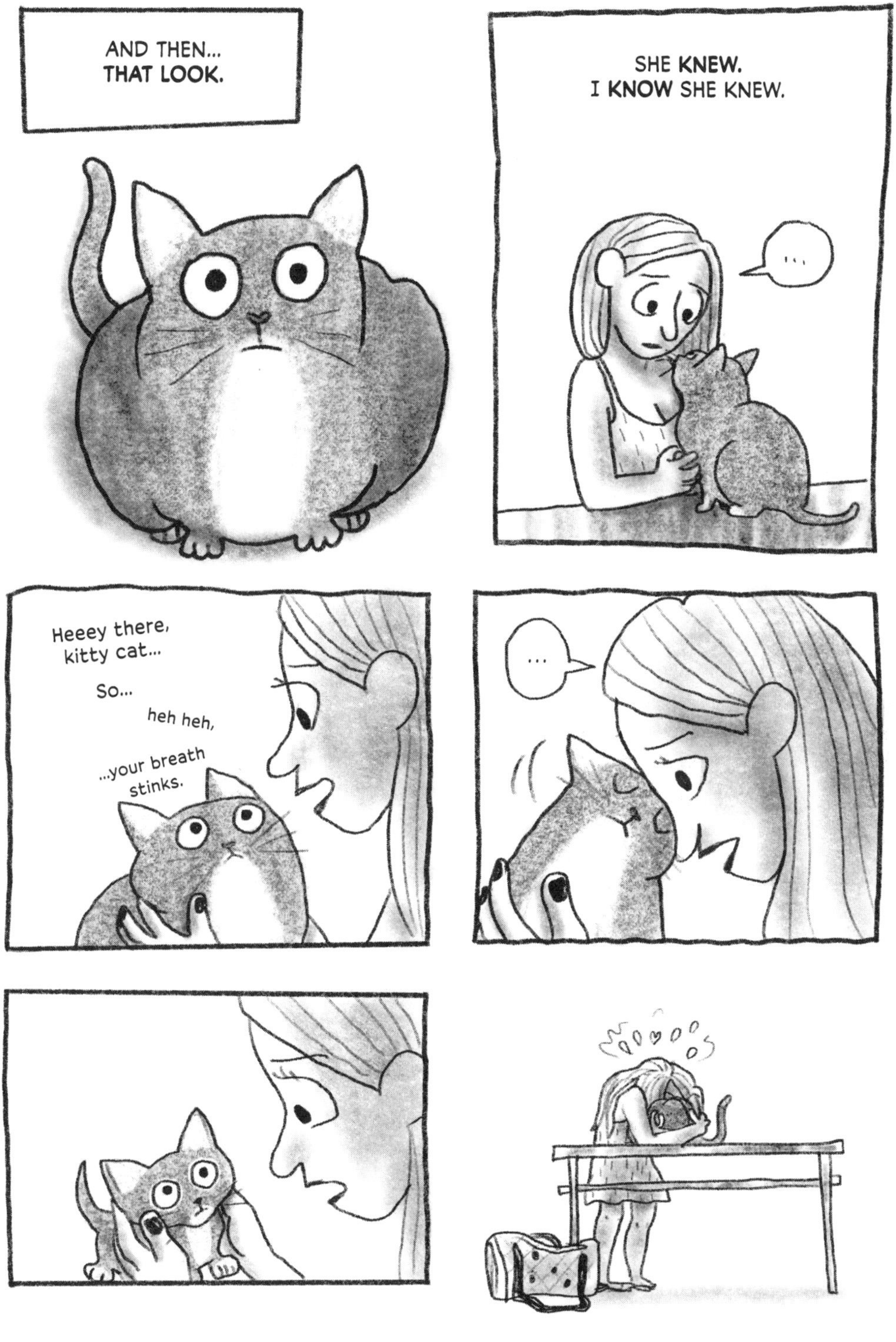
AND THEN...
THAT LOOK.
SHE KNEW.
I KNOW SHE KNEW.
...
Heeey there,
kitty cat...
So...
heh heh,
...your breath
stinks.
...

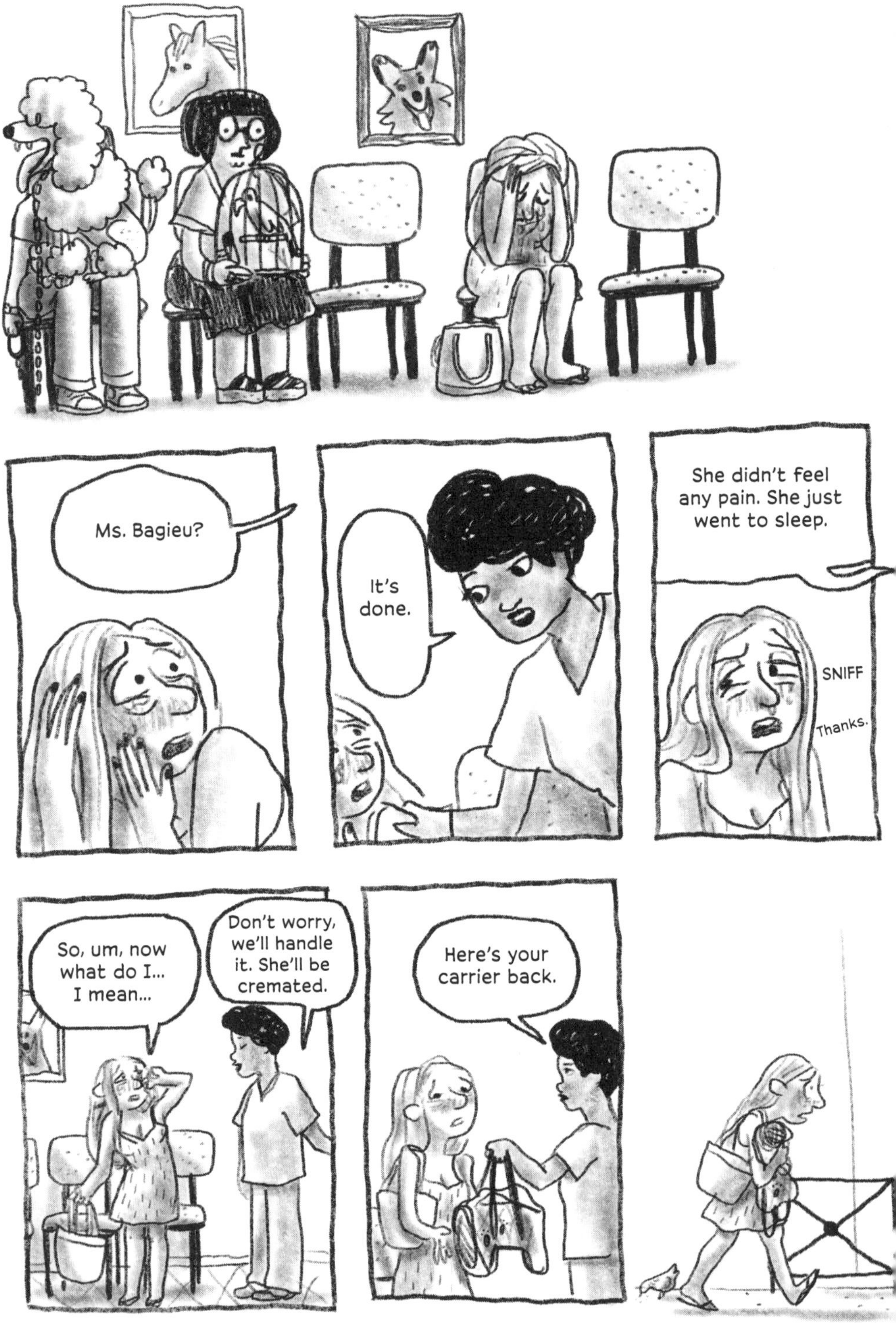
Ms. Bagieu?
It's done.
She didn't feel any pain. She just went to sleep.
SNIFF
Thanks.
So, um, now what do I... I mean...
Don't worry, we'll handle it. She'll be cremated.
Here's your carrier back.

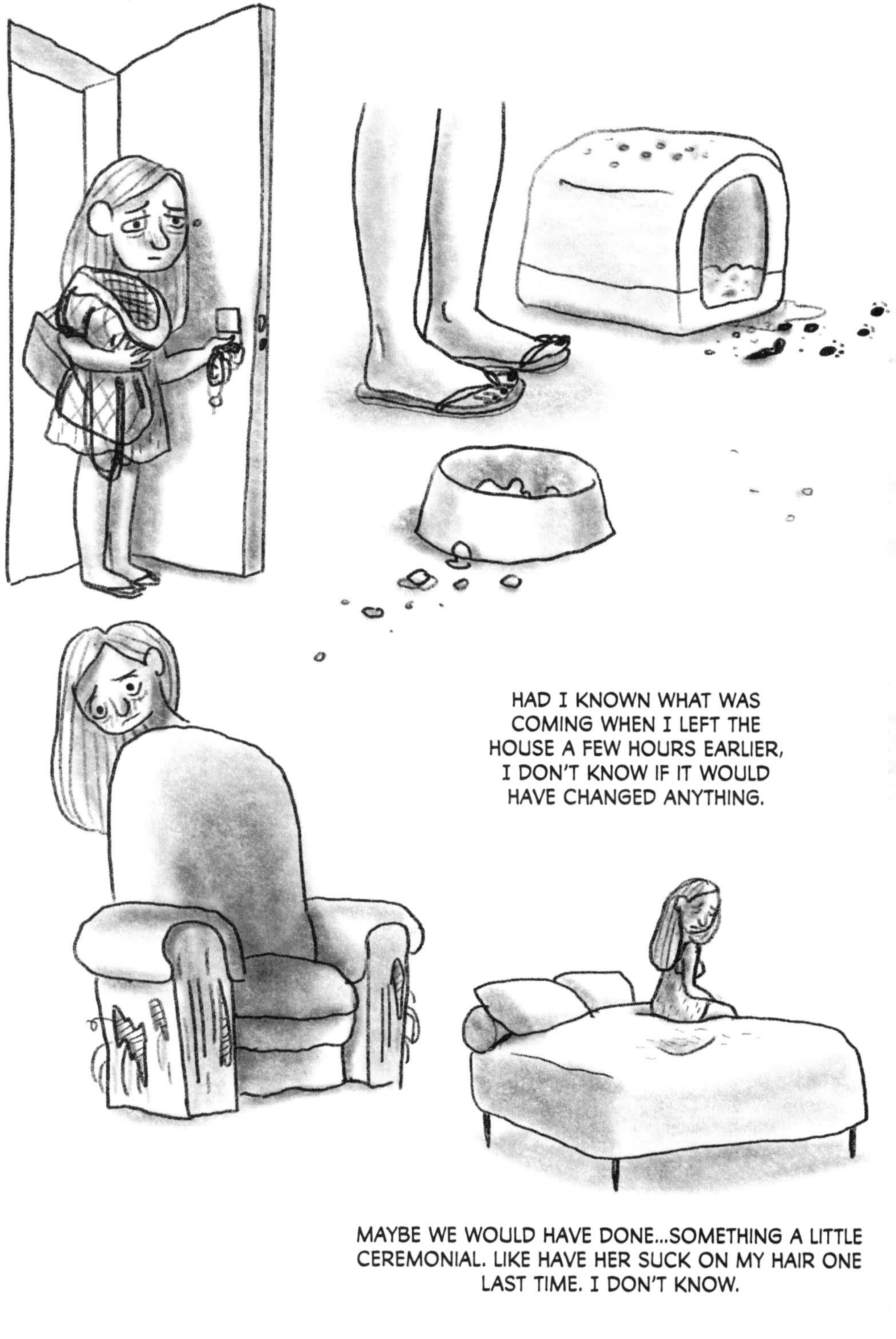
HAD I KNOWN WHAT WAS COMING WHEN I LEFT THE HOUSE A FEW HOURS EARLIER, I DON'T KNOW IF IT WOULD HAVE CHANGED ANYTHING.
MAYBE WE WOULD HAVE DONE...SOMETHING A LITTLE CEREMONIAL. LIKE HAVE HER SUCK ON MY HAIR ONE LAST TIME. I DON'T KNOW.

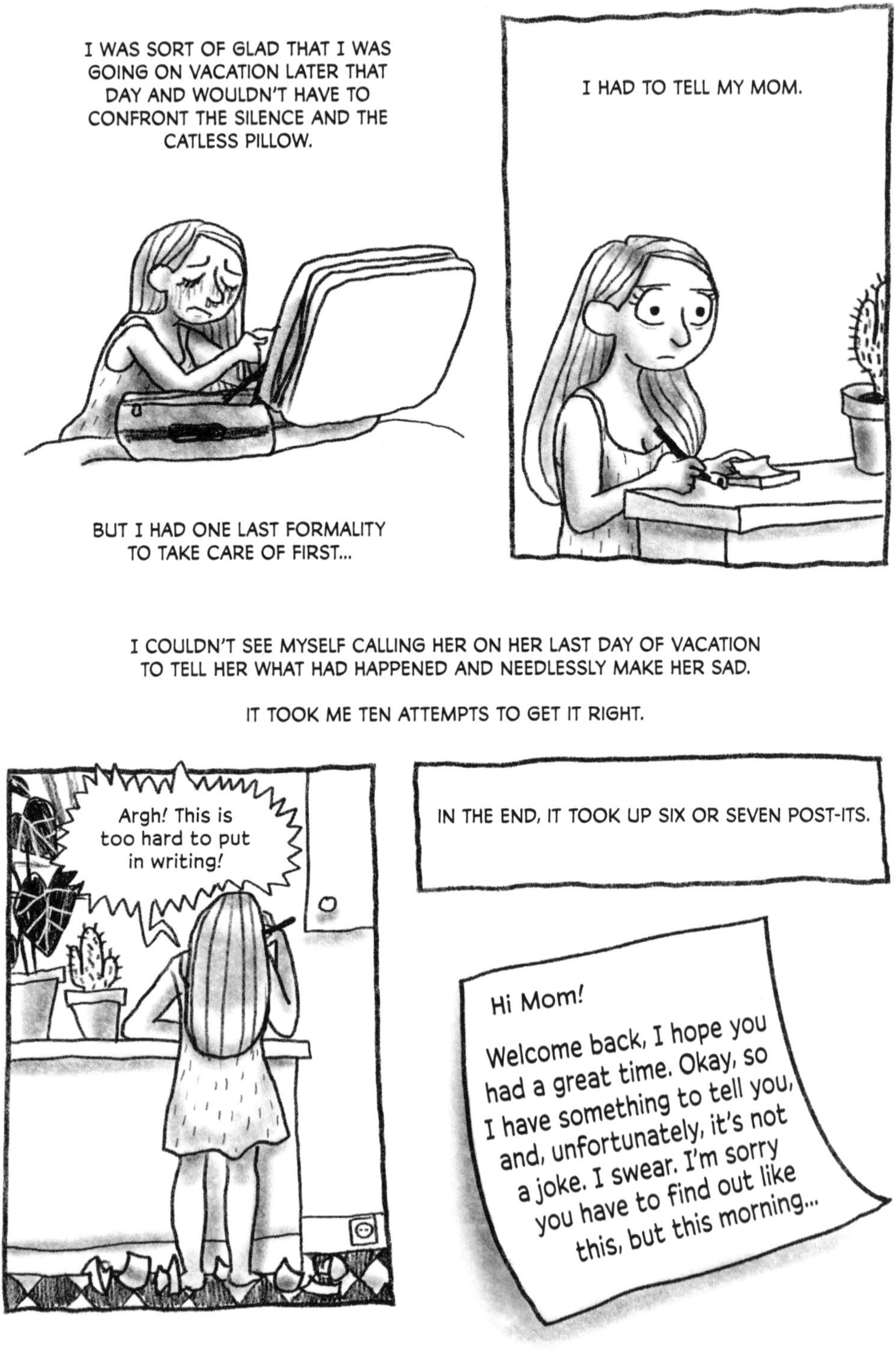
I WAS SORT OF GLAD THAT I WAS GOING ON VACATION LATER THAT DAY AND WOULDN'T HAVE TO CONFRONT THE SILENCE AND THE CATLESS PILLOW.
BUT I HAD ONE LAST FORMALITY TO TAKE CARE OF FIRST...
I HAD TO TELL MY MOM.
I COULDN'T SEE MYSELF CALLING HER ON HER LAST DAY OF VACATION TO TELL HER WHAT HAD HAPPENED AND NEEDLESSLY MAKE HER SAD.
IT TOOK ME TEN ATTEMPTS TO GET IT RIGHT.
Argh! This is too hard to put in writing!
IN THE END, IT TOOK UP SIX OR SEVEN POST-ITS.
Hi Mom!
Welcome back, I hope you had a great time. Okay, so I have something to tell you, and, unfortunately, it's not a joke. I swear. I'm sorry you have to find out like this, but this morning...

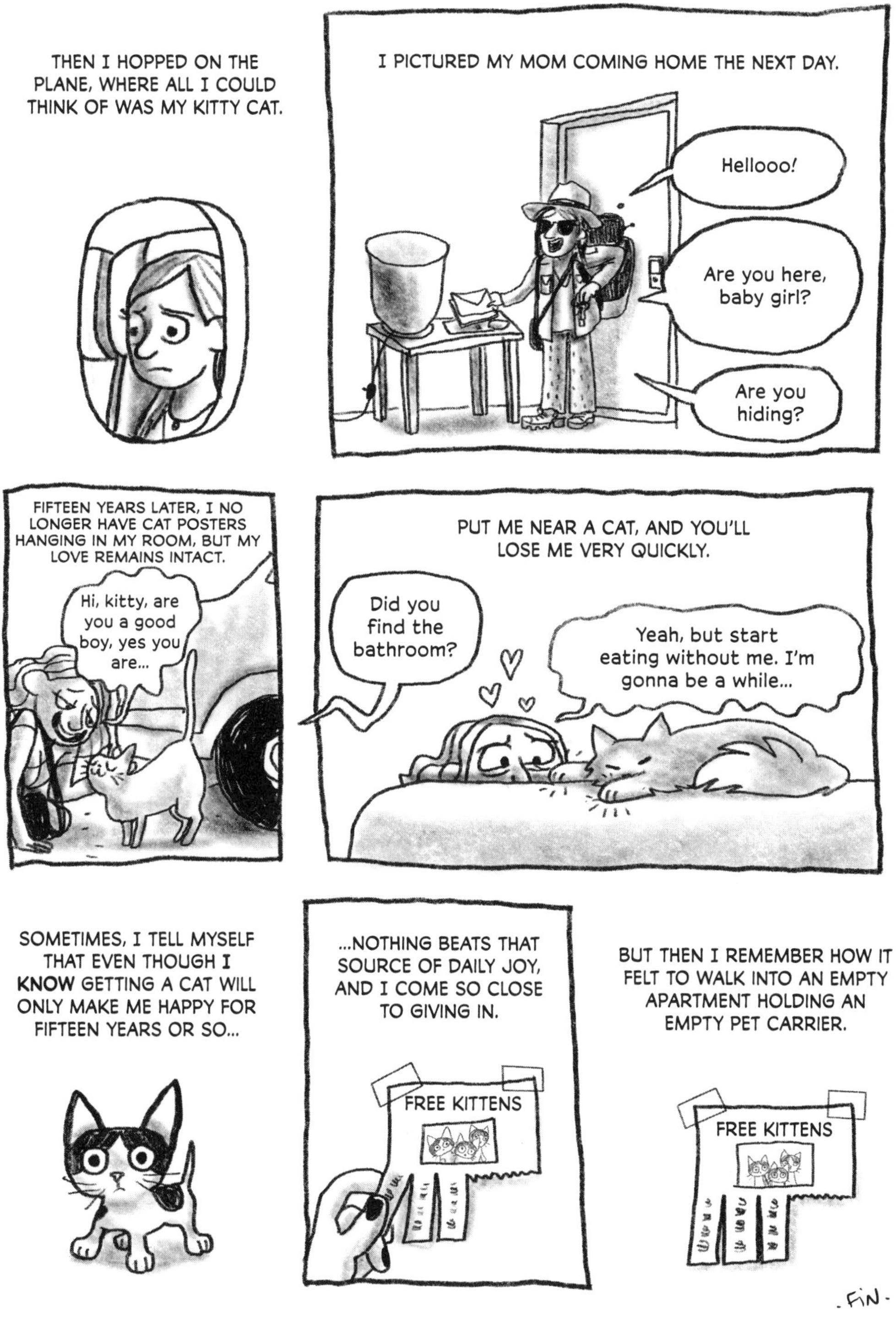
THEN I HOPPED ON THE PLANE, WHERE ALL I COULD THINK OF WAS MY KITTY CAT.
I PICTURED MY MOM COMING HOME THE NEXT DAY.
Hellooo!
Are you here, baby girl?
Are you hiding?
FIFTEEN YEARS LATER, I NO LONGER HAVE CAT POSTERS HANGING IN MY ROOM, BUT MY LOVE REMAINS INTACT.
Hi, kitty, are you a good boy, yes you are...
PUT ME NEAR A CAT, AND YOU'LL LOSE ME VERY QUICKLY.
Did you find the bathroom?
Yeah, but start eating without me. I'm gonna be a while...
SOMETIMES, I TELL MYSELF THAT EVEN THOUGH I **KNOW** GETTING A CAT WILL ONLY MAKE ME HAPPY FOR FIFTEEN YEARS OR SO...
...NOTHING BEATS THAT SOURCE OF DAILY JOY, AND I COME SO CLOSE TO GIVING IN.
FREE KITTENS
BUT THEN I REMEMBER HOW IT FELT TO WALK INTO AN EMPTY APARTMENT HOLDING AN EMPTY PET CARRIER.
FREE KITTENS
- FIN -

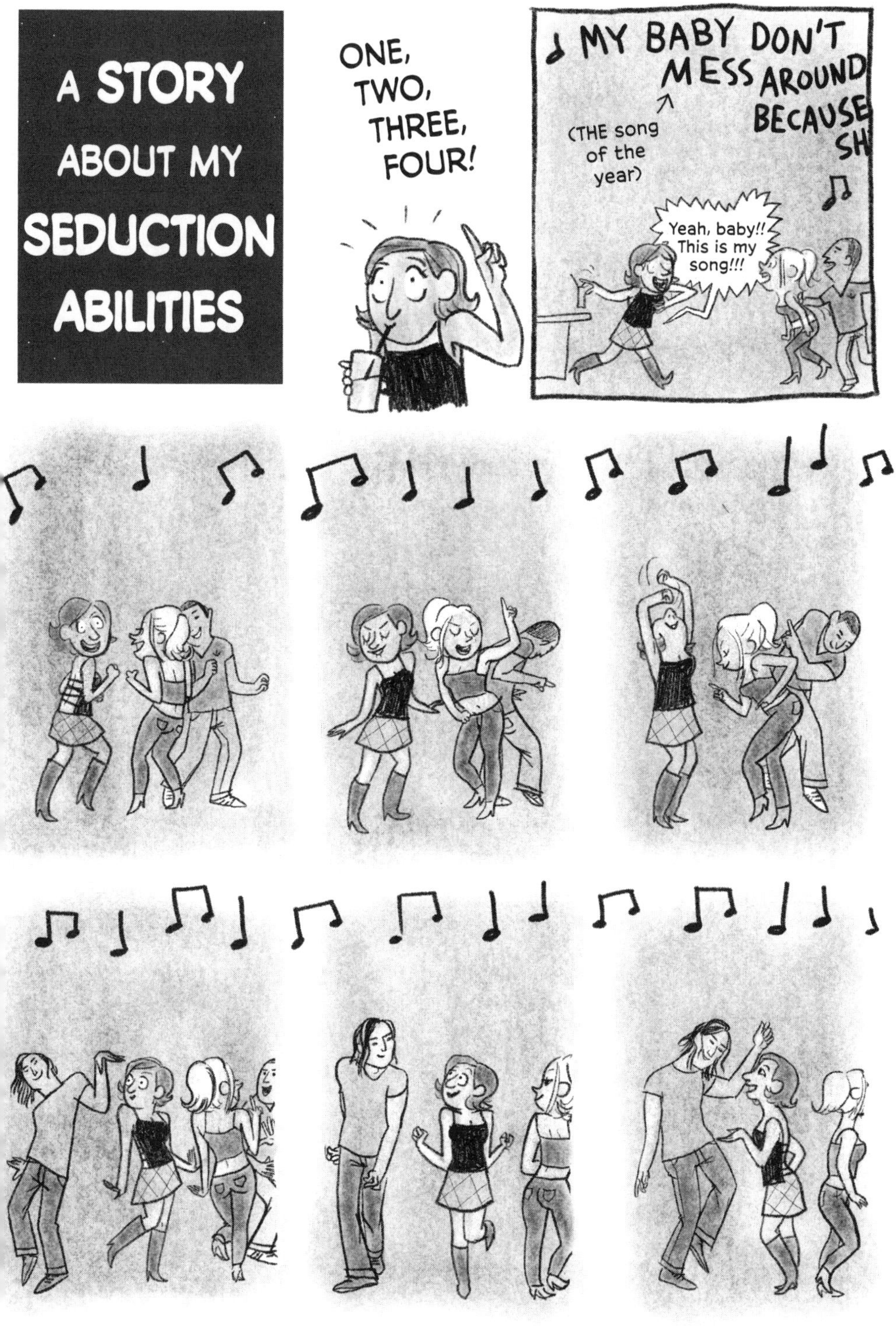
A STORY ABOUT MY SEDUCTION ABILITIES
ONE, TWO, THREE, FOUR!
MY BABY DON'T MESS AROUND BECAUSE SH
(THE song of the year)
Yeah, baby!! This is my song!!!

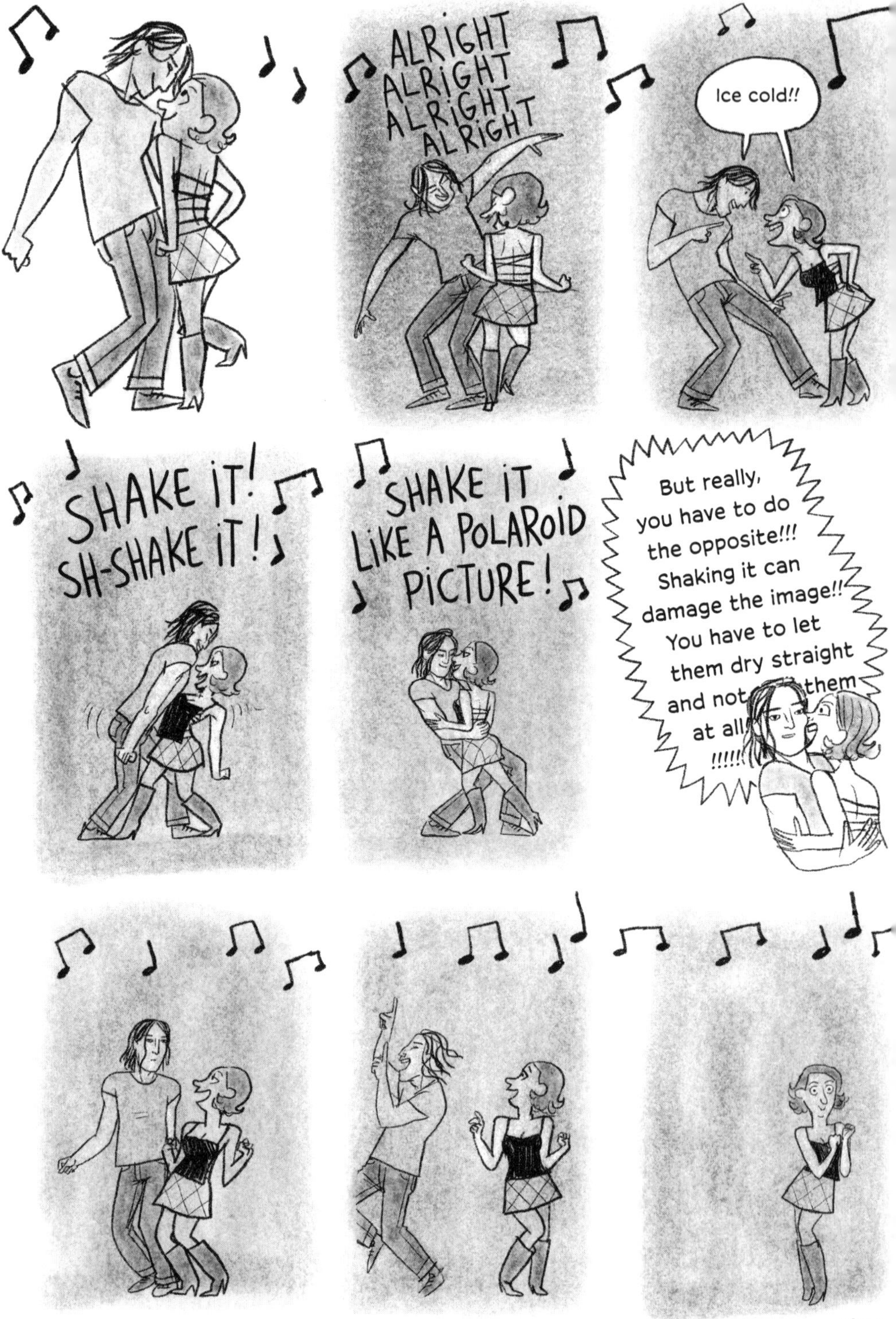
ALRIGHT ALRIGHT ALRIGHT ALRIGHT
Ice cold!!
SHAKE IT! SH-SHAKE IT!
SHAKE IT LIKE A POLAROID PICTURE!
But really, you have to do the opposite!!! Shaking it can damage the image!! You have to let them dry straight and not them at all !!!!!
-FIN-

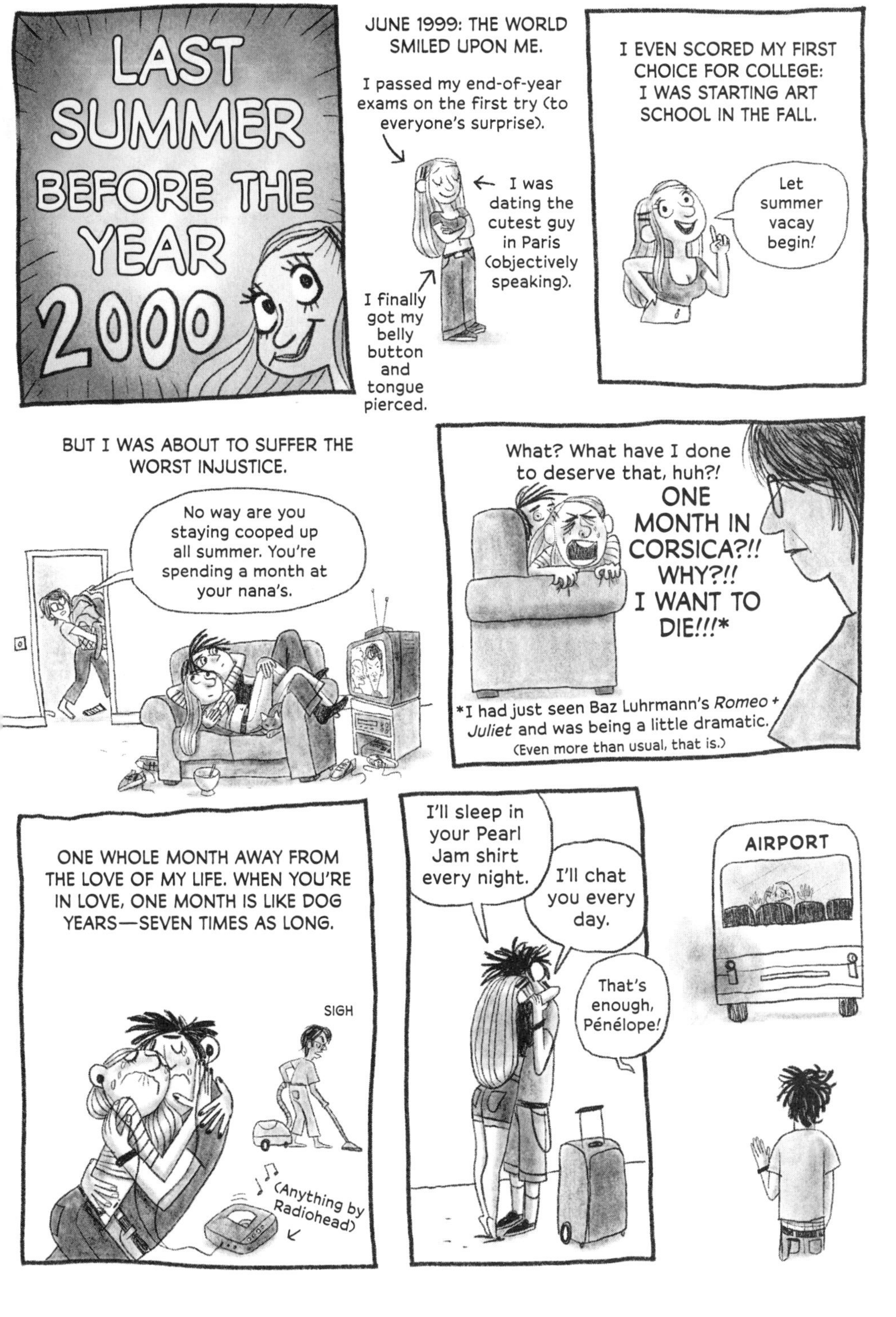
LAST SUMMER BEFORE THE YEAR 2000
JUNE 1999: THE WORLD SMILED UPON ME.
I passed my end-of-year exams on the first try (to everyone's surprise).
I was dating the cutest guy in Paris (objectively speaking).
I finally got my belly button and tongue pierced.
I EVEN SCORED MY FIRST CHOICE FOR COLLEGE: I WAS STARTING ART SCHOOL IN THE FALL.
Let summer vacay begin!
BUT I WAS ABOUT TO SUFFER THE WORST INJUSTICE.
No way are you staying cooped up all summer. You're spending a month at your nana's.
What? What have I done to deserve that, huh?!
ONE MONTH IN CORSICA?!! WHY?!! I WANT TO DIE!!!*
*I had just seen Baz Luhrmann's *Romeo + Juliet* and was being a little dramatic.
(Even more than usual, that is.)
ONE WHOLE MONTH AWAY FROM THE LOVE OF MY LIFE. WHEN YOU'RE IN LOVE, ONE MONTH IS LIKE DOG YEARS—SEVEN TIMES AS LONG.
SIGH
(Anything by Radiohead)
I'll sleep in your Pearl Jam shirt every night.
I'll chat you every day.
That's enough, Pénélope!
AIRPORT

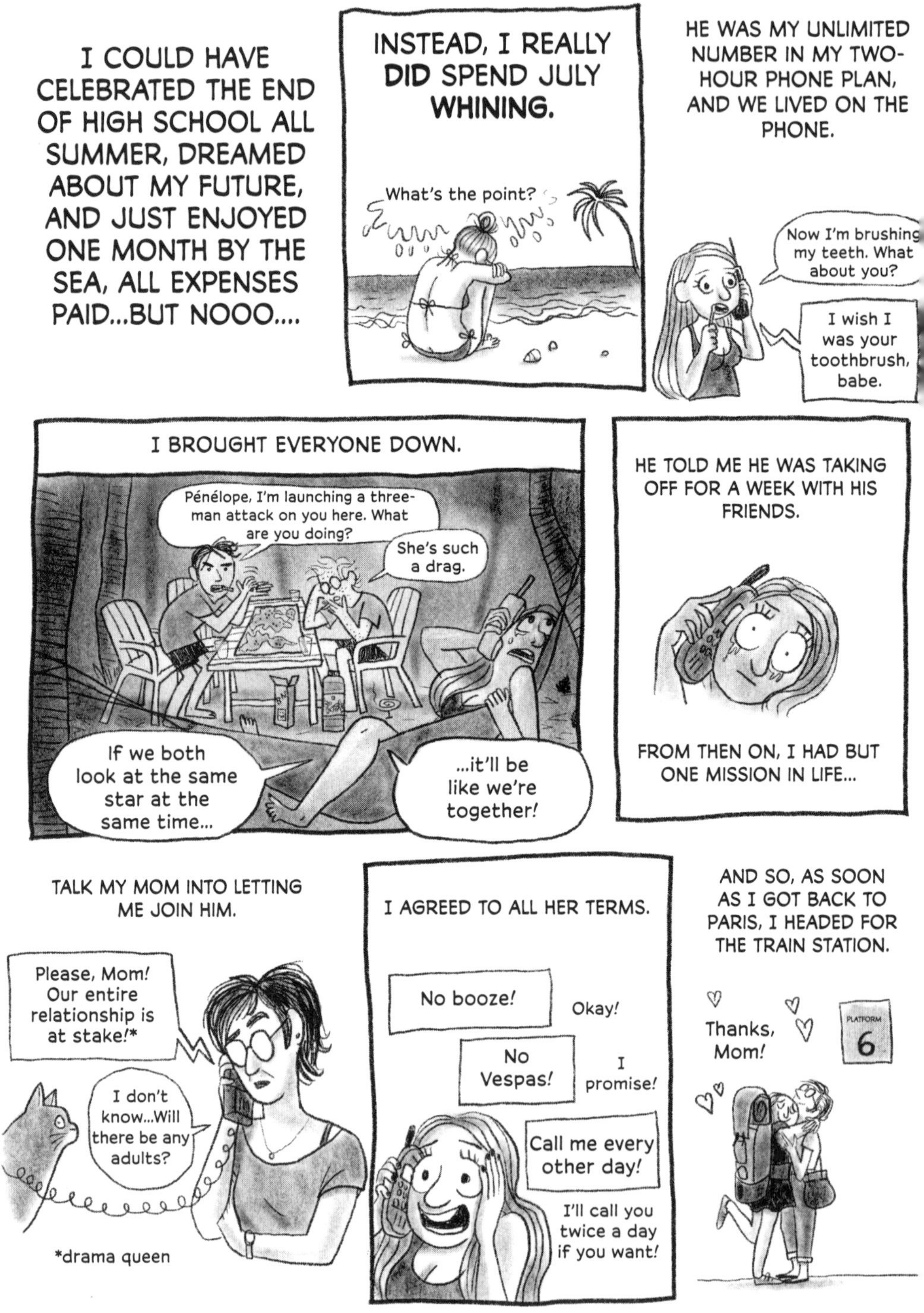
I COULD HAVE CELEBRATED THE END OF HIGH SCHOOL ALL SUMMER, DREAMED ABOUT MY FUTURE, AND JUST ENJOYED ONE MONTH BY THE SEA, ALL EXPENSES PAID...BUT NOOO....
INSTEAD, I REALLY DID SPEND JULY WHINING.
What's the point?
HE WAS MY UNLIMITED NUMBER IN MY TWO-HOUR PHONE PLAN, AND WE LIVED ON THE PHONE.
Now I'm brushing my teeth. What about you?
I wish I was your toothbrush, babe.
I BROUGHT EVERYONE DOWN.
Pénélope, I'm launching a three-man attack on you here. What are you doing?
She's such a drag.
If we both look at the same star at the same time...
...it'll be like we're together!
HE TOLD ME HE WAS TAKING OFF FOR A WEEK WITH HIS FRIENDS.
FROM THEN ON, I HAD BUT ONE MISSION IN LIFE...
TALK MY MOM INTO LETTING ME JOIN HIM.
Please, Mom! Our entire relationship is at stake!*
I don't know...Will there be any adults?
*drama queen
I AGREED TO ALL HER TERMS.
No booze!
Okay!
No Vespas!
I promise!
Call me every other day!
I'll call you twice a day if you want!
AND SO, AS SOON AS I GOT BACK TO PARIS, I HEADED FOR THE TRAIN STATION.
Thanks, Mom!
PLATFORM
6

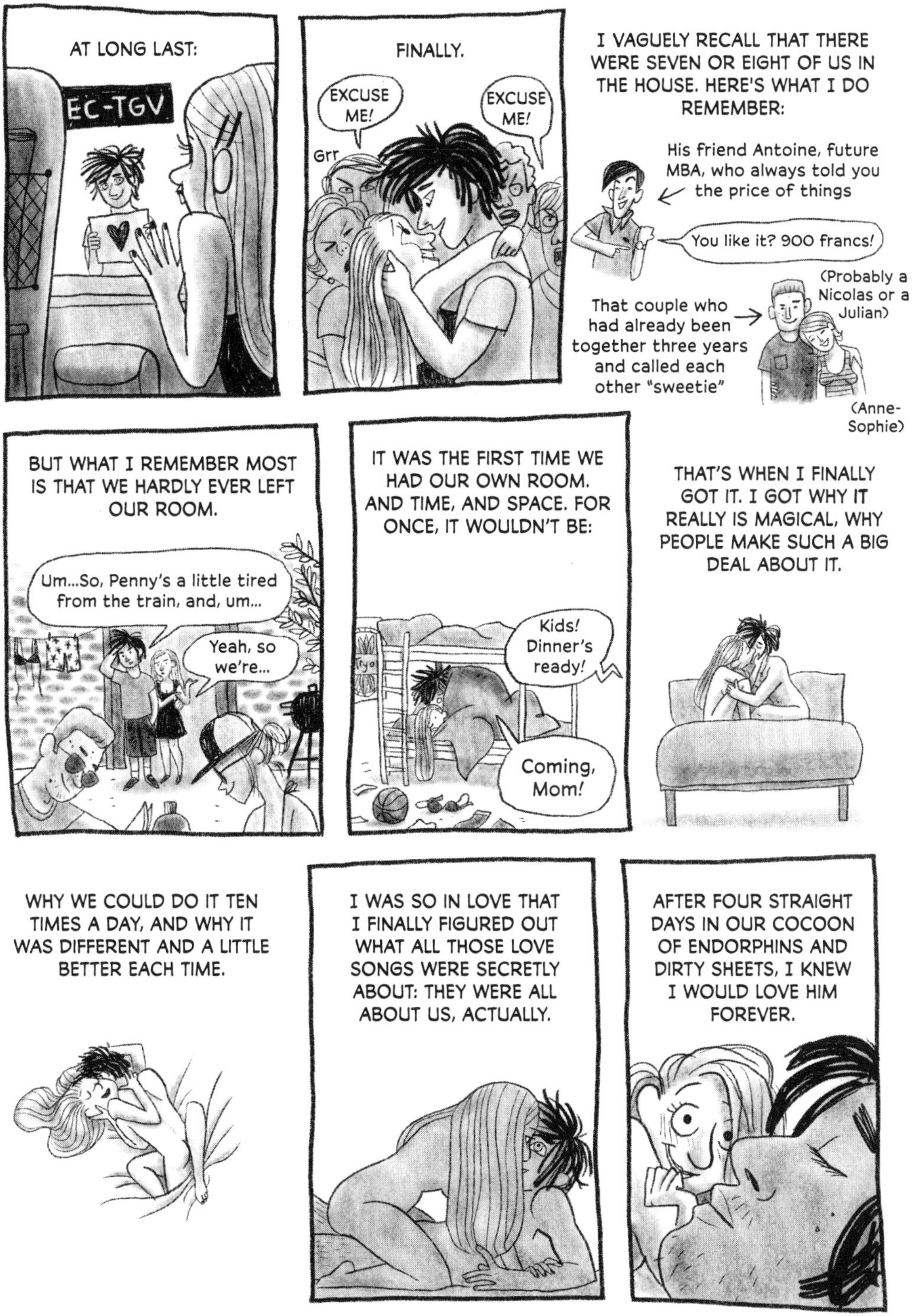
AT LONG LAST:
EC-TGV
FINALLY.
EXCUSE ME!
Grr
EXCUSE ME!
I VAGUELY RECALL THAT THERE WERE SEVEN OR EIGHT OF US IN THE HOUSE. HERE'S WHAT I DO REMEMBER:
His friend Antoine, future MBA, who always told you the price of things
You like it? 900 francs!
That couple who had already been together three years and called each other "sweetie"
(Probably a Nicolas or a Julian)
(Anne-Sophie)
BUT WHAT I REMEMBER MOST IS THAT WE HARDLY EVER LEFT OUR ROOM.
Um...So, Penny's a little tired from the train, and, um...
Yeah, so we're...
IT WAS THE FIRST TIME WE HAD OUR OWN ROOM. AND TIME, AND SPACE. FOR ONCE, IT WOULDN'T BE:
Kids! Dinner's ready!
Coming, Mom!
THAT'S WHEN I FINALLY GOT IT. I GOT WHY IT REALLY IS MAGICAL, WHY PEOPLE MAKE SUCH A BIG DEAL ABOUT IT.
WHY WE COULD DO IT TEN TIMES A DAY, AND WHY IT WAS DIFFERENT AND A LITTLE BETTER EACH TIME.
I WAS SO IN LOVE THAT I FINALLY FIGURED OUT WHAT ALL THOSE LOVE SONGS WERE SECRETLY ABOUT: THEY WERE ALL ABOUT US, ACTUALLY.
AFTER FOUR STRAIGHT DAYS IN OUR COCOON OF ENDORPHINS AND DIRTY SHEETS, I KNEW I WOULD LOVE HIM FOREVER.

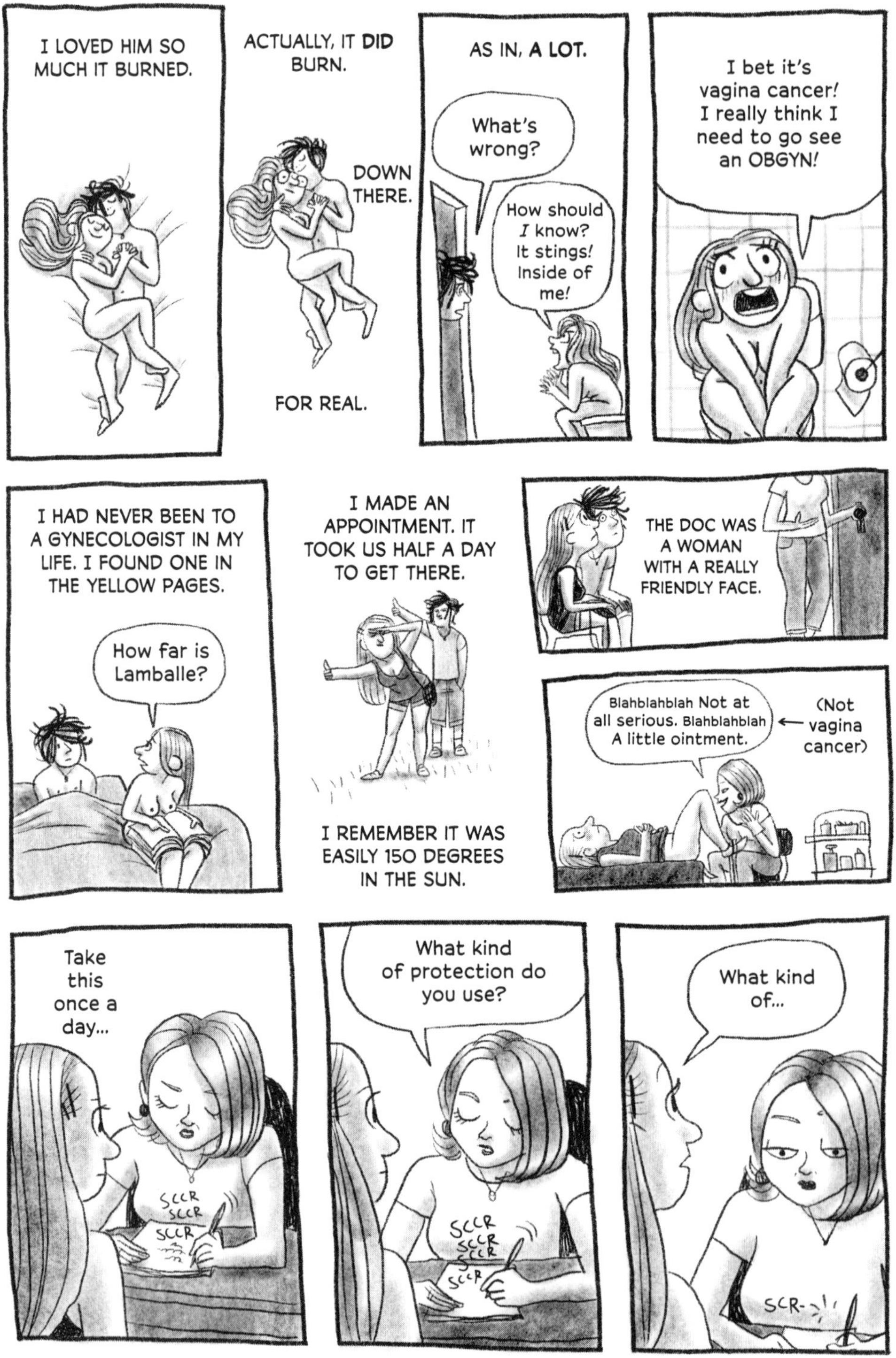
I LOVED HIM SO MUCH IT BURNED.
ACTUALLY, IT **DID** BURN.
DOWN THERE.
FOR REAL.
AS IN, **A LOT.**
What's wrong?
How should *I* know? It stings! Inside of me!
I bet it's vagina cancer! I really think I need to go see an OBGYN!
I HAD NEVER BEEN TO A GYNECOLOGIST IN MY LIFE. I FOUND ONE IN THE YELLOW PAGES.
How far is Lamballe?
I MADE AN APPOINTMENT. IT TOOK US HALF A DAY TO GET THERE.
I REMEMBER IT WAS EASILY 150 DEGREES IN THE SUN.
THE DOC WAS A WOMAN WITH A REALLY FRIENDLY FACE.
Blahblahblah Not at all serious. Blahblahblah A little ointment.
(Not vagina cancer)
Take this once a day...
SCCR SCCR SCCR
What kind of protection do you use?
SCCR SCCR SCCR SCCR
What kind of...
SCR-

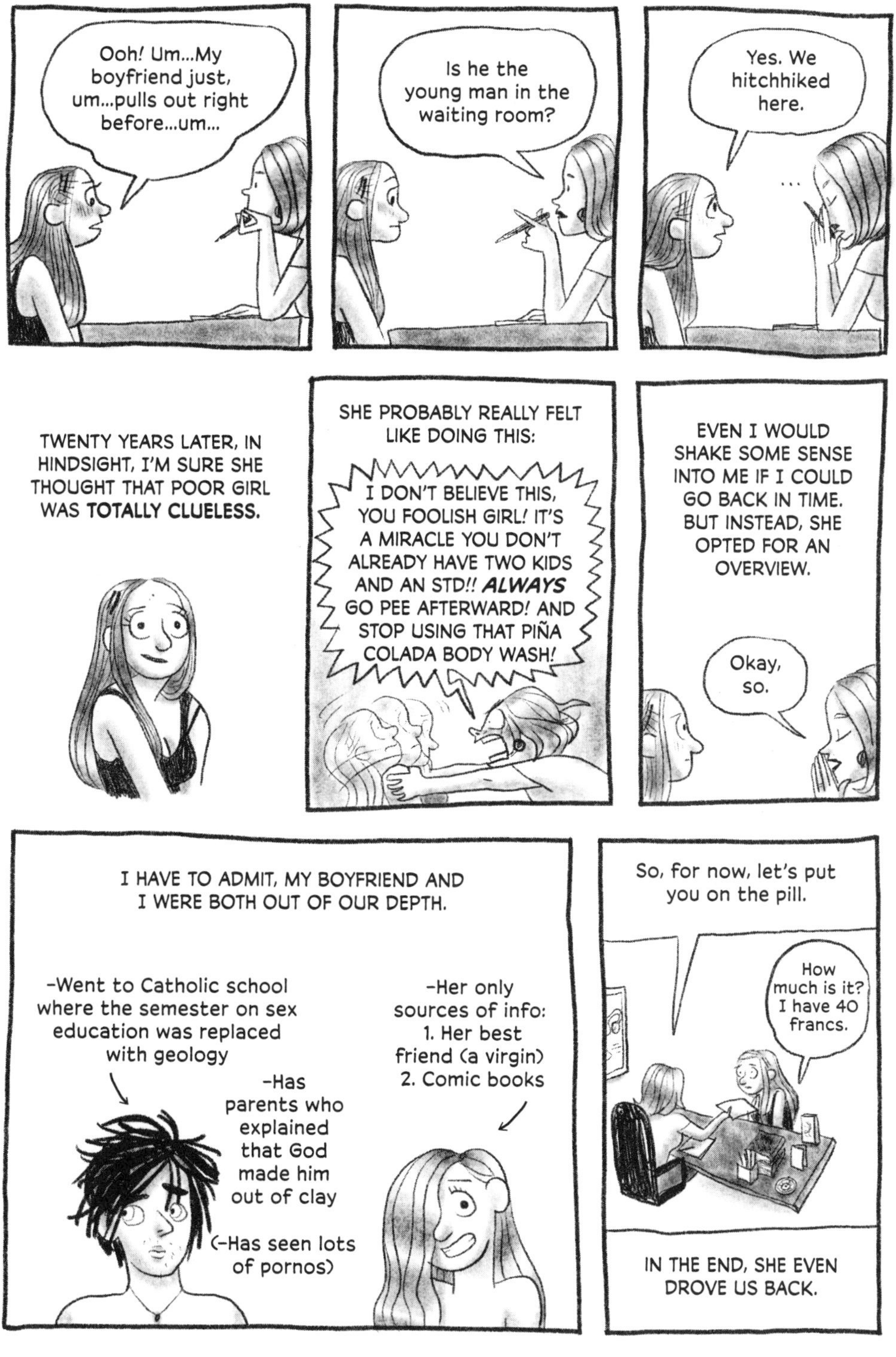
Ooh! Um...My boyfriend just, um...pulls out right before...um...
Is he the young man in the waiting room?
Yes. We hitchhiked here.
...
TWENTY YEARS LATER, IN HINDSIGHT, I'M SURE SHE THOUGHT THAT POOR GIRL WAS **TOTALLY CLUELESS.**
SHE PROBABLY REALLY FELT LIKE DOING THIS:
I DON'T BELIEVE THIS, YOU FOOLISH GIRL! IT'S A MIRACLE YOU DON'T ALREADY HAVE TWO KIDS AND AN STD!! ***ALWAYS*** GO PEE AFTERWARD! AND STOP USING THAT PIÑA COLADA BODY WASH!
EVEN I WOULD SHAKE SOME SENSE INTO ME IF I COULD GO BACK IN TIME. BUT INSTEAD, SHE OPTED FOR AN OVERVIEW.
Okay, so.
I HAVE TO ADMIT, MY BOYFRIEND AND I WERE BOTH OUT OF OUR DEPTH.
-Went to Catholic school where the semester on sex education was replaced with geology
-Has parents who explained that God made him out of clay
(-Has seen lots of pornos)
-Her only sources of info:
1. Her best friend (a virgin)
2. Comic books
So, for now, let's put you on the pill.
How much is it? I have 40 francs.
IN THE END, SHE EVEN DROVE US BACK.

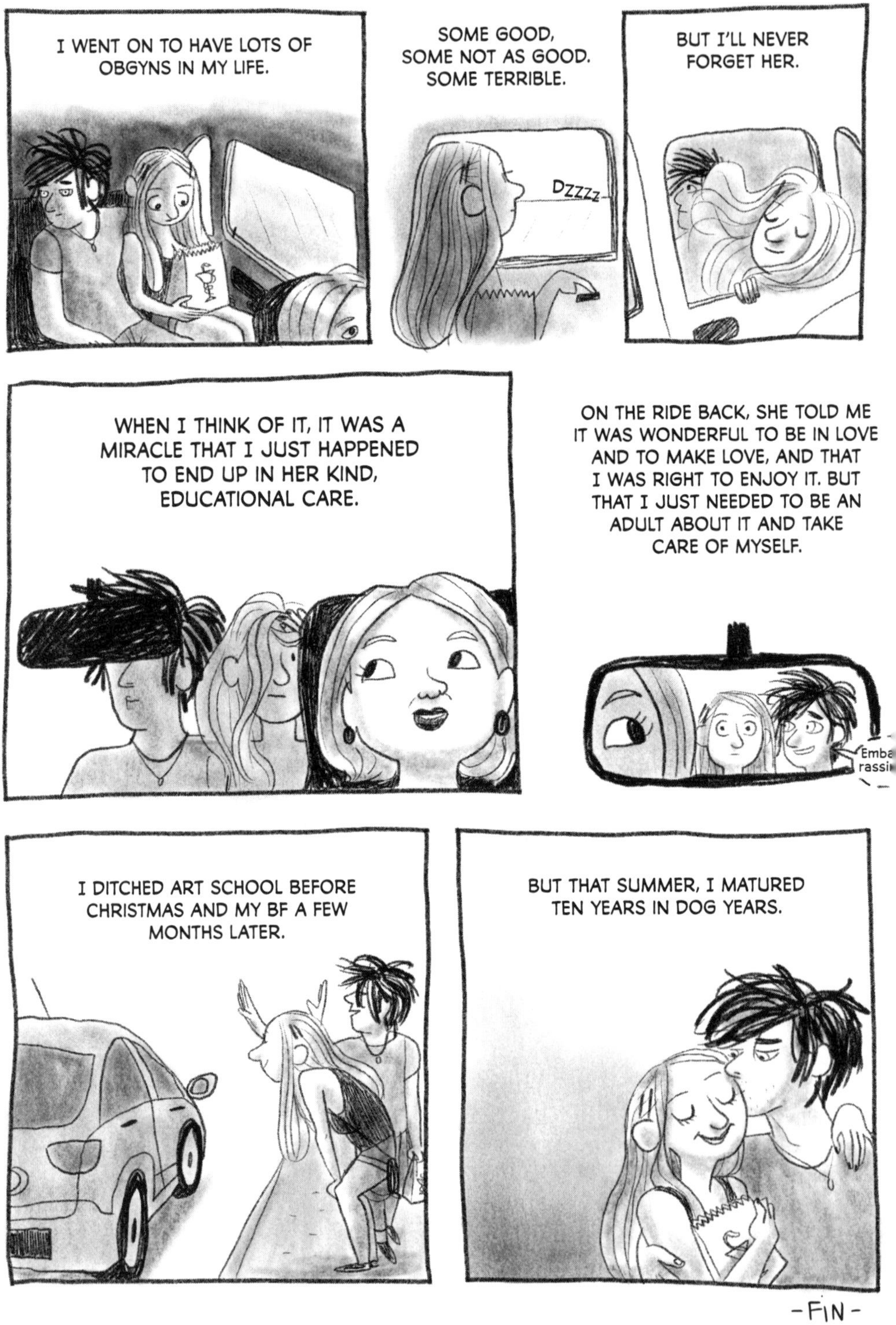
I WENT ON TO HAVE LOTS OF OBGYNS IN MY LIFE.
SOME GOOD, SOME NOT AS GOOD. SOME TERRIBLE.
DZZZZ
BUT I'LL NEVER FORGET HER.
WHEN I THINK OF IT, IT WAS A MIRACLE THAT I JUST HAPPENED TO END UP IN HER KIND, EDUCATIONAL CARE.
ON THE RIDE BACK, SHE TOLD ME IT WAS WONDERFUL TO BE IN LOVE AND TO MAKE LOVE, AND THAT I WAS RIGHT TO ENJOY IT. BUT THAT I JUST NEEDED TO BE AN ADULT ABOUT IT AND TAKE CARE OF MYSELF.
I DITCHED ART SCHOOL BEFORE CHRISTMAS AND MY BF A FEW MONTHS LATER.
BUT THAT SUMMER, I MATURED TEN YEARS IN DOG YEARS.
-FIN-

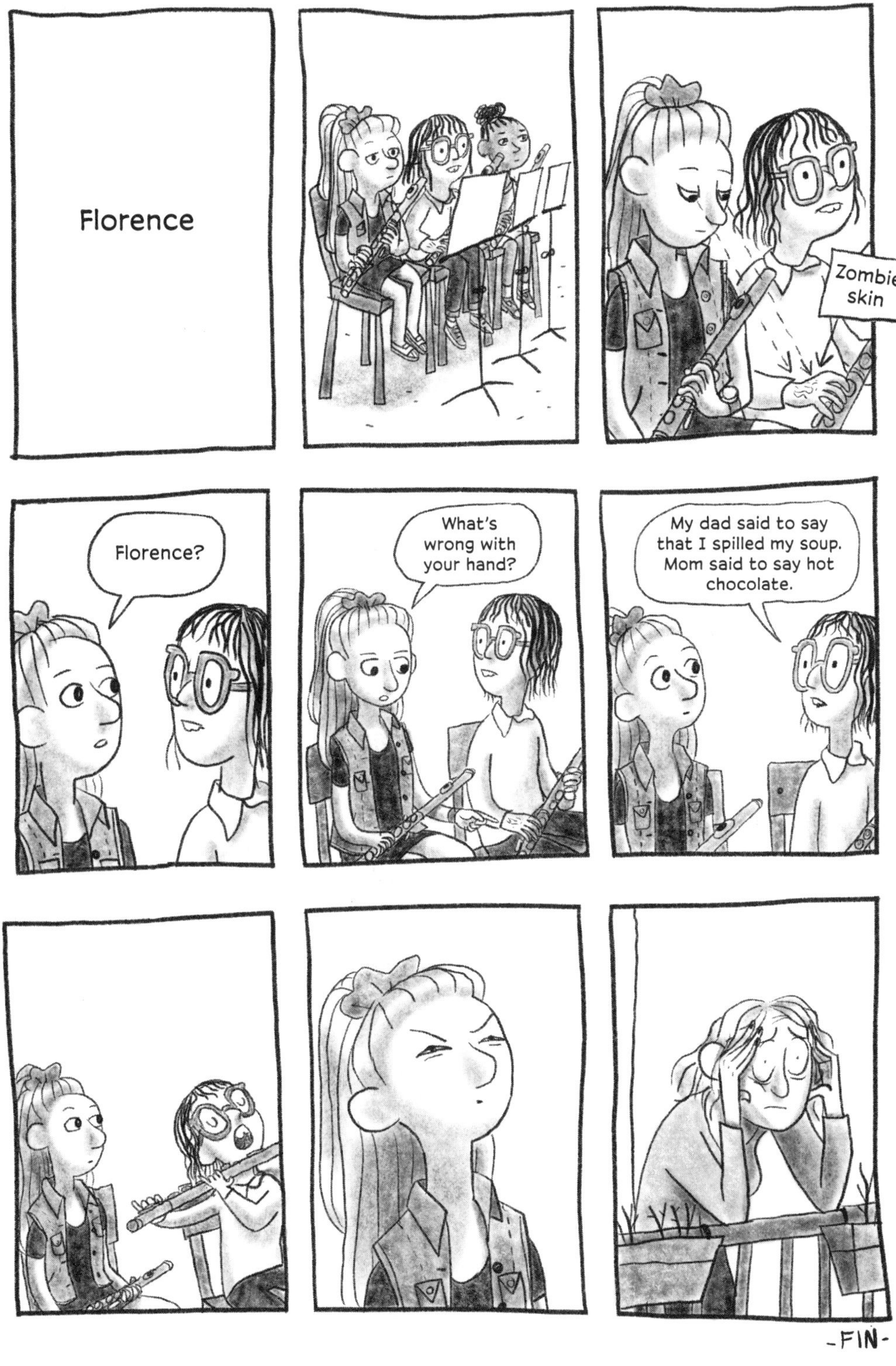
Florence
Zombie skin
Florence?
What's wrong with your hand?
My dad said to say that I spilled my soup. Mom said to say hot chocolate.
-FIN-

The TEDDY BEAR Effect

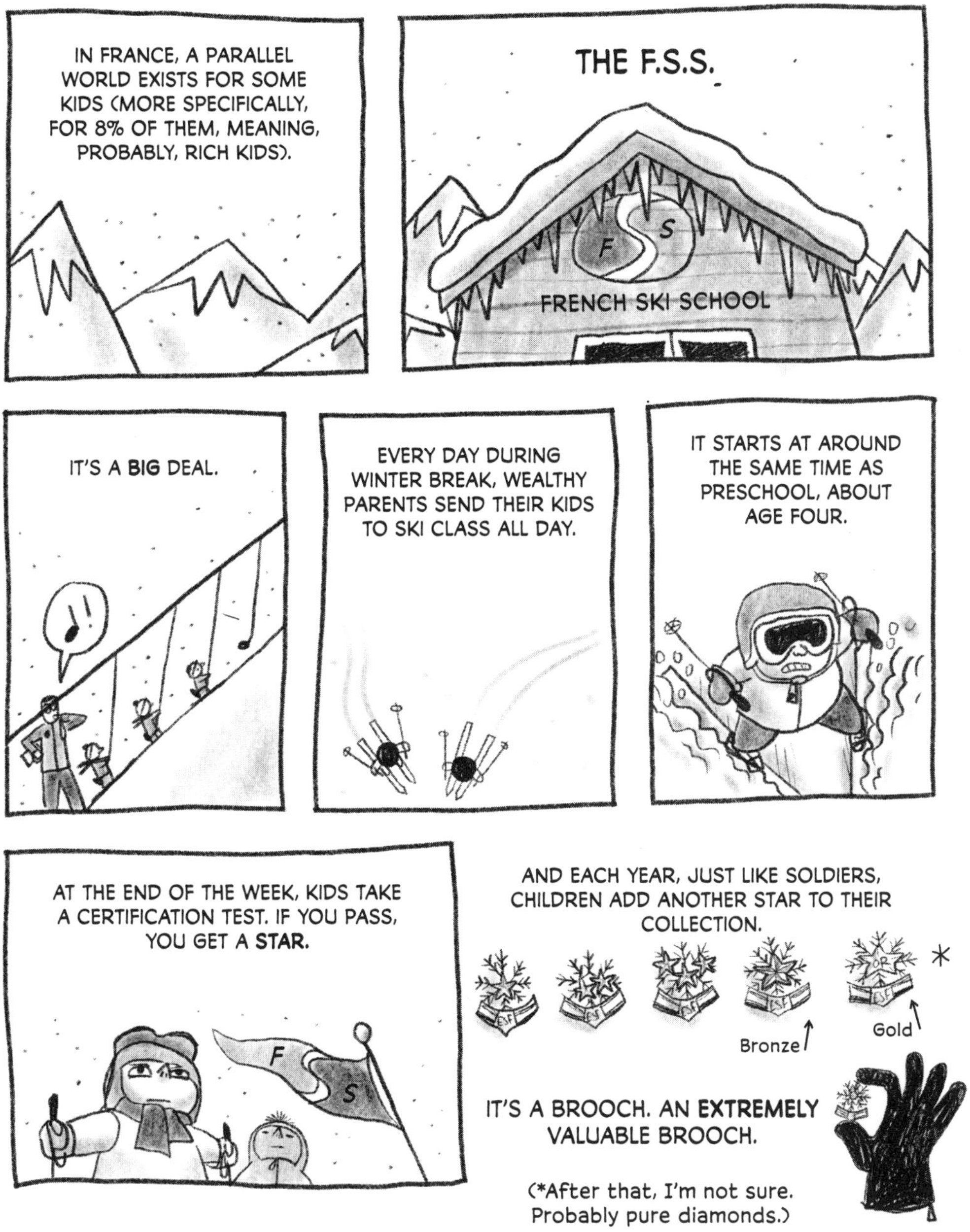

IN FRANCE, A PARALLEL WORLD EXISTS FOR SOME KIDS (MORE SPECIFICALLY, FOR 8% OF THEM, MEANING, PROBABLY, RICH KIDS).
THE F.S.S.
F S
FRENCH SKI SCHOOL
IT'S A **BIG** DEAL.
♪!
EVERY DAY DURING WINTER BREAK, WEALTHY PARENTS SEND THEIR KIDS TO SKI CLASS ALL DAY.
IT STARTS AT AROUND THE SAME TIME AS PRESCHOOL, ABOUT AGE FOUR.
AT THE END OF THE WEEK, KIDS TAKE A CERTIFICATION TEST. IF YOU PASS, YOU GET A **STAR.**
F S
AND EACH YEAR, JUST LIKE SOLDIERS, CHILDREN ADD ANOTHER STAR TO THEIR COLLECTION.
*
Bronze
Gold
IT'S A BROOCH. AN **EXTREMELY** VALUABLE BROOCH.
(*After that, I'm not sure. Probably pure diamonds.)

WHEN SCHOOL RESUMES, THE CHOSEN ONES PROUDLY DISPLAY THEIR DECORATIONS.

NOT WEARING YOUR STAR IS AKIN TO ADMITTING YOUR OWN MEDIOCRITY.

I...I left it on the train! I swear!

FOR TWO OR THREE YEARS, BEFORE THEY SPLIT UP (WHEN WE HAD MONEY), OUR PARENTS SENT US TO SKI SCHOOL, TOO.

WHAT A MAGICAL MEMORY.

THE FIRST SKI SCHOOL TEST, THE ONE I HAD TO TAKE THAT YEAR, EARNS YOU YOUR VERY FIRST BROOCH. BEFORE THE STARS, THERE'S

THE SNOWFLAKE.

F.S.S.

THERE WAS **NO WAY** I WAS SHOWING UP AT SCHOOL ON MONDAY WITHOUT THAT FREAKING PIN.

It's go time.

HOWEVER, ONCE THE TEST WAS OVER, AND DESPITE PROMISES OF REWARDS, NO SNOWFLAKE FOR ME.

INSTEAD, A DIFFERENT BROOCH:

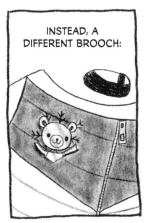

A TEDDY BEAR.

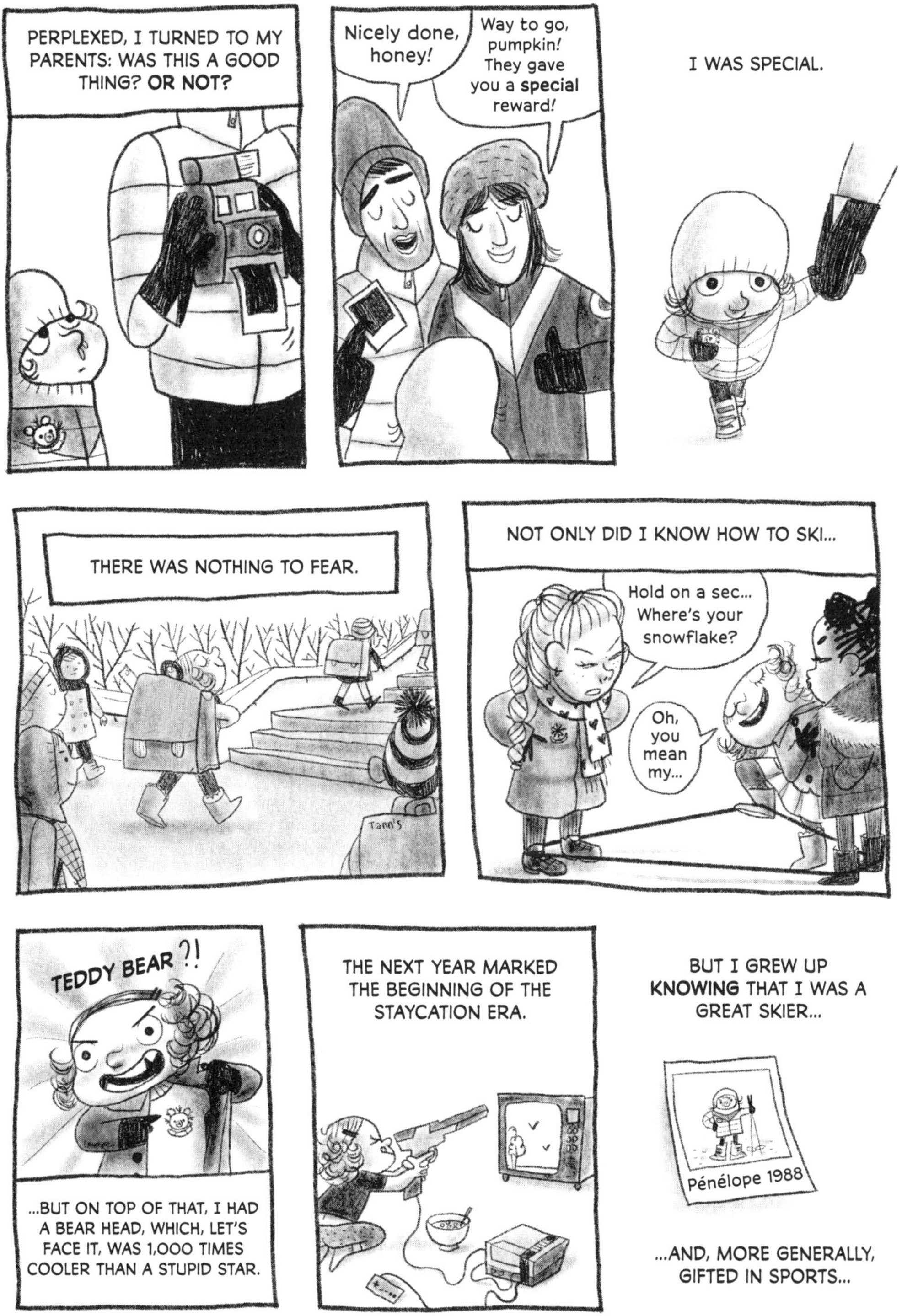
PERPLEXED, I TURNED TO MY PARENTS: WAS THIS A GOOD THING? **OR NOT?**
Nicely done, honey!
Way to go, pumpkin! They gave you a **special** reward!
I WAS SPECIAL.
THERE WAS NOTHING TO FEAR.
Tann's
NOT ONLY DID I KNOW HOW TO SKI...
Hold on a sec... Where's your snowflake?
Oh, you mean my...
TEDDY BEAR ?!
...BUT ON TOP OF THAT, I HAD A BEAR HEAD, WHICH, LET'S FACE IT, WAS 1,000 TIMES COOLER THAN A STUPID STAR.
THE NEXT YEAR MARKED THE BEGINNING OF THE STAYCATION ERA.
BUT I GREW UP **KNOWING** THAT I WAS A GREAT SKIER...
Pénélope 1988
...AND, MORE GENERALLY, GIFTED IN SPORTS...

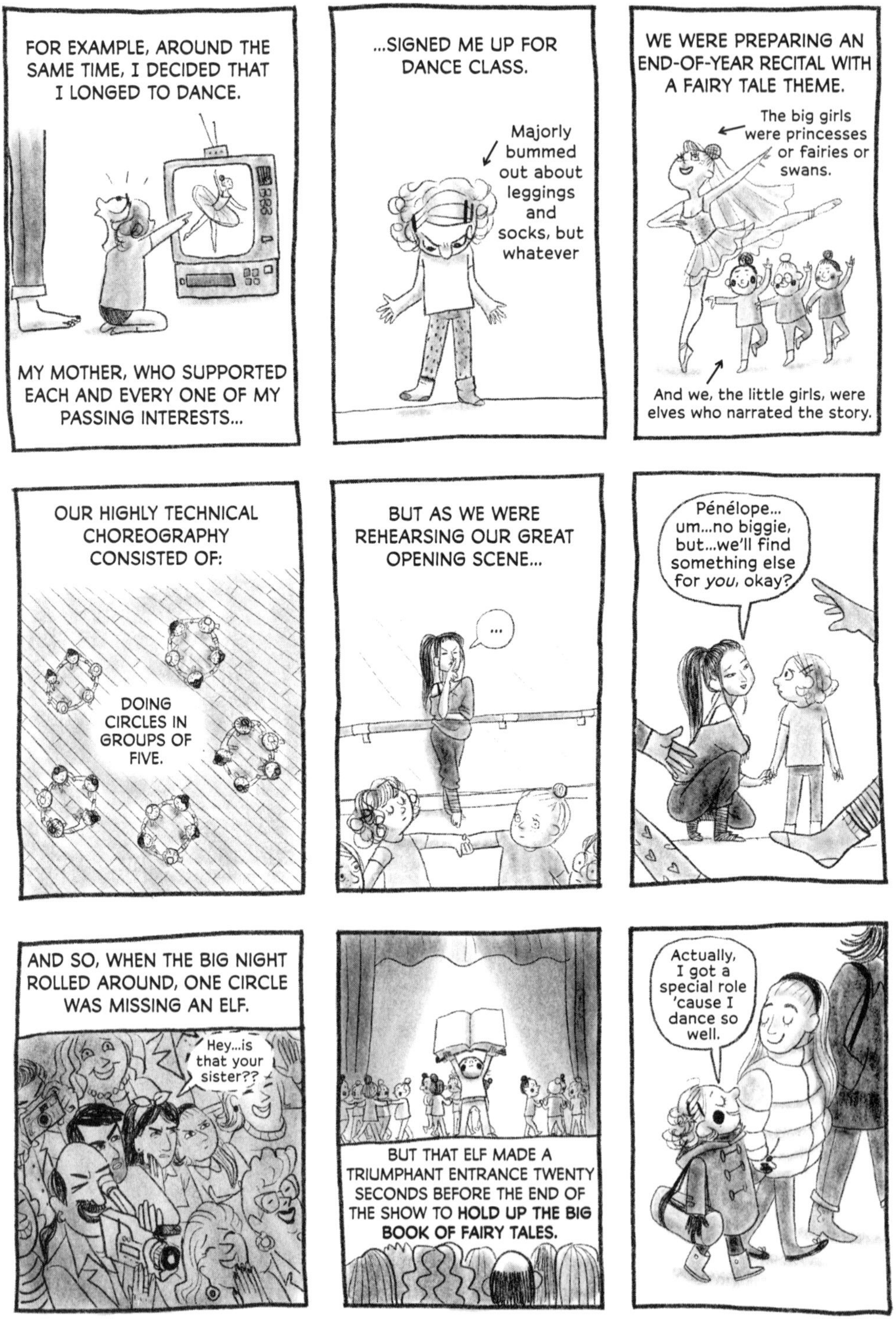
FOR EXAMPLE, AROUND THE SAME TIME, I DECIDED THAT I LONGED TO DANCE.
MY MOTHER, WHO SUPPORTED EACH AND EVERY ONE OF MY PASSING INTERESTS...
...SIGNED ME UP FOR DANCE CLASS.
Majorly bummed out about leggings and socks, but whatever
WE WERE PREPARING AN END-OF-YEAR RECITAL WITH A FAIRY TALE THEME.
The big girls were princesses or fairies or swans.
And we, the little girls, were elves who narrated the story.
OUR HIGHLY TECHNICAL CHOREOGRAPHY CONSISTED OF:
DOING CIRCLES IN GROUPS OF FIVE.
BUT AS WE WERE REHEARSING OUR GREAT OPENING SCENE...
...
Pénélope... um...no biggie, but...we'll find something else for *you*, okay?
AND SO, WHEN THE BIG NIGHT ROLLED AROUND, ONE CIRCLE WAS MISSING AN ELF.
Hey...is that your sister??
BUT THAT ELF MADE A TRIUMPHANT ENTRANCE TWENTY SECONDS BEFORE THE END OF THE SHOW TO **HOLD UP THE BIG BOOK OF FAIRY TALES.**
Actually, I got a special role 'cause I dance so well.

NEVERTHELESS, I SPENT THE REST OF MY LIFE CAREFULLY **AVOIDING** SPORTS. NO CLASSICAL DANCE AT TEN.

I'm sick of this thing, it's giving me a migraine.

ULTIMATELY, NOT MUCH PARTICIPATION IN HIGH SCHOOL GYM CLASS...

You've had your period during swim class four times this month. Maybe go see a doctor.

...AND ADMIRABLE CONSISTENCY AS AN ADULT.

You want to go where? *Pilates??* You think I have *time* for that? I mean seriously!

BUT THEN MY SISTER STARTED RUNNING IN THE MORNINGS, RIGHT PAST MY PLACE, AND IT BECAME A NICE WAY TO SPEND TIME TOGETHER.

First experience of physical exertion (at age thirty)

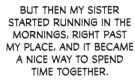

NEEDLESS TO SAY, I HAD NEVER RUN, OR EVEN BROKEN A SWEAT, EXCEPT TO CATCH A BUS. MY BODY HAD LESS THAN 5% MUSCLE MASS, **BUT:**

Yeah, but...I have this... natural ability...for sports... see...

If I really invest myself, I automatically do great.

WHICH IS WHY ONE NIGHT, MY SISTER (DRUNK) ASKED ME:

Hey about we sign up for a marathon

marathon

matrathon

INSTEAD OF SUGGESTING SHE QUIT DRINKING, I REPLIED:

You're on! Let's do it!

(How many miles is that, again?)

12?

AFTER ALL, HOW DIFFERENT COULD IT BE FROM THE SNOWFLAKE?

Double dragon

C

P

ALL I NEEDED TO DO WAS **FOCUS.**

WE TRAINED. WE DID INTERVAL TRAINING AT 7 A.M. IN THE RAIN. WE RAN, AND WE CROSSED THE FINISH LINE TOGETHER.

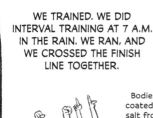

Bodies coated in salt from evaporated sweat

I ALMOST DIED, I ALMOST PUKED, MY RUN TIME WAS LOUSY, MY POOR JELL-O BODY DIDN'T UNDERSTAND WHY I WAS PUNISHING IT.

One month in a splint

BUT TO BE PERFECTLY HONEST, I NEVER ONCE DOUBTED I COULD DO IT—NOT FOR A **SINGLE MOMENT.**

(A month with that on, too)

How could I fail? It's simple. Sports is all about mindset.... My mind's stronger than my body. Makes sense, right...?

ONE DAY, I HIT THE SLOPES AGAIN WITH SOME FRIENDS.

Did you guys go to ski school?

A little. Yeah.

Remember how **proud** we were with our snowflakes?

Even though it was so easy, you mean?

Haha, yeah, you just had to, like, put on your skis, take them off, and do the plow!

Haha, totally, they practically **gave** it to you!

Oh, and remember that fake prize they made up for the losers? What was it called, again?

Ha ha, oh, yeaah, wait.

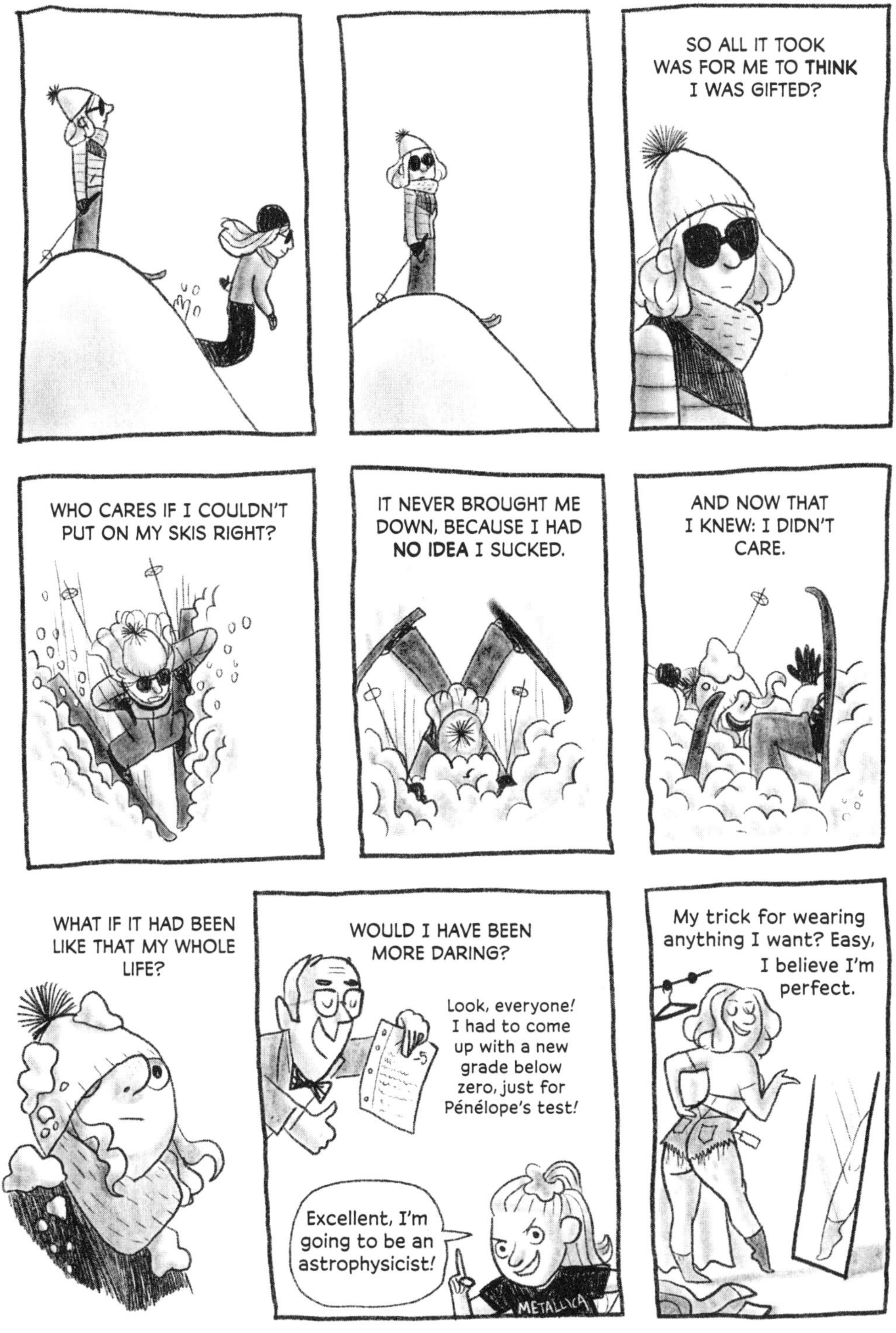
SO ALL IT TOOK WAS FOR ME TO **THINK** I WAS GIFTED?
WHO CARES IF I COULDN'T PUT ON MY SKIS RIGHT?
IT NEVER BROUGHT ME DOWN, BECAUSE I HAD **NO IDEA** I SUCKED.
AND NOW THAT I KNEW: I DIDN'T CARE.
WHAT IF IT HAD BEEN LIKE THAT MY WHOLE LIFE?
WOULD I HAVE BEEN MORE DARING?
Look, everyone! I had to come up with a new grade below zero, just for Pénélope's test!
-5
Excellent, I'm going to be an astrophysicist!
METALLICA
My trick for wearing anything I want? Easy, I believe I'm perfect.

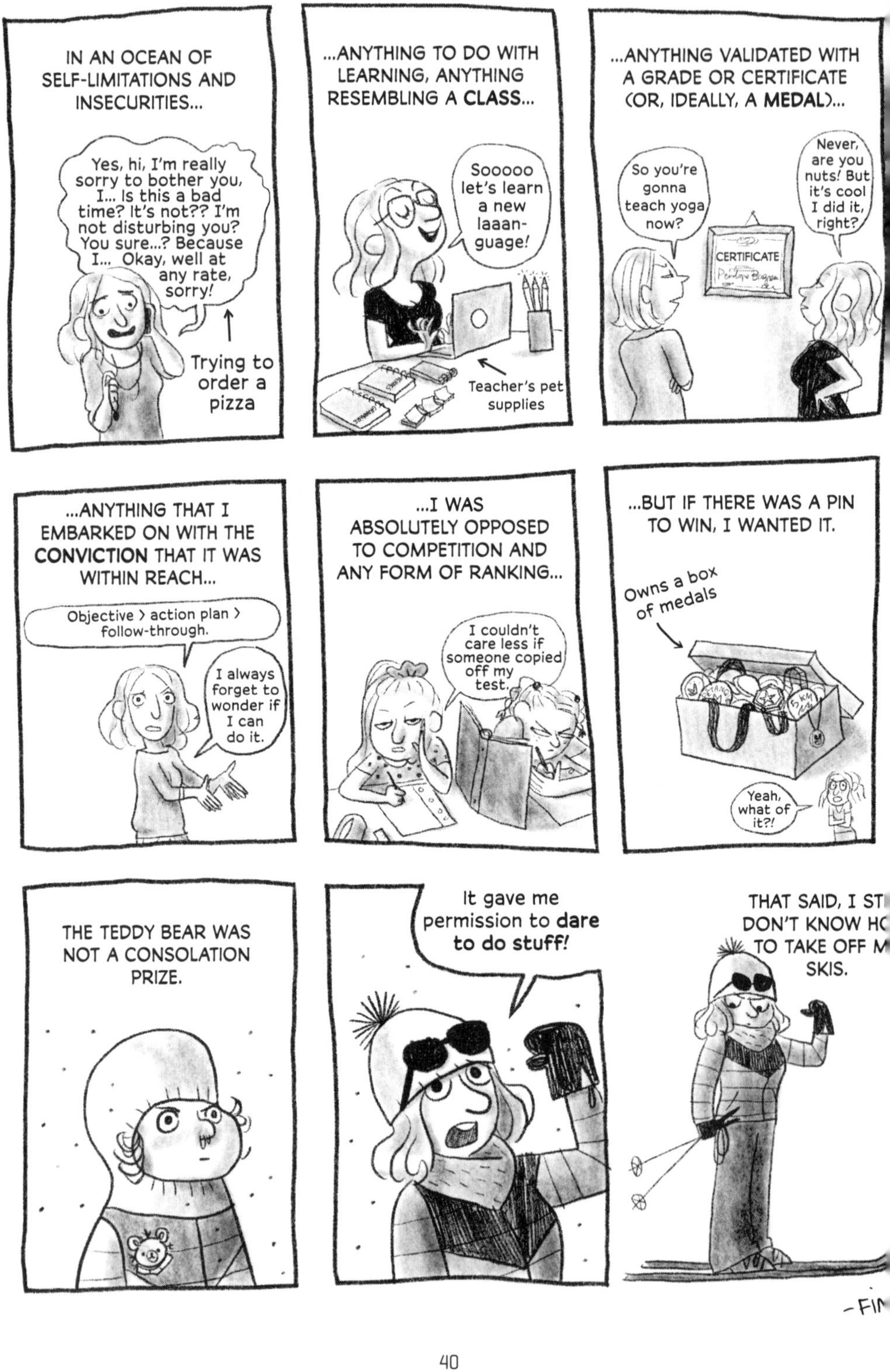
IN AN OCEAN OF SELF-LIMITATIONS AND INSECURITIES...
Yes, hi, I'm really sorry to bother you, I... Is this a bad time? It's not?? I'm not disturbing you? You sure...? Because I... Okay, well at any rate, sorry!
Trying to order a pizza
...ANYTHING TO DO WITH LEARNING, ANYTHING RESEMBLING A CLASS...
Sooooo let's learn a new laaan-guage!
Teacher's pet supplies
...ANYTHING VALIDATED WITH A GRADE OR CERTIFICATE (OR, IDEALLY, A MEDAL)...
So you're gonna teach yoga now?
CERTIFICATE
Never, are you nuts! But it's cool I did it, right?
...ANYTHING THAT I EMBARKED ON WITH THE CONVICTION THAT IT WAS WITHIN REACH...
Objective › action plan › follow-through.
I always forget to wonder if I can do it.
...I WAS ABSOLUTELY OPPOSED TO COMPETITION AND ANY FORM OF RANKING...
I couldn't care less if someone copied off my test.
...BUT IF THERE WAS A PIN TO WIN, I WANTED IT.
Owns a box of medals
Yeah, what of it?!
THE TEDDY BEAR WAS NOT A CONSOLATION PRIZE.
It gave me permission to dare to do stuff!
THAT SAID, I ST DON'T KNOW HC TO TAKE OFF M SKIS.
-FIN

DÉJÀ VU

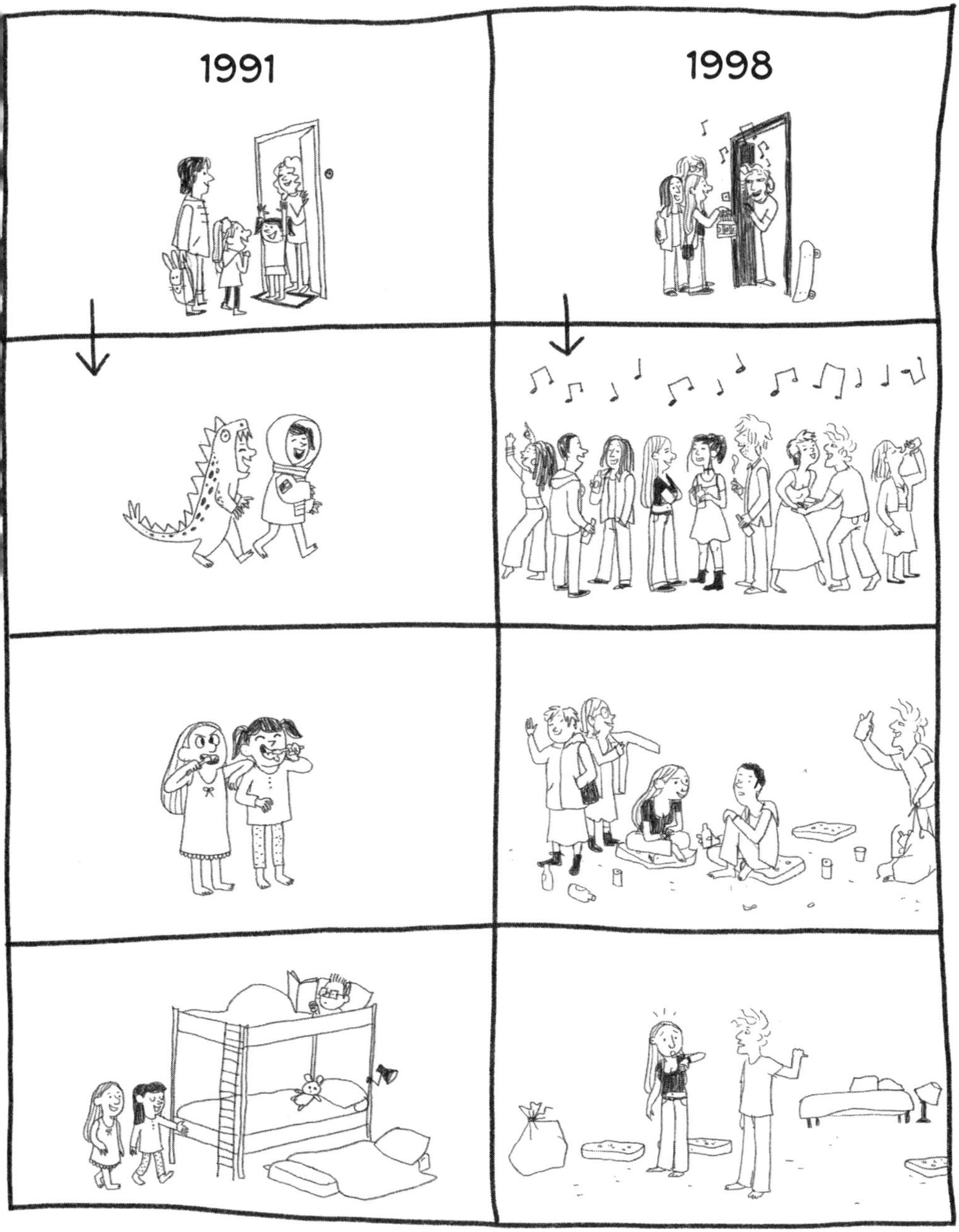
1991
1998

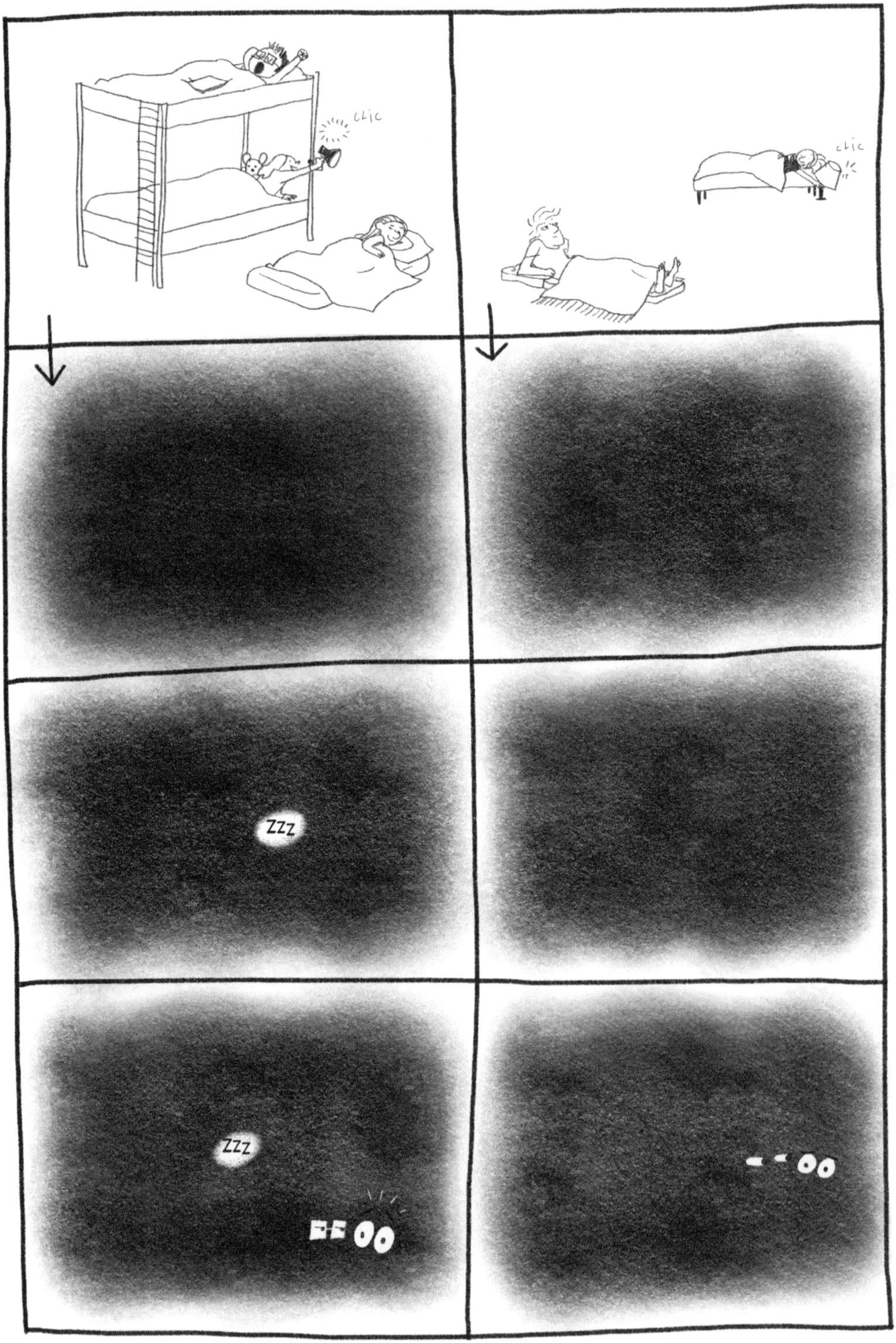
CLIC
CLIC
ZZZ
ZZZ

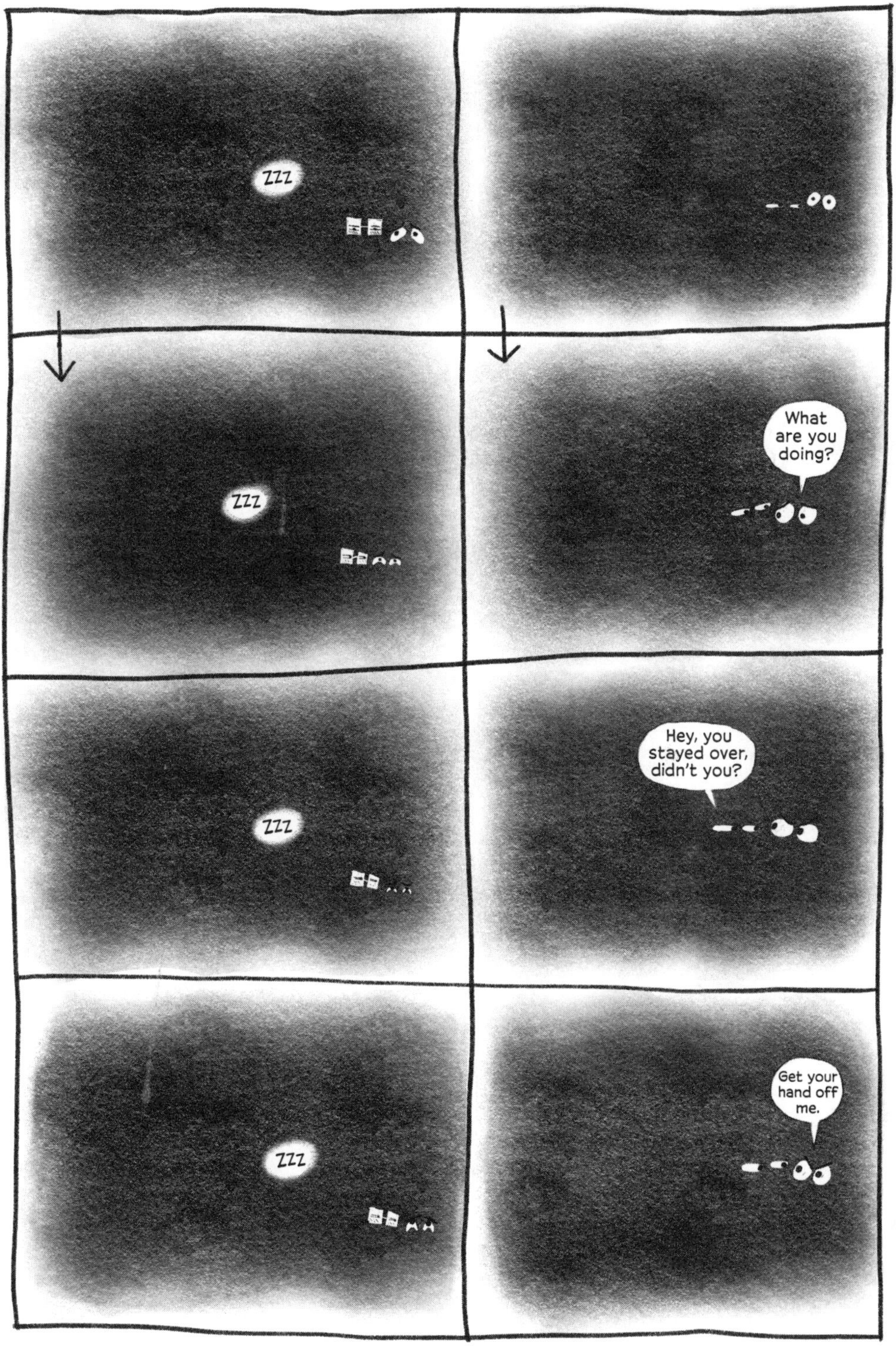
ZZZ
ZZZ
What are you doing?
ZZZ
Hey, you stayed over, didn't you?
ZZZ
Get your hand off me.

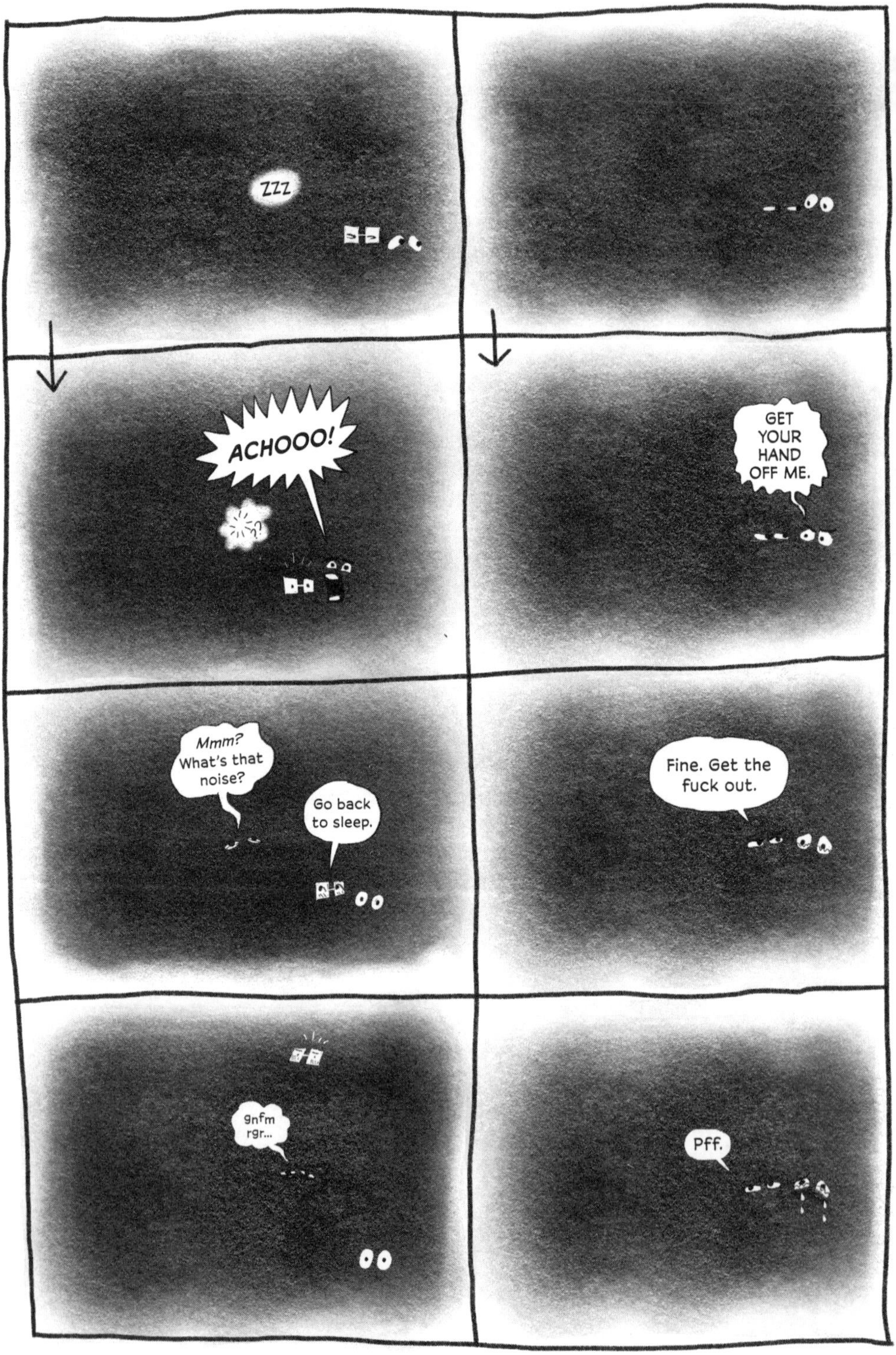

ZZZ
ACHOOO!
GET YOUR HAND OFF ME.
Mmm? What's that noise?
Go back to sleep.
Fine. Get the fuck out.
gnfm rgr...
Pff.

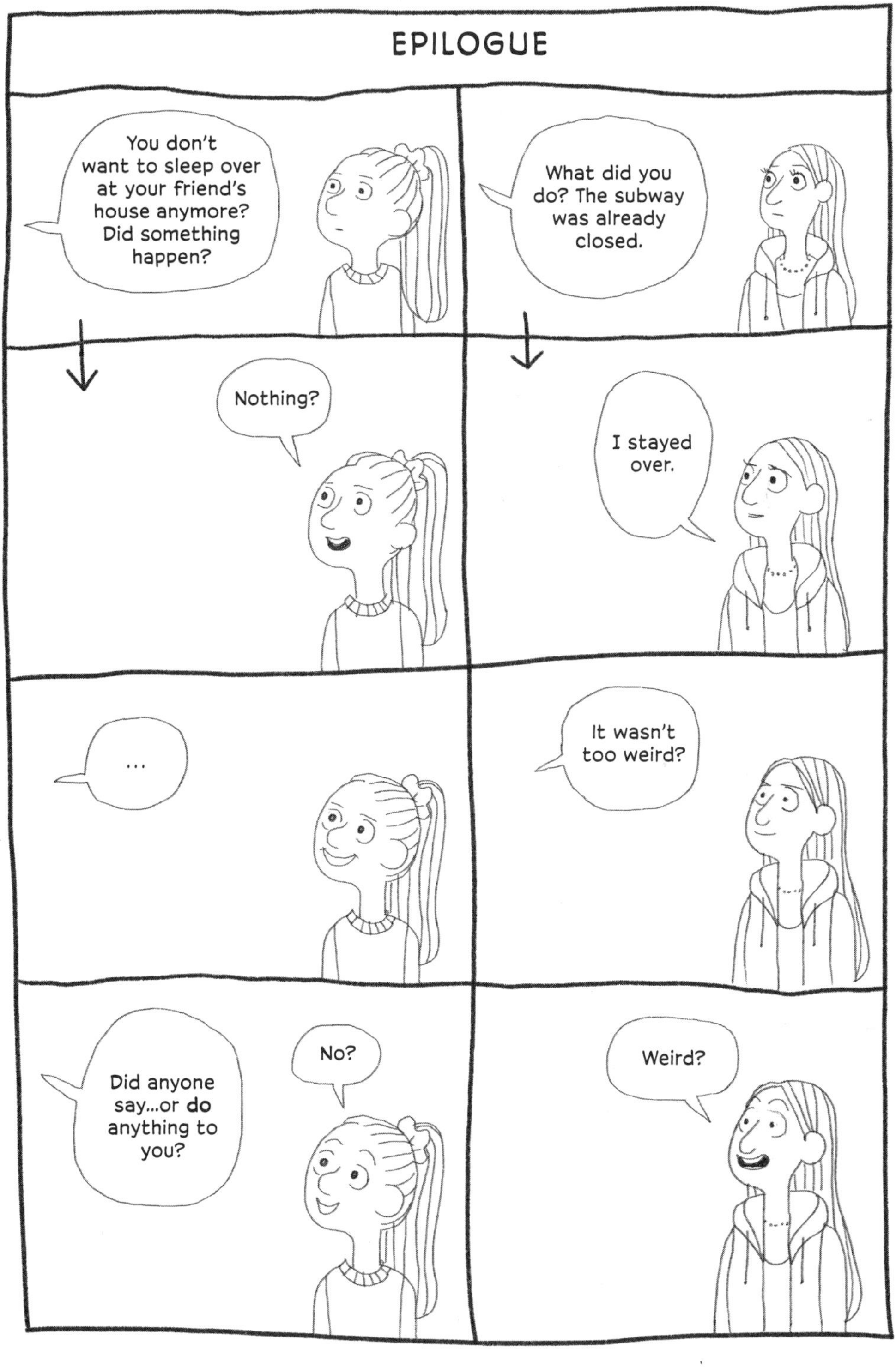
EPILOGUE
You don't want to sleep over at your friend's house anymore? Did something happen?
Nothing?
What did you do? The subway was already closed.
I stayed over.
...
It wasn't too weird?
Did anyone say...or do anything to you?
No?
Weird?

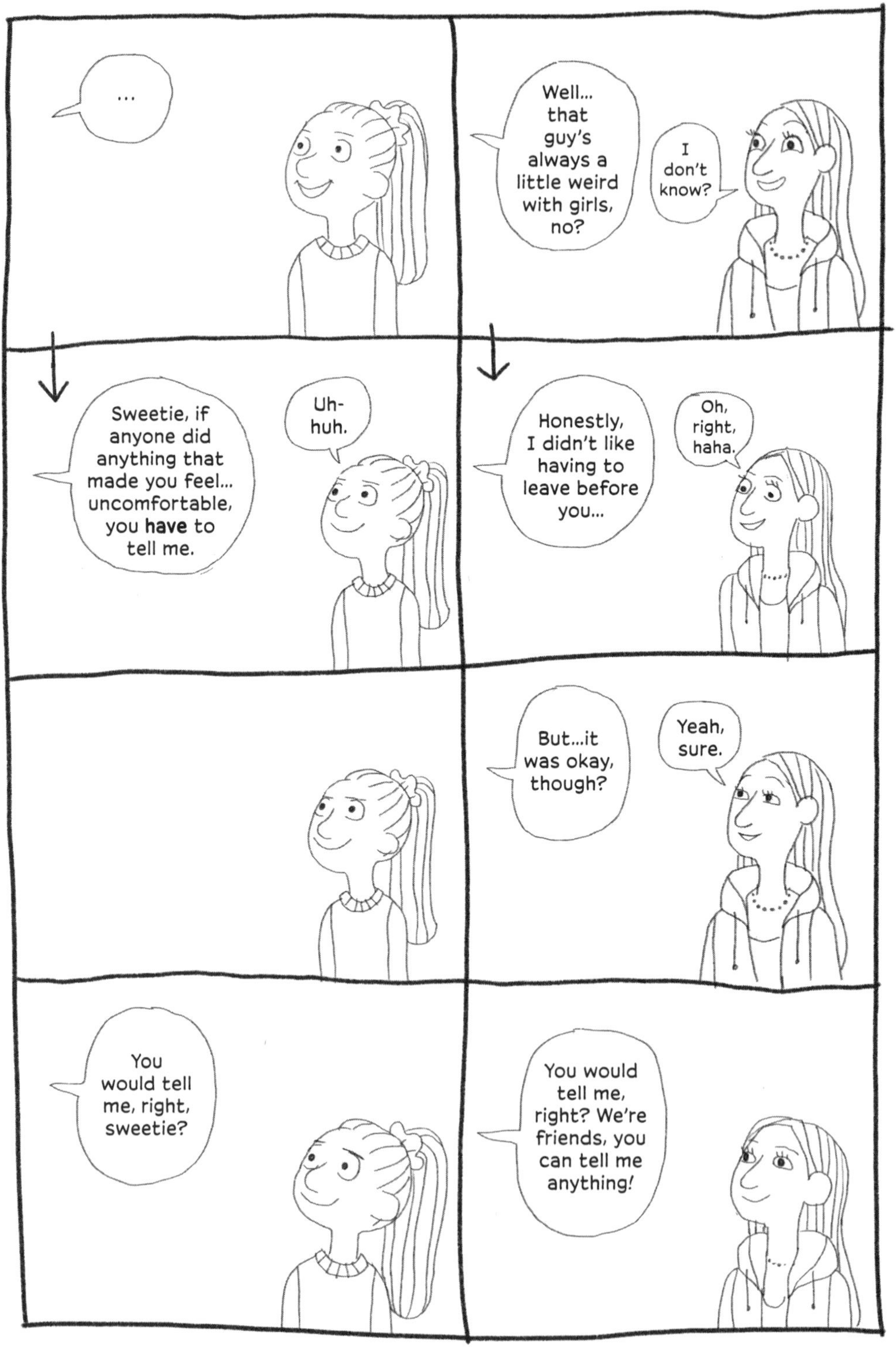
...
Well... that guy's always a little weird with girls, no?
I don't know?
Sweetie, if anyone did anything that made you feel... uncomfortable, you **have** to tell me.
Uh-huh.
Honestly, I didn't like having to leave before you...
Oh, right, haha.
But...it was okay, though?
Yeah, sure.
You would tell me, right, sweetie?
You would tell me, right? We're friends, you can tell me anything!

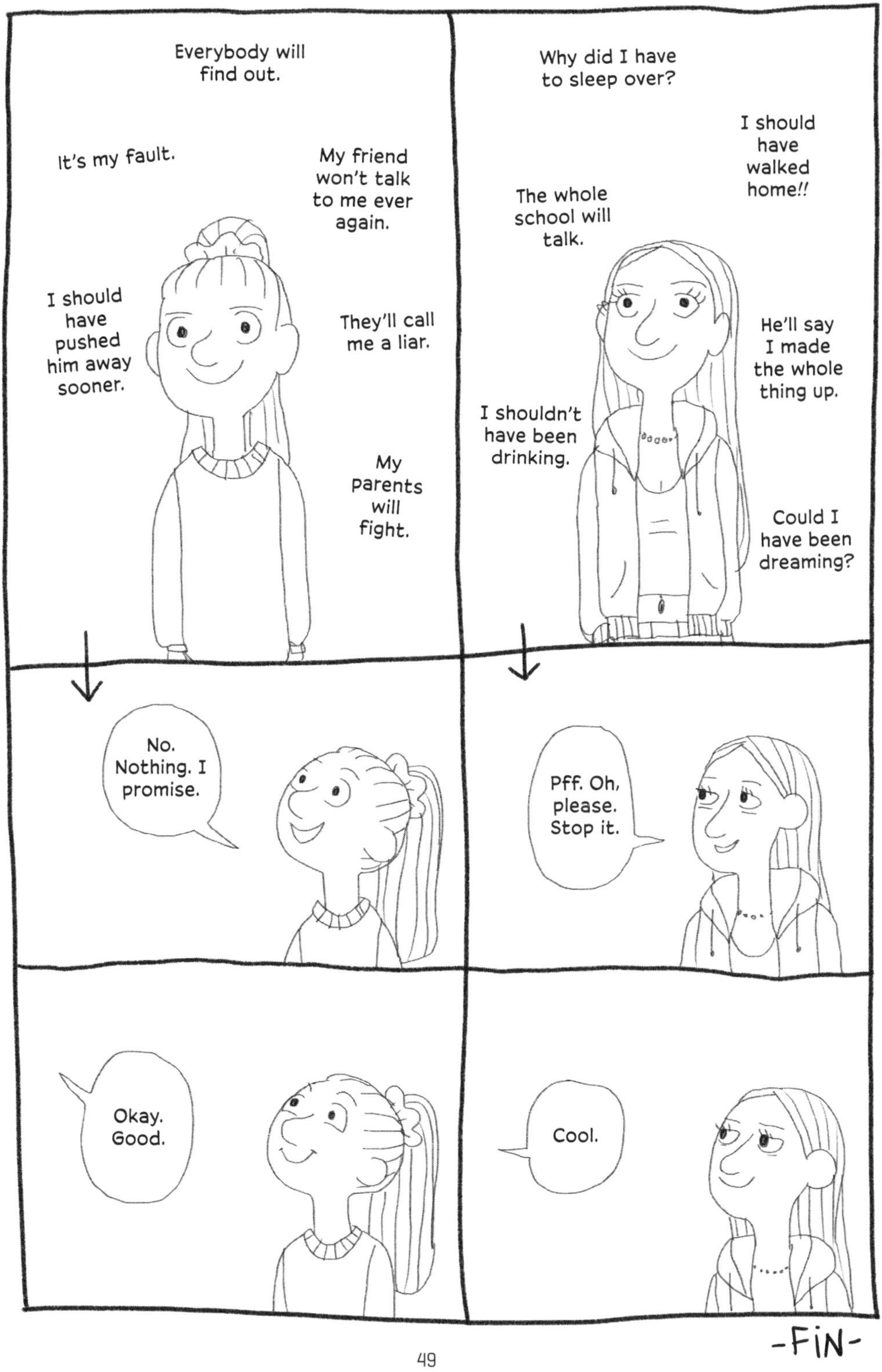
Everybody will find out.
It's my fault.
My friend won't talk to me ever again.
I should have pushed him away sooner.
They'll call me a liar.
My parents will fight.
Why did I have to sleep over?
I should have walked home!!
The whole school will talk.
He'll say I made the whole thing up.
I shouldn't have been drinking.
Could I have been dreaming?
No. Nothing. I promise.
Pff. Oh, please. Stop it.
Okay. Good.
Cool.
-FiN-

A STORY ABOUT MY FINGERS

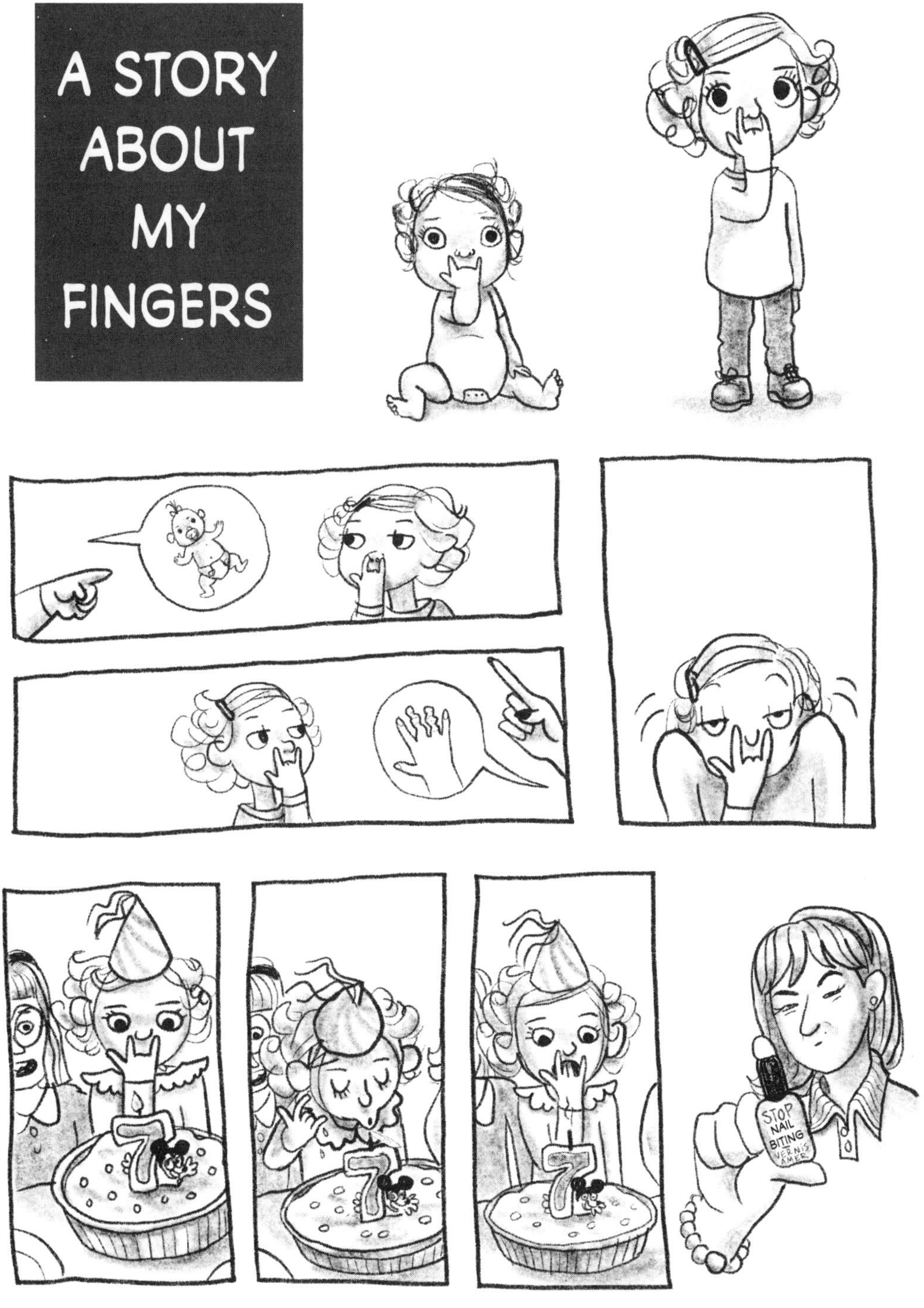
STOP NAIL BITING
VERNIS AMER

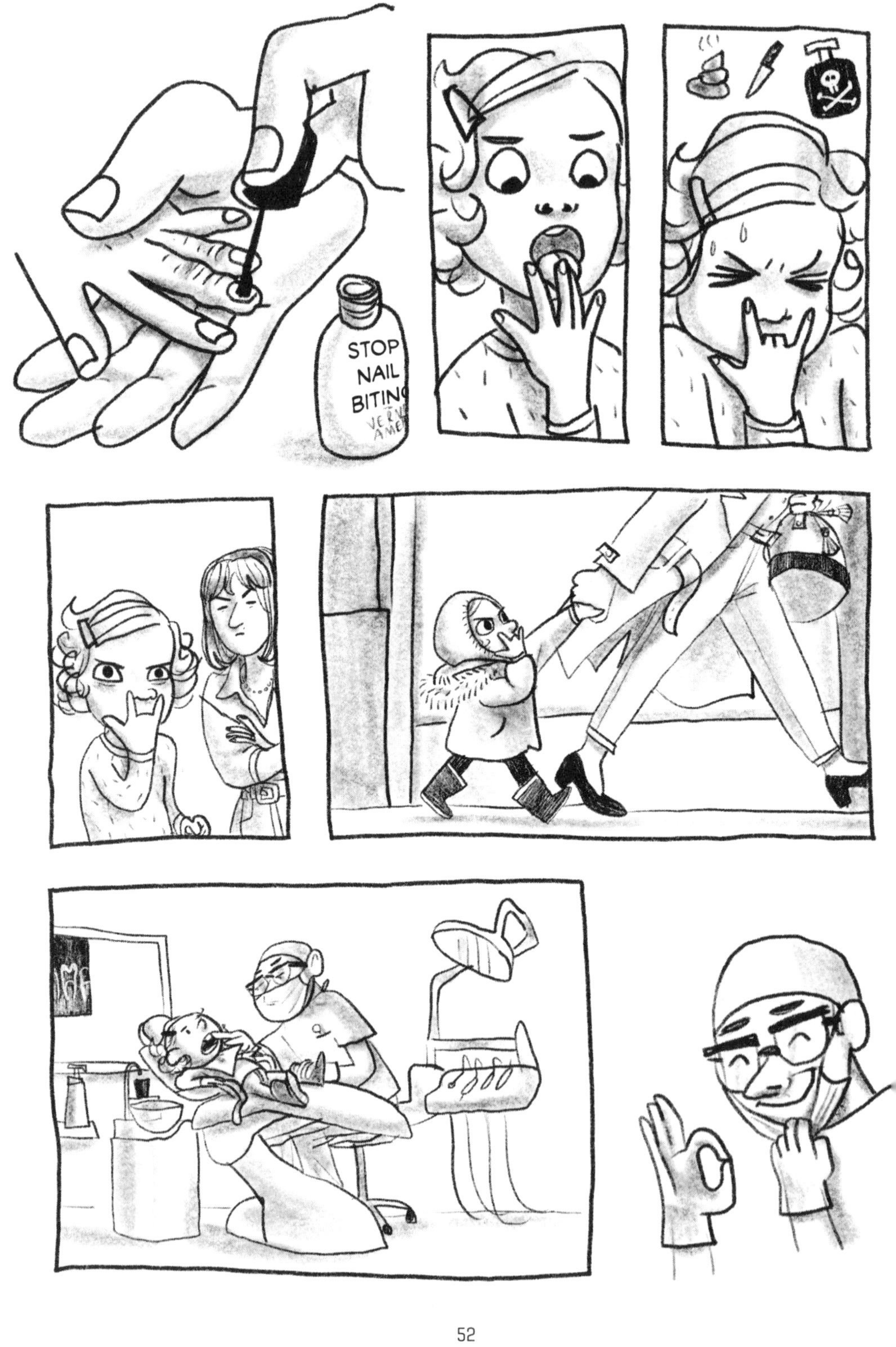
STOP
NAIL
BITING

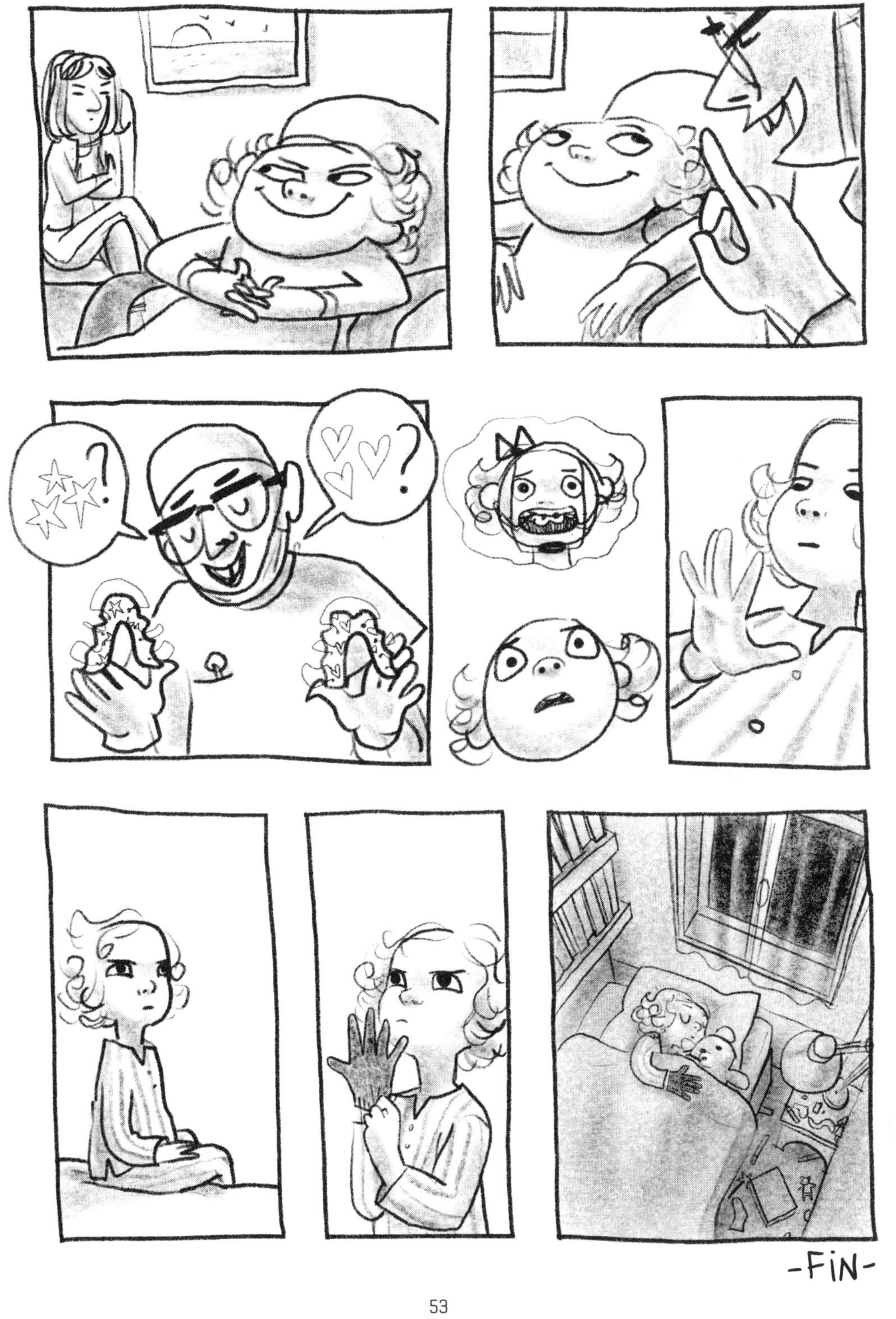
?
?

-FIN-

VALIDATION

EVERY ERA HAS ITS FORM OF SOCIETAL PRESSURE INFLICTED ON YOUNG GIRLS. ME, I GREW UP WITH THE 32C.

Your not-so-secret weapon. The one and only WonderBra.

OK!

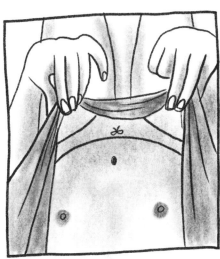

BOYS IN SCHOOL RANKED US BY BOOB SIZE.

Girls in 8th grade Class B

I DIDN'T EVEN MAKE THE FLIP SIDE OF THE LIST.

THE GIRLS WHO WORE BRAS MADE SURE THEY WERE VISIBLE.

LONG SIGH

MEANWHILE, UNDER MY OWN T-SHIRT: **ZILCH.** NOT THE SLIGHTEST LITTLE BUMP.

Big baby belly (unfortunate)

DON'T TOUCH

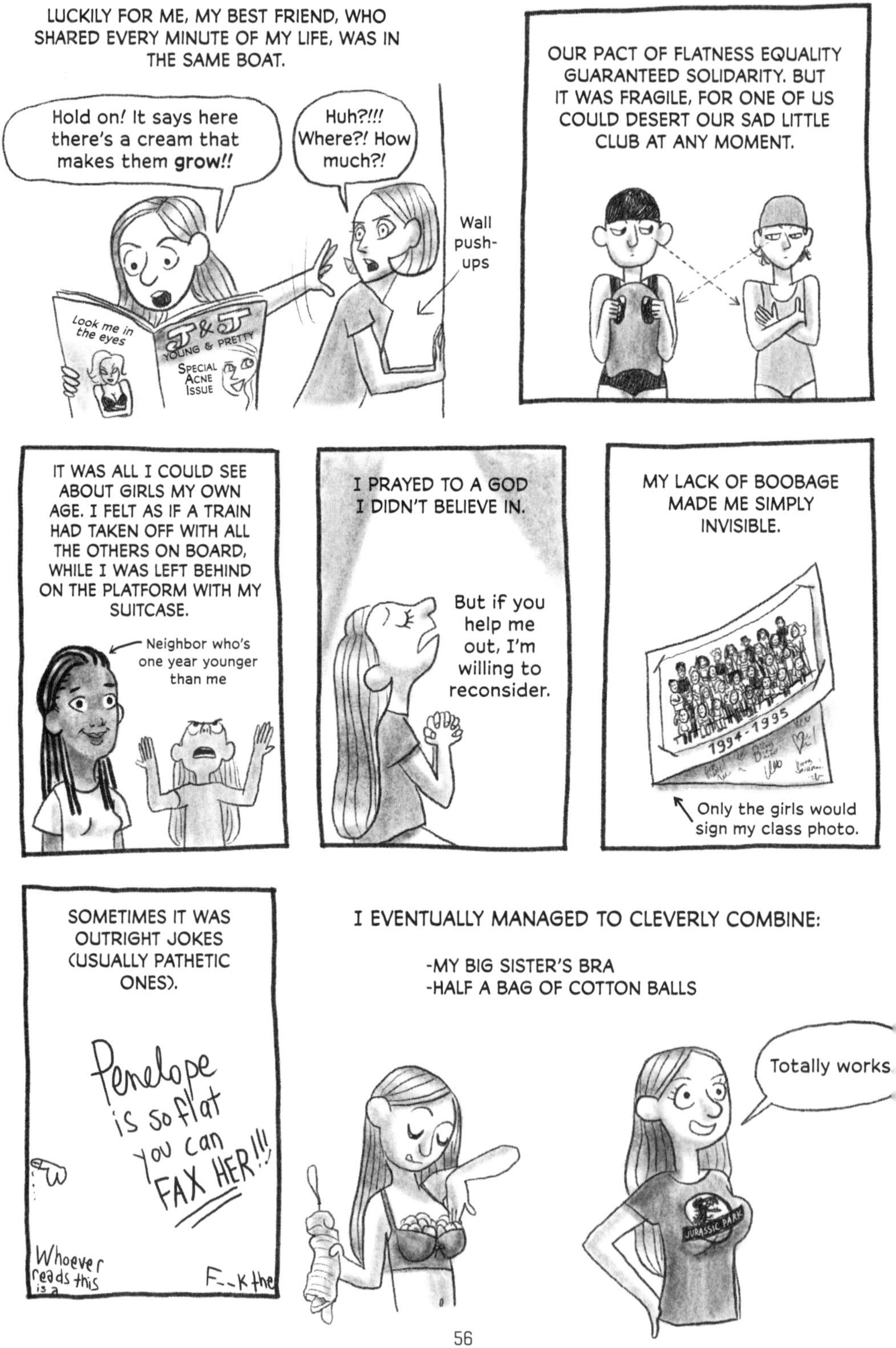

LUCKILY FOR ME, MY BEST FRIEND, WHO SHARED EVERY MINUTE OF MY LIFE, WAS IN THE SAME BOAT.
Hold on! It says here there's a cream that makes them **grow**!!
Huh?!!! Where?! How much?!
Look me in the eyes
J&J YOUNG & PRETTY
SPECIAL ACNE ISSUE
Wall push-ups
OUR PACT OF FLATNESS EQUALITY GUARANTEED SOLIDARITY. BUT IT WAS FRAGILE, FOR ONE OF US COULD DESERT OUR SAD LITTLE CLUB AT ANY MOMENT.
IT WAS ALL I COULD SEE ABOUT GIRLS MY OWN AGE. I FELT AS IF A TRAIN HAD TAKEN OFF WITH ALL THE OTHERS ON BOARD, WHILE I WAS LEFT BEHIND ON THE PLATFORM WITH MY SUITCASE.
Neighbor who's one year younger than me
I PRAYED TO A GOD I DIDN'T BELIEVE IN.
But if you help me out, I'm willing to reconsider.
MY LACK OF BOOBAGE MADE ME SIMPLY INVISIBLE.
1994-1995
Only the girls would sign my class photo.
SOMETIMES IT WAS OUTRIGHT JOKES (USUALLY PATHETIC ONES).
Penelope is so flat you can FAX HER!!!
Whoever reads this is a
F--k the
I EVENTUALLY MANAGED TO CLEVERLY COMBINE:
-MY BIG SISTER'S BRA
-HALF A BAG OF COTTON BALLS
Totally works.
JURASSIC PARK

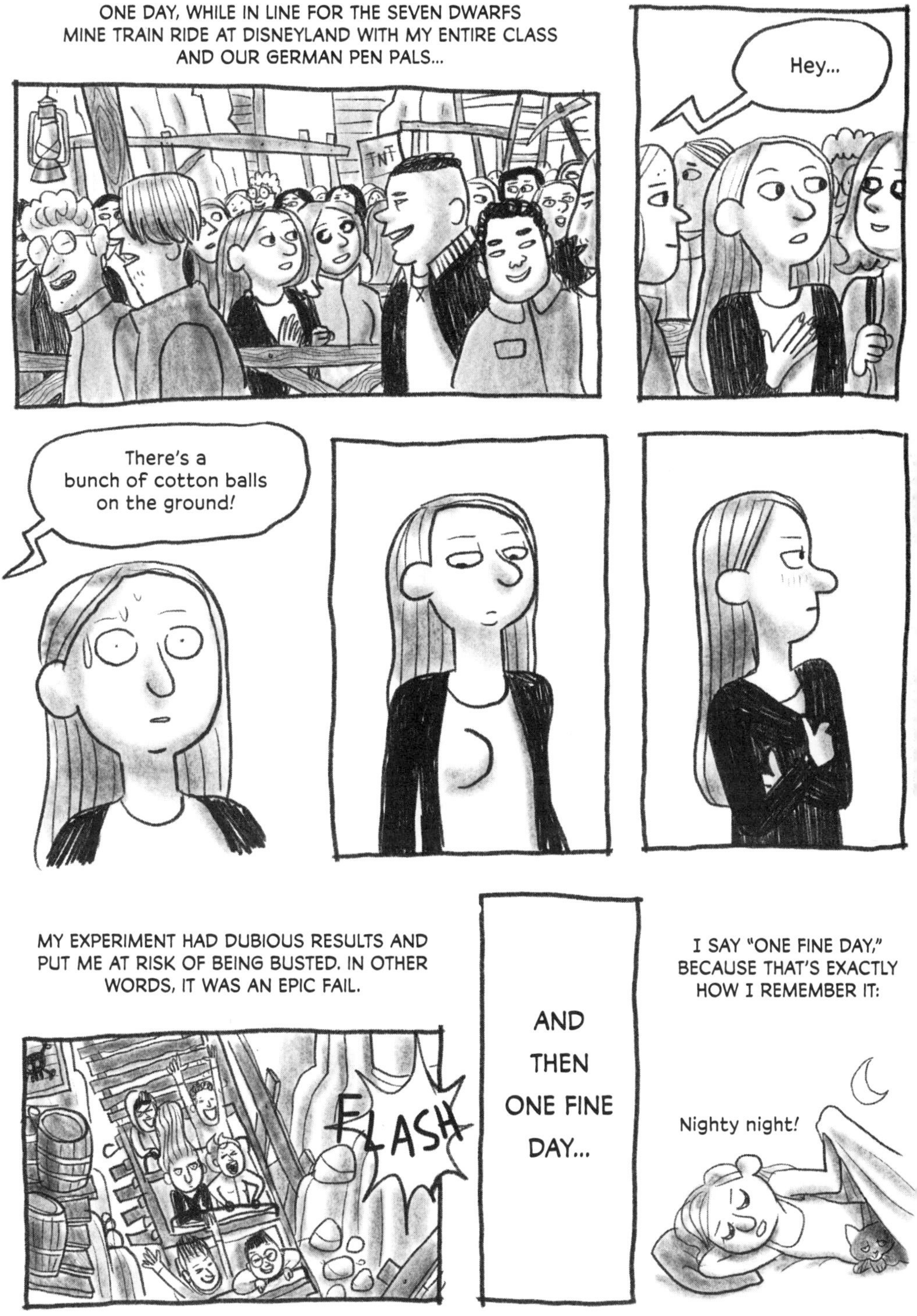
ONE DAY, WHILE IN LINE FOR THE SEVEN DWARFS MINE TRAIN RIDE AT DISNEYLAND WITH MY ENTIRE CLASS AND OUR GERMAN PEN PALS...
TNT
Hey...
There's a bunch of cotton balls on the ground!
MY EXPERIMENT HAD DUBIOUS RESULTS AND PUT ME AT RISK OF BEING BUSTED. IN OTHER WORDS, IT WAS AN EPIC FAIL.
FLASH
AND THEN ONE FINE DAY...
I SAY "ONE FINE DAY," BECAUSE THAT'S EXACTLY HOW I REMEMBER IT:
Nighty night!

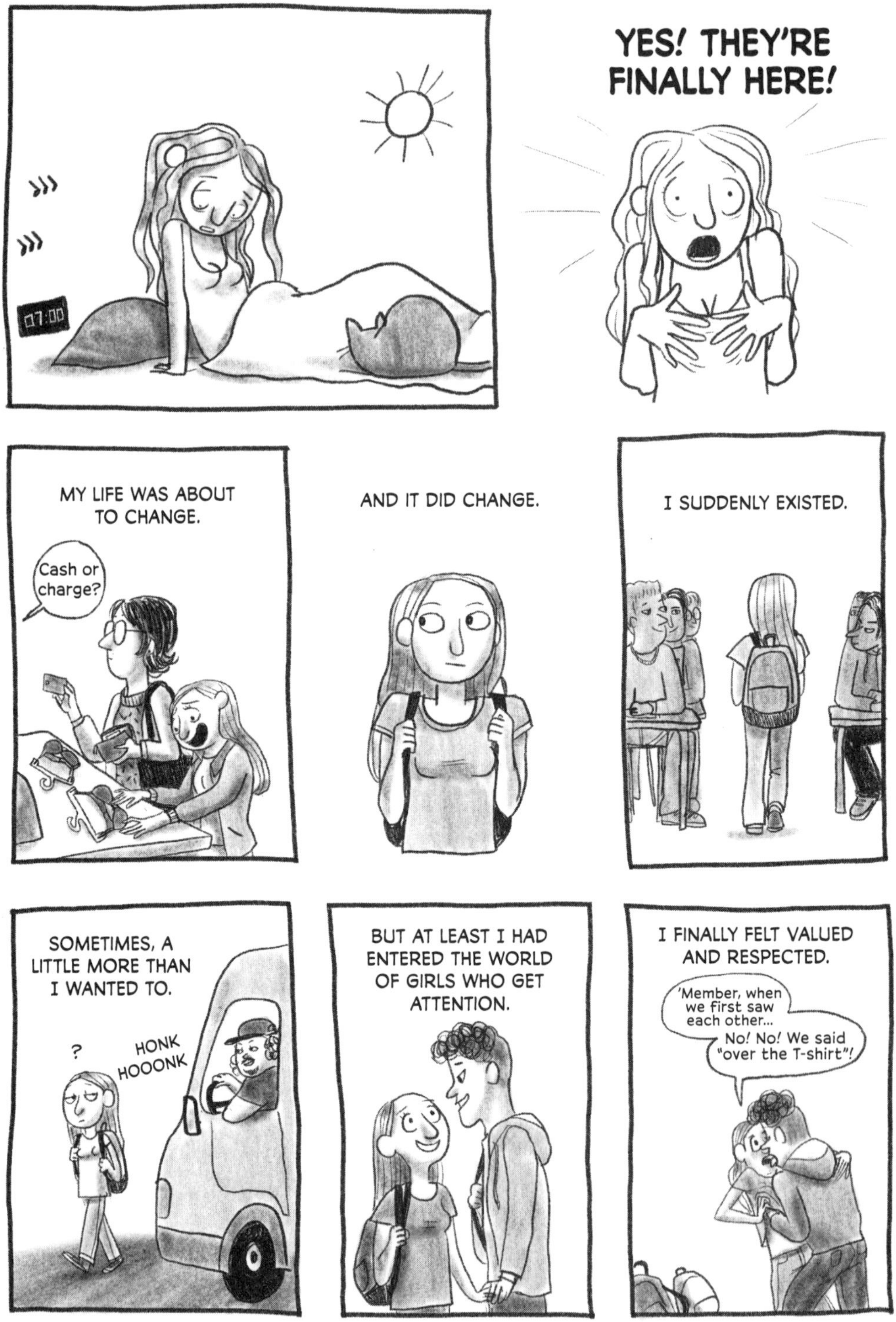

07:00
YES! THEY'RE FINALLY HERE!
MY LIFE WAS ABOUT TO CHANGE.
Cash or charge?
AND IT DID CHANGE.
I SUDDENLY EXISTED.
SOMETIMES, A LITTLE MORE THAN I WANTED TO.
?
HONK HOOONK
BUT AT LEAST I HAD ENTERED THE WORLD OF GIRLS WHO GET ATTENTION.
I FINALLY FELT VALUED AND RESPECTED.
'Member, when we first saw each other...
No! No! We said "over the T-shirt"!

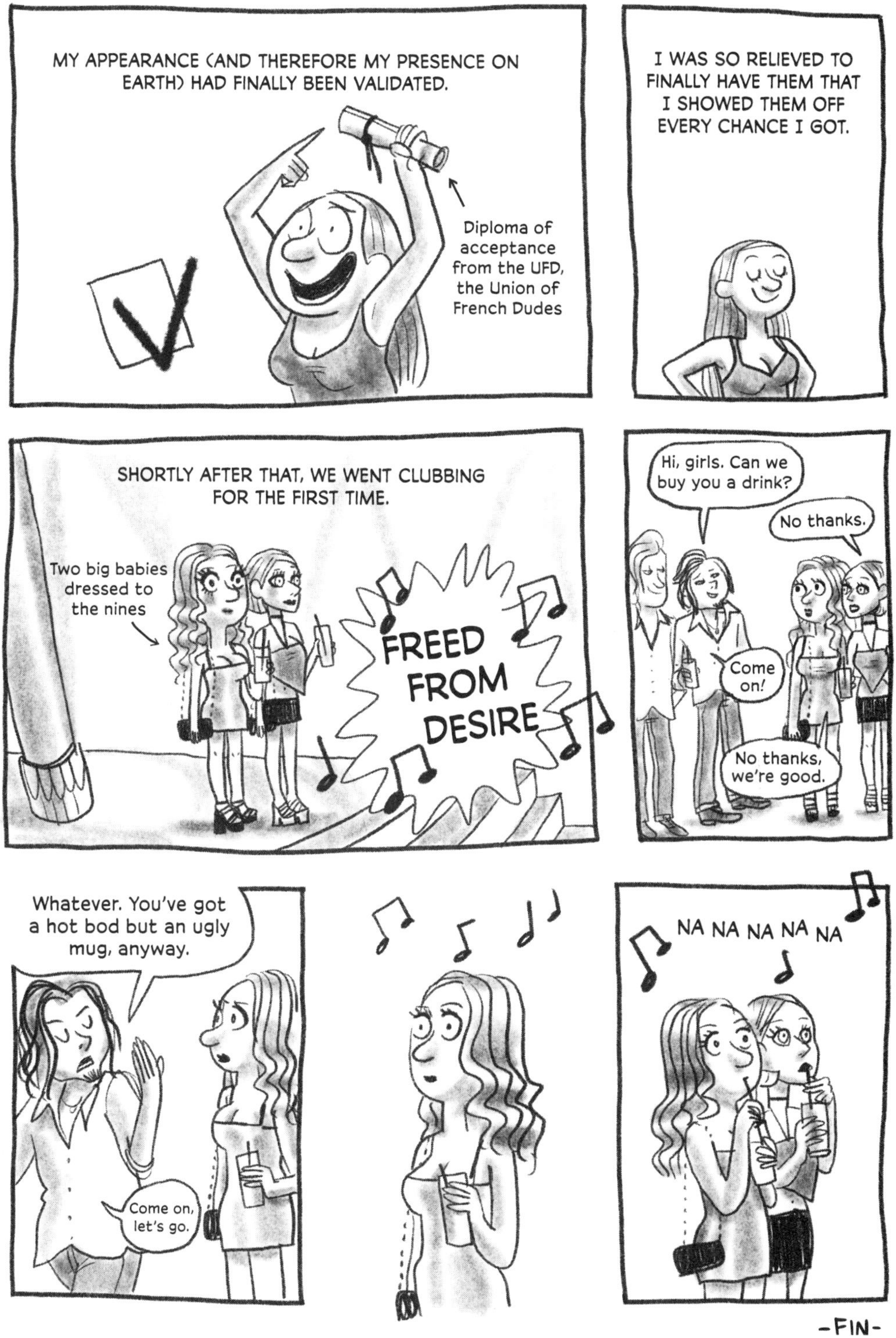

MY APPEARANCE (AND THEREFORE MY PRESENCE ON EARTH) HAD FINALLY BEEN VALIDATED.
Diploma of acceptance from the UFD, the Union of French Dudes
I WAS SO RELIEVED TO FINALLY HAVE THEM THAT I SHOWED THEM OFF EVERY CHANCE I GOT.
SHORTLY AFTER THAT, WE WENT CLUBBING FOR THE FIRST TIME.
Two big babies dressed to the nines
FREED FROM DESIRE
Hi, girls. Can we buy you a drink?
No thanks.
Come on!
No thanks, we're good.
Whatever. You've got a hot bod but an ugly mug, anyway.
Come on, let's go.
NA NA NA NA NA
-FIN-

Three Days

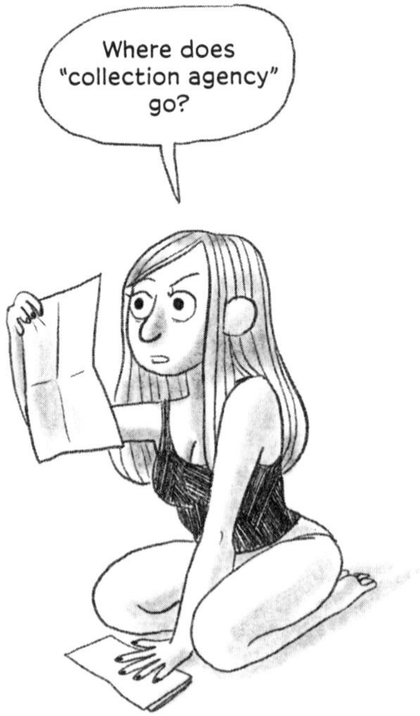
Where does "collection agency" go?

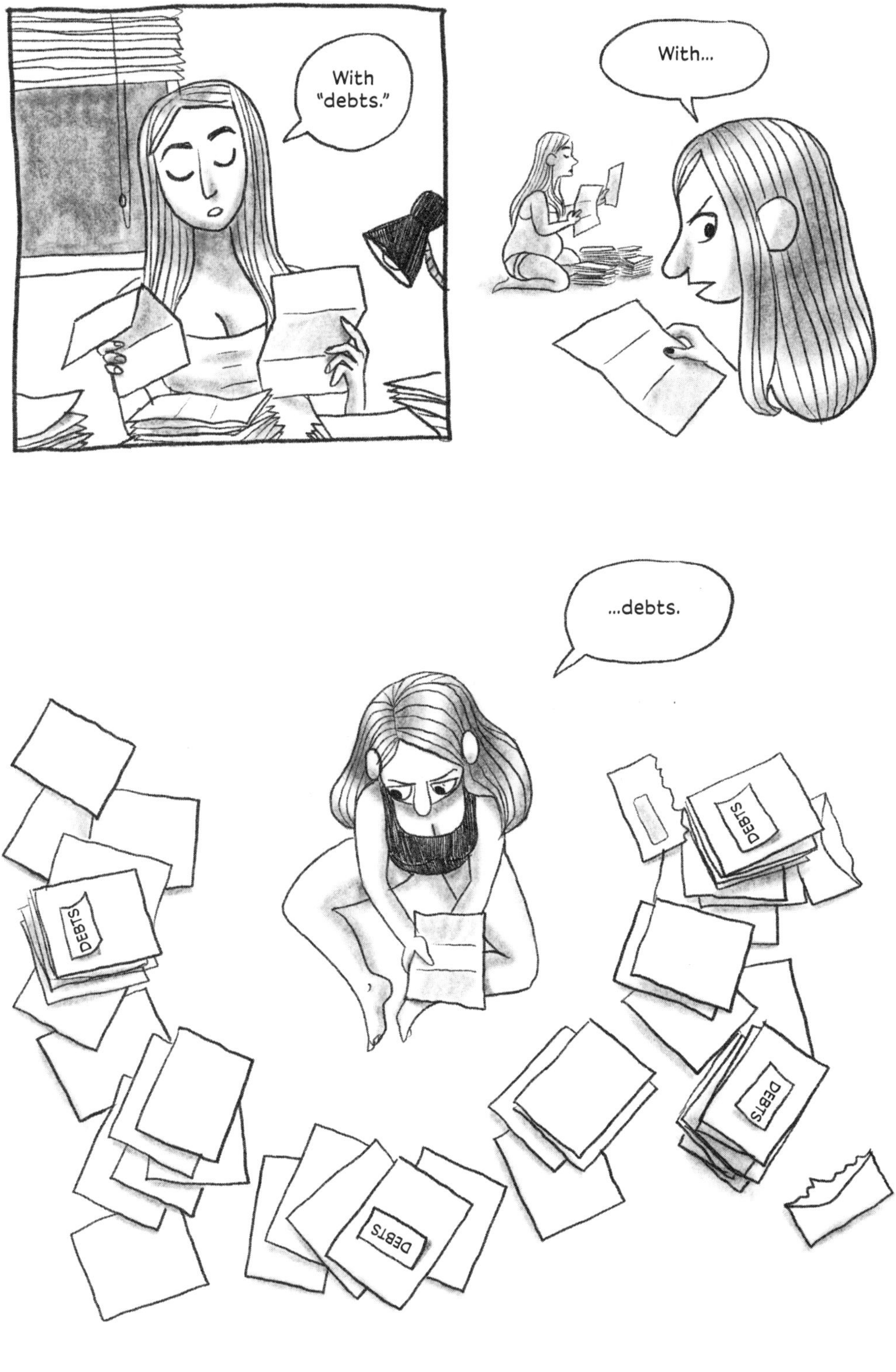
With "debts."
With...
...debts.
DEBTS
DEBTS
DEBTS
DEBTS

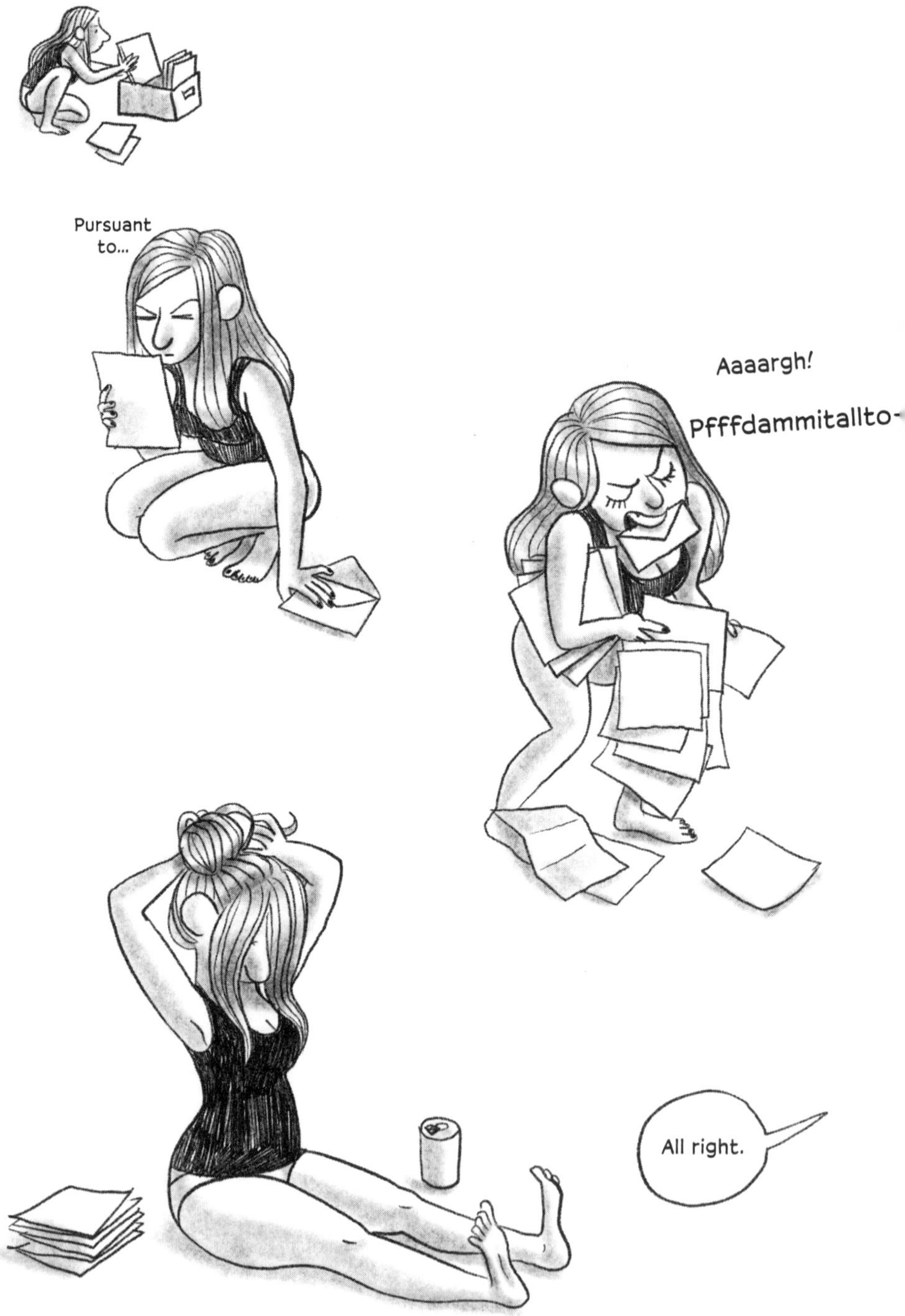
Pursuant to...
Aaaargh!
Pfffdammitallto-
All right.

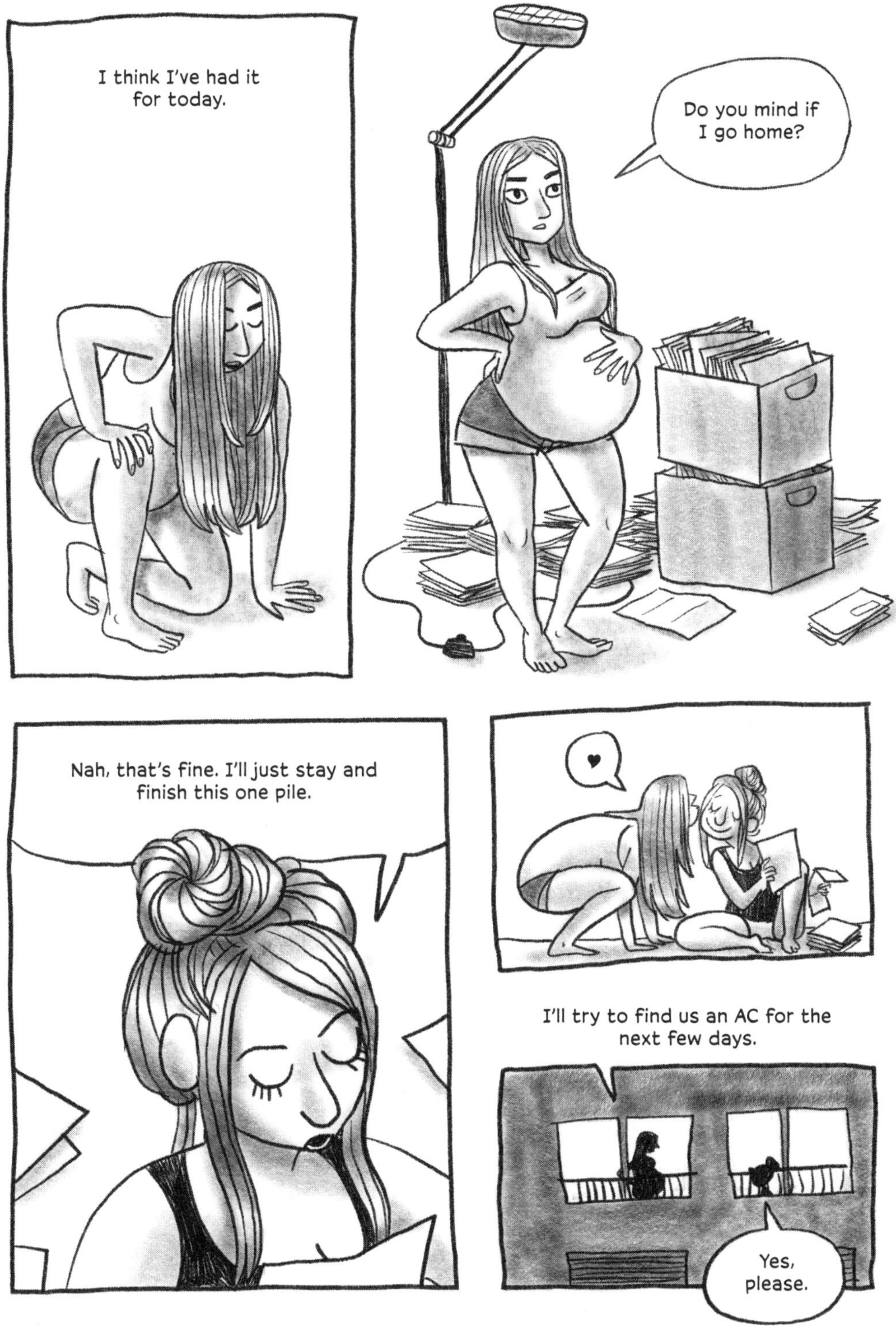
I think I've had it for today.
Do you mind if I go home?
Nah, that's fine. I'll just stay and finish this one pile.
I'll try to find us an AC for the next few days.
Yes, please.

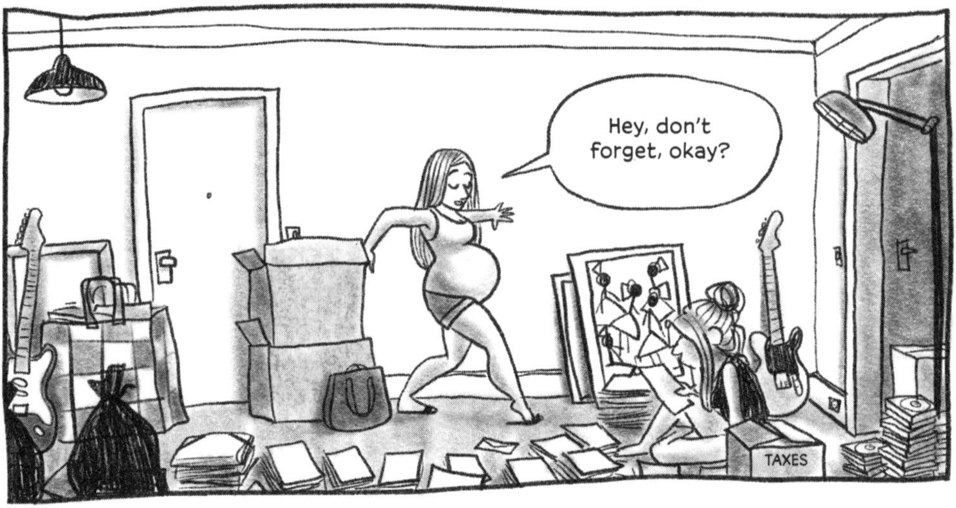
Hey, don't
forget, okay?
TAXES

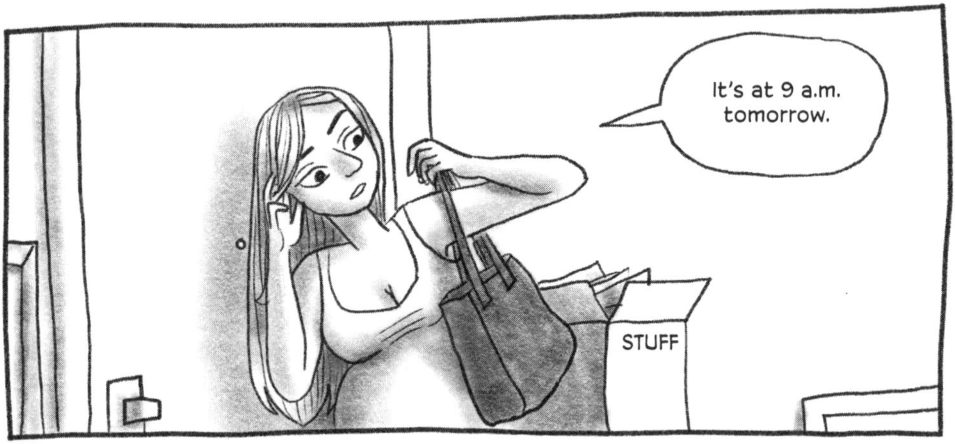
It's at 9 a.m.
tomorrow.
STUFF

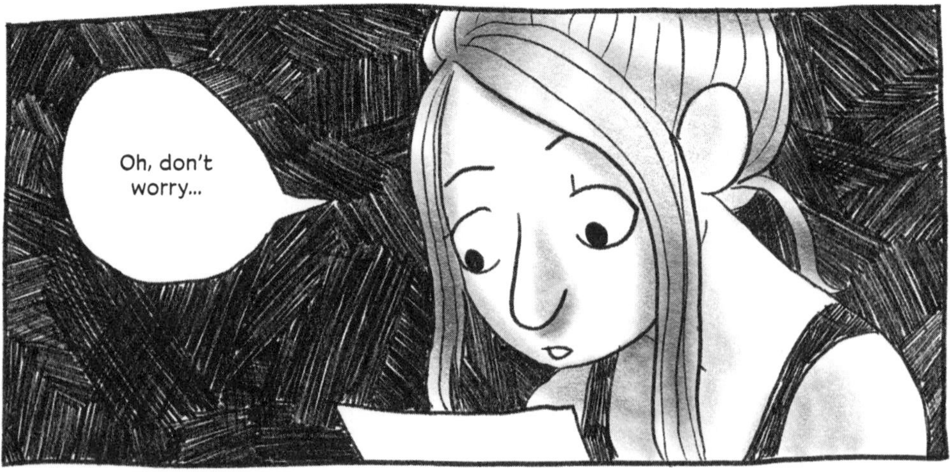
Oh, don't
worry...

How could I possibly
forget?

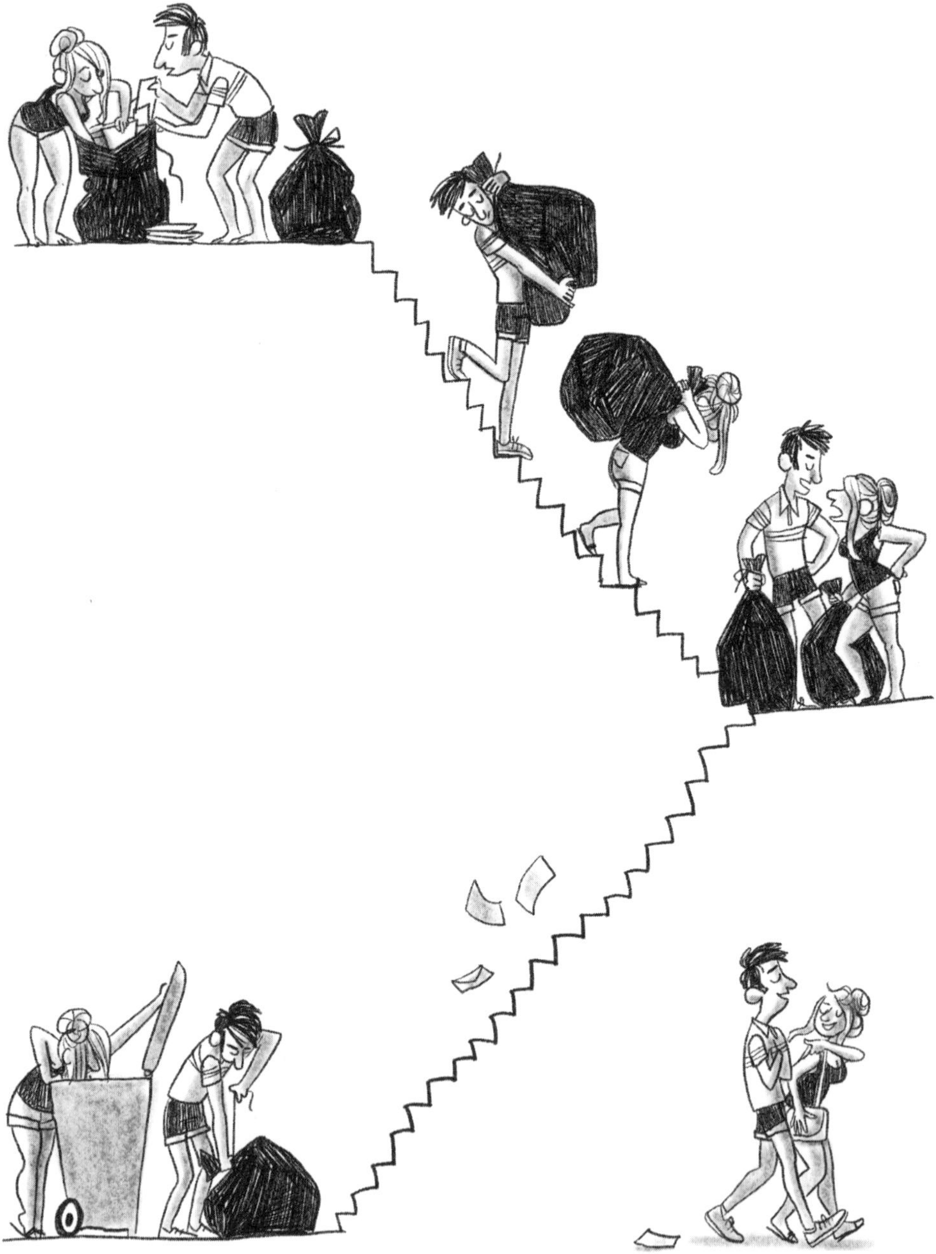

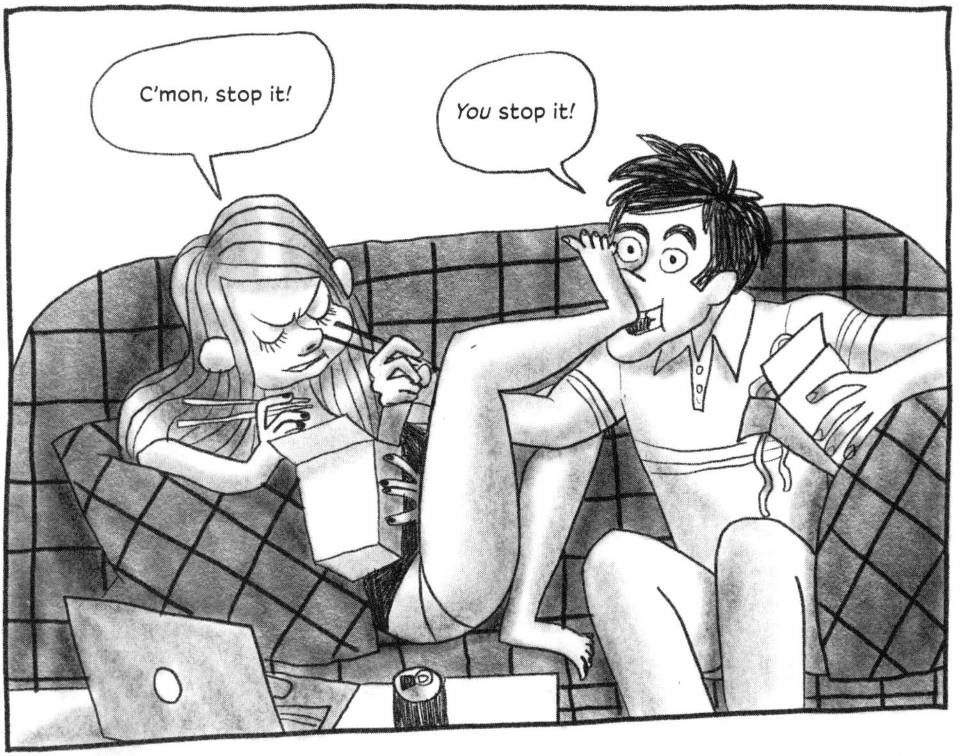
C'mon, stop it!
You stop it!

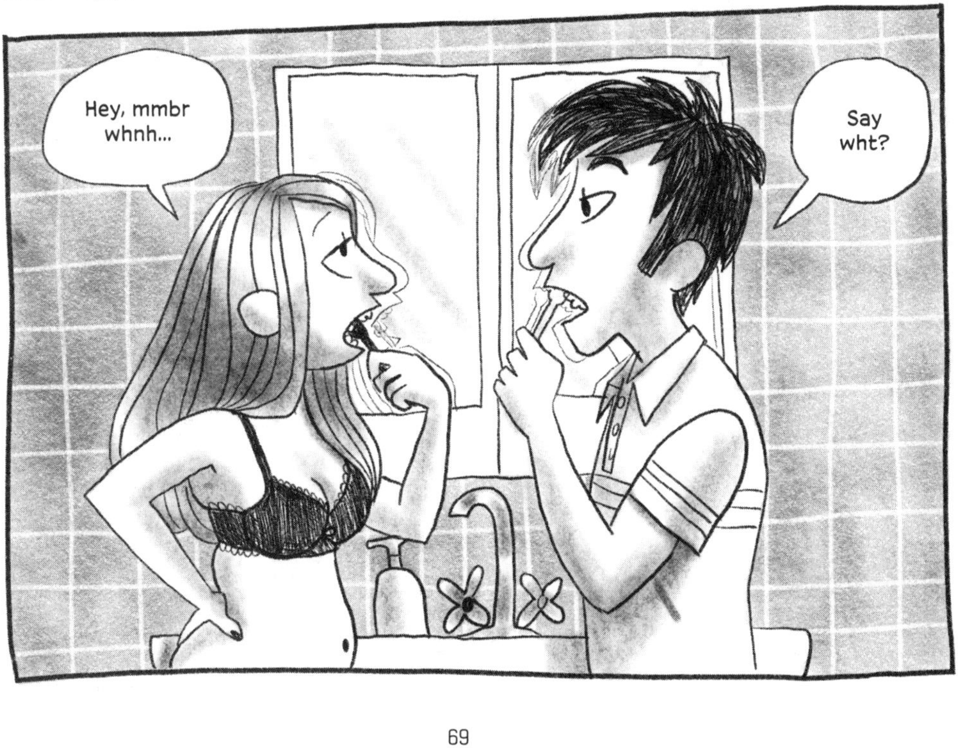
Hey, mmbr whnh...
Say wht?

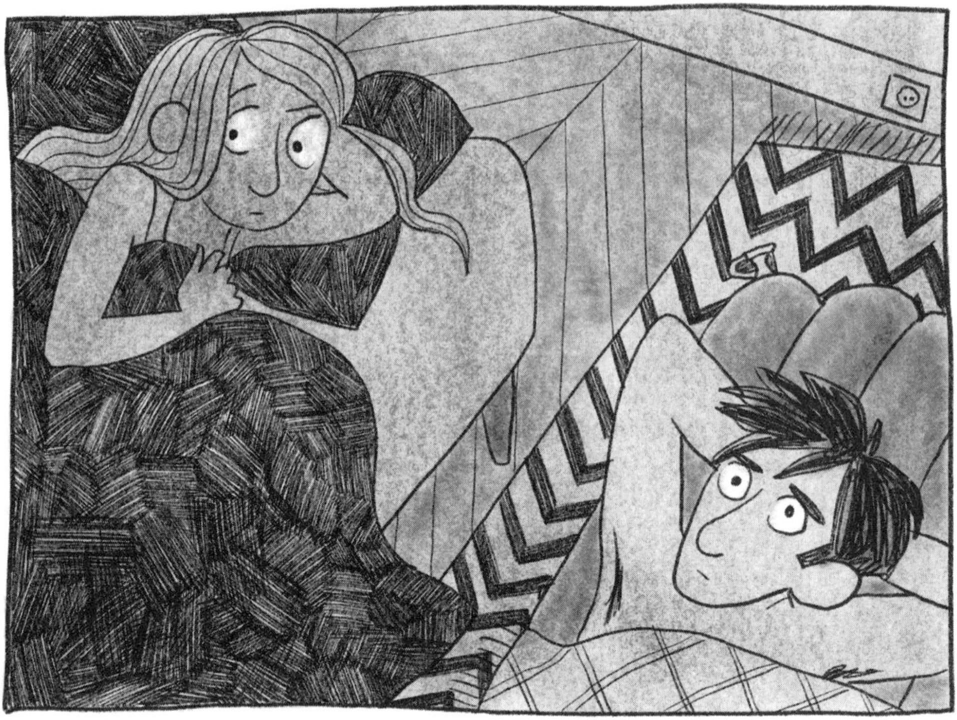

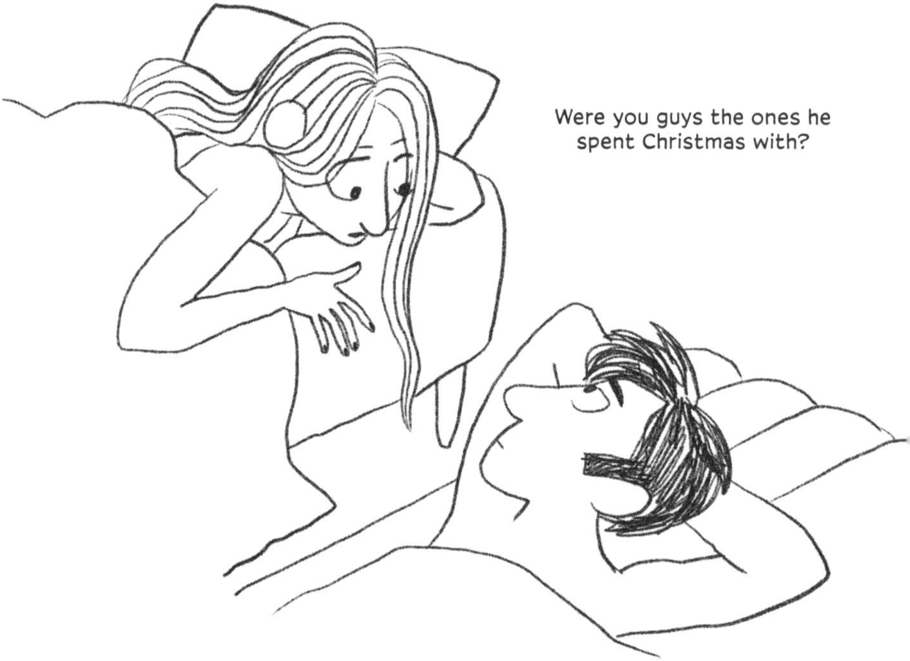
Were you guys the ones he spent Christmas with?

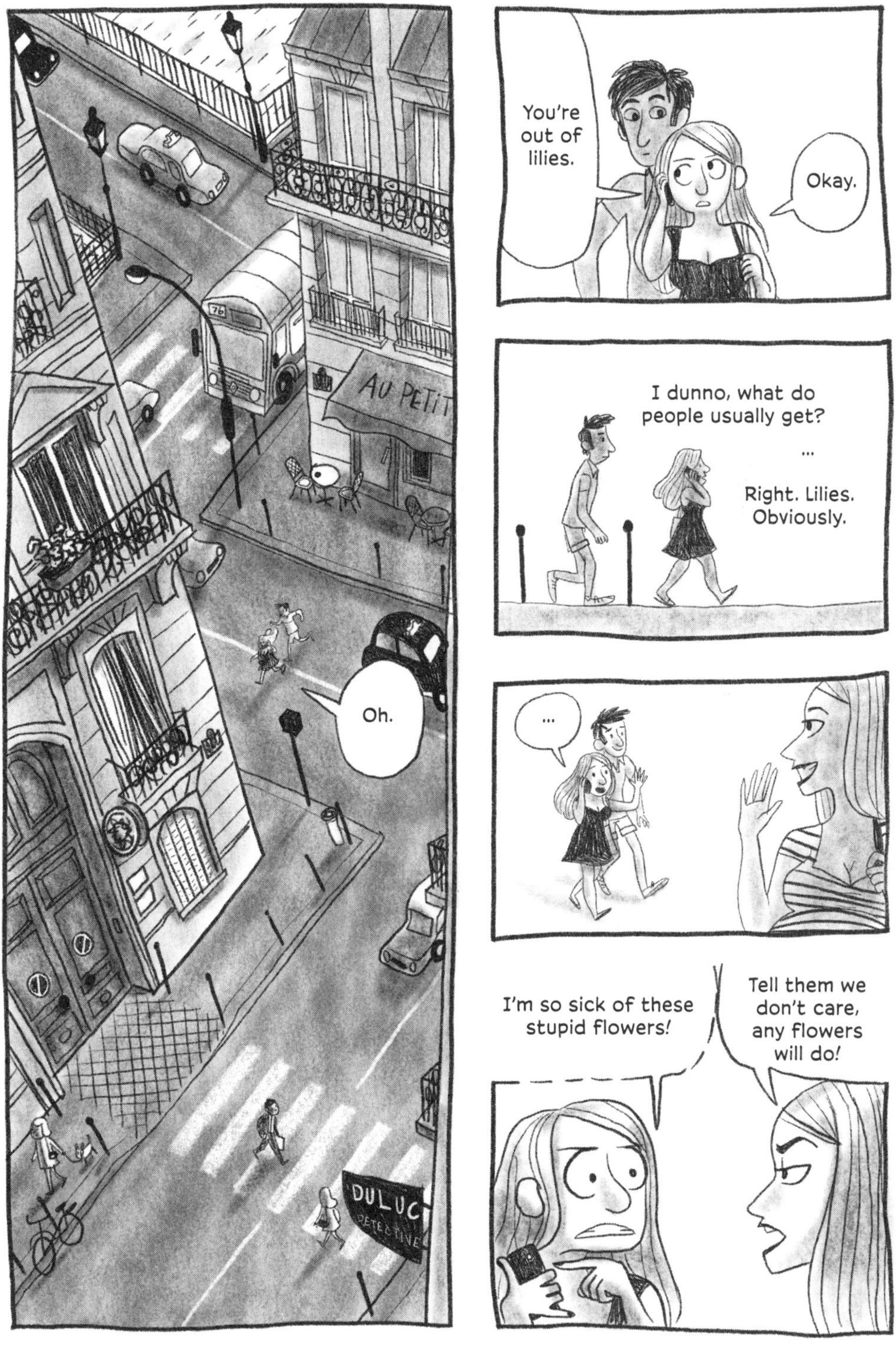
AU PETIT
Oh.
DULUC
DETECTIVE
You're out of lilies.
Okay.
I dunno, what do people usually get?
...
Right. Lilies. Obviously.
...
I'm so sick of these stupid flowers!
Tell them we don't care, any flowers will do!

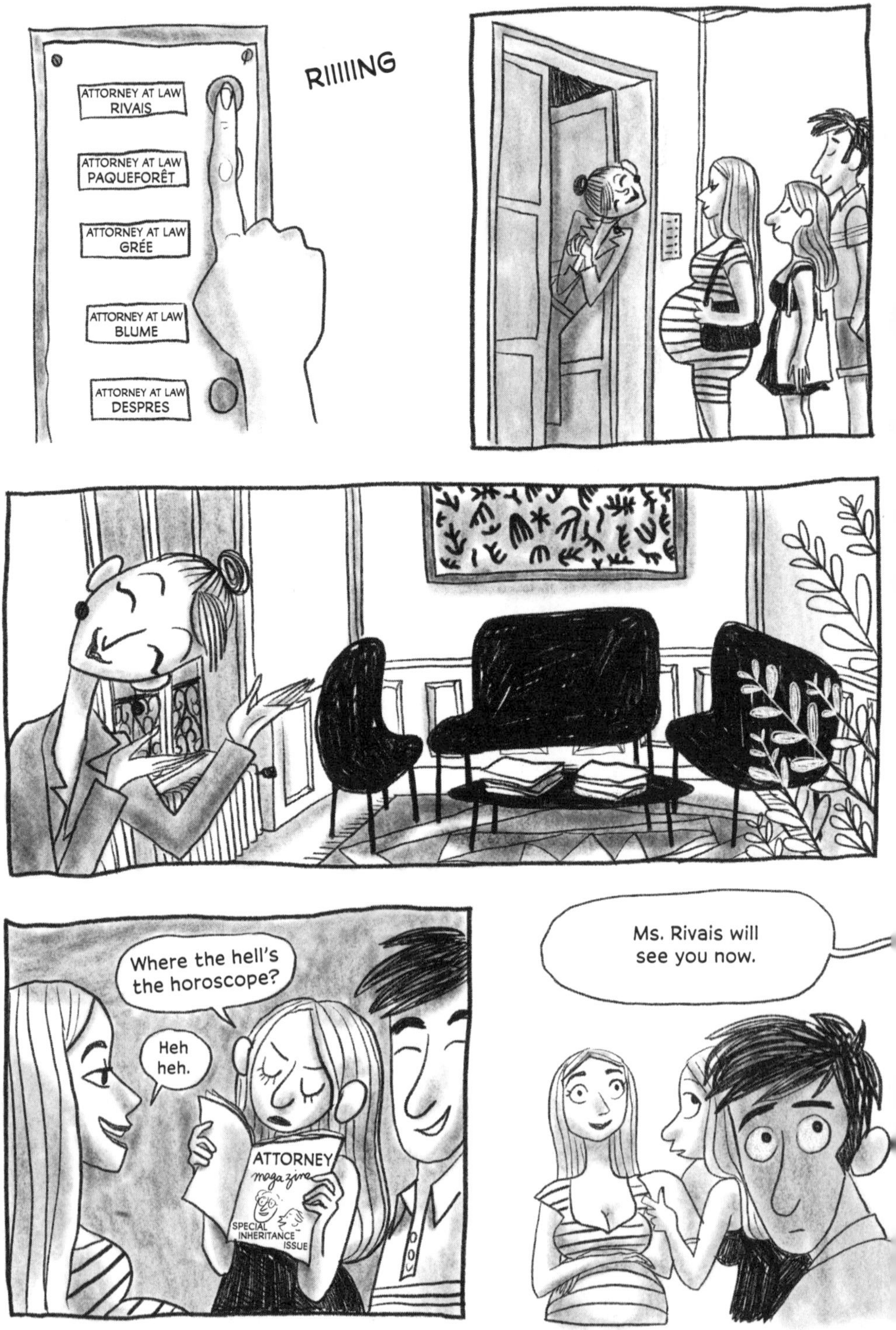
ATTORNEY AT LAW RIVAIS
ATTORNEY AT LAW PAQUEFORÊT
ATTORNEY AT LAW GRÉE
ATTORNEY AT LAW BLUME
ATTORNEY AT LAW DESPRES
RIIIIING
Where the hell's the horoscope?
Heh heh.
ATTORNEY magazine
SPECIAL INHERITANCE ISSUE
Ms. Rivais will see you now.

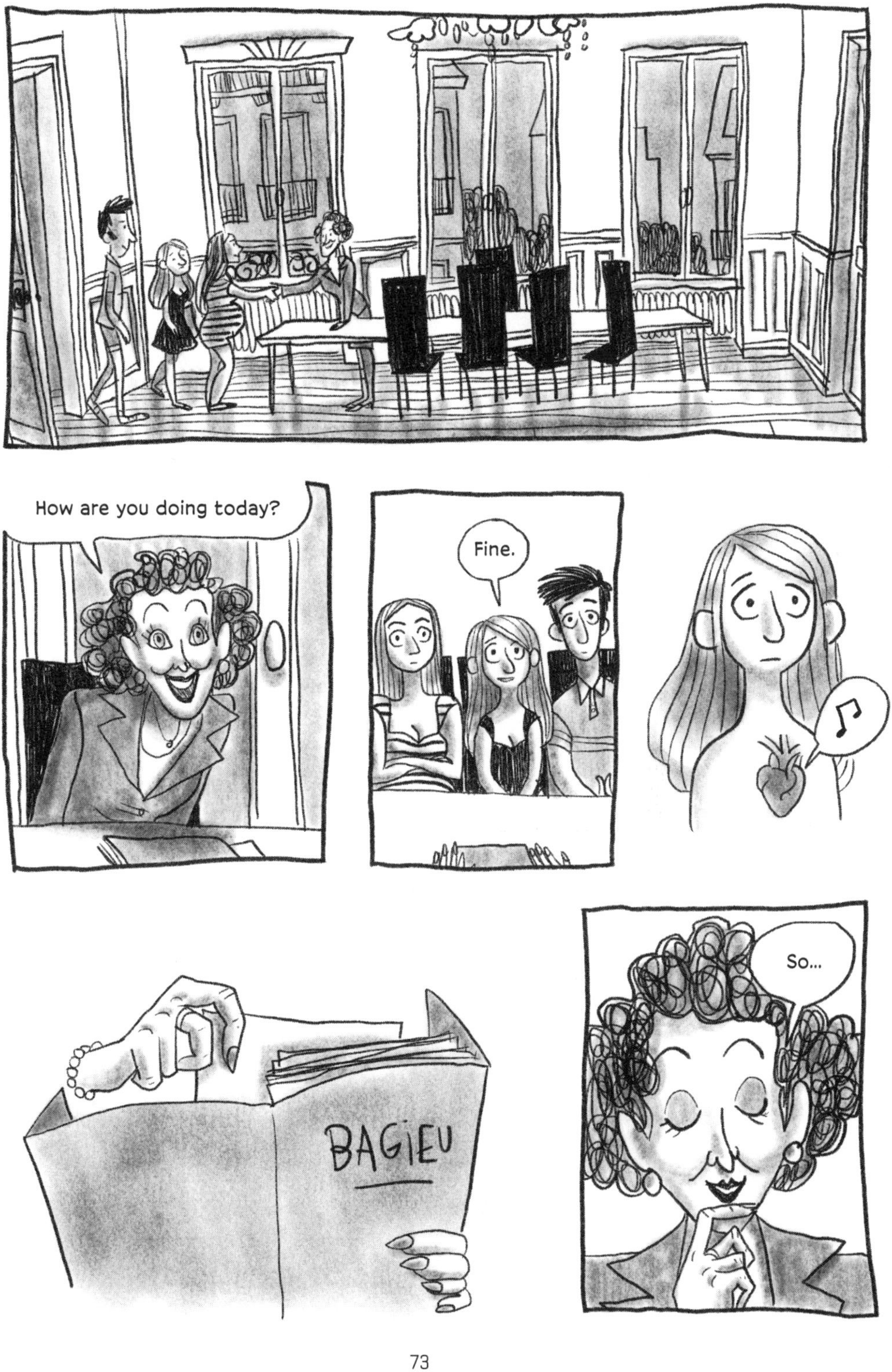
How are you doing today?
Fine.
BAGIEU
So...

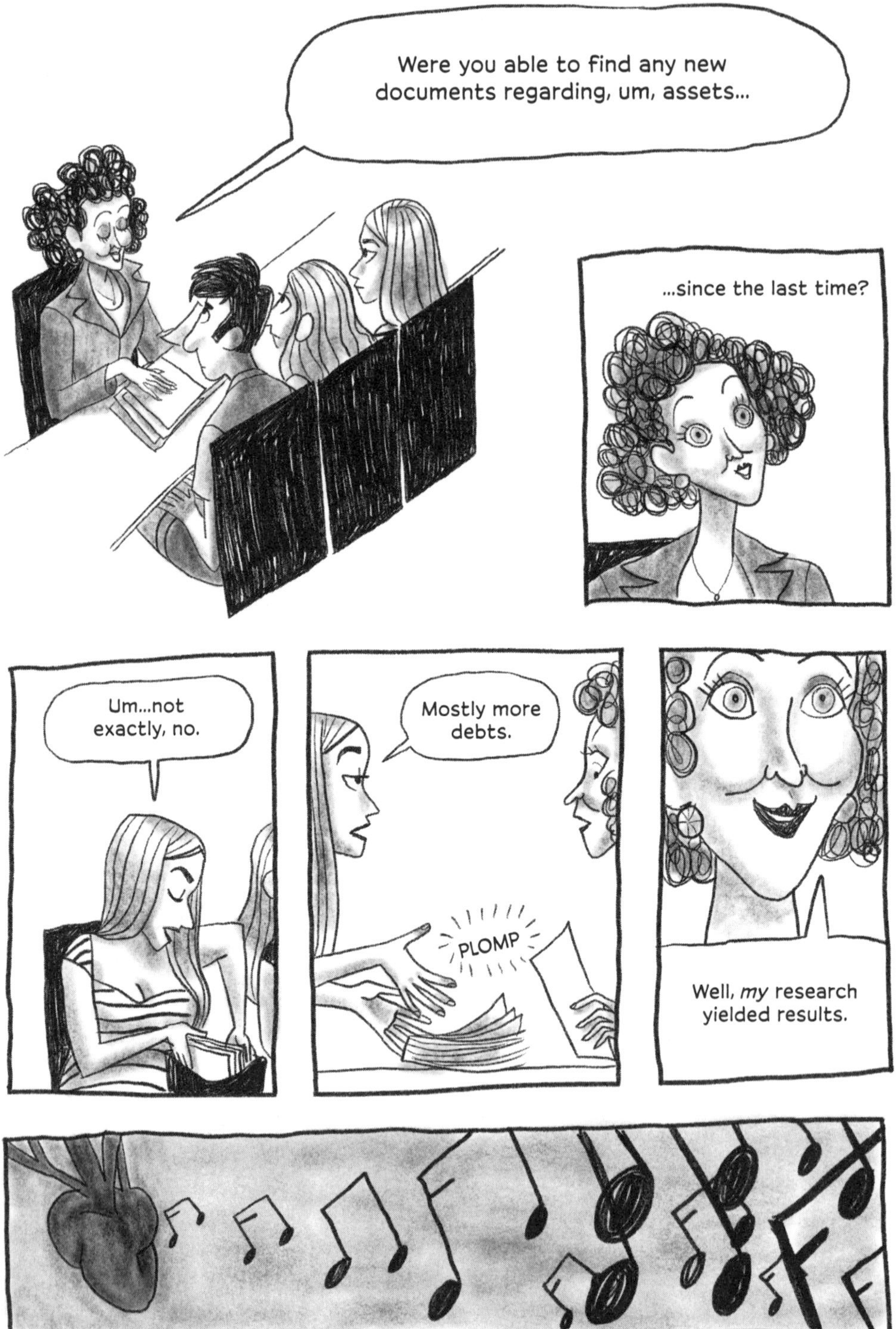
Were you able to find any new documents regarding, um, assets...
...since the last time?
Um...not exactly, no.
Mostly more debts.
PLOMP
Well, *my* research yielded results.

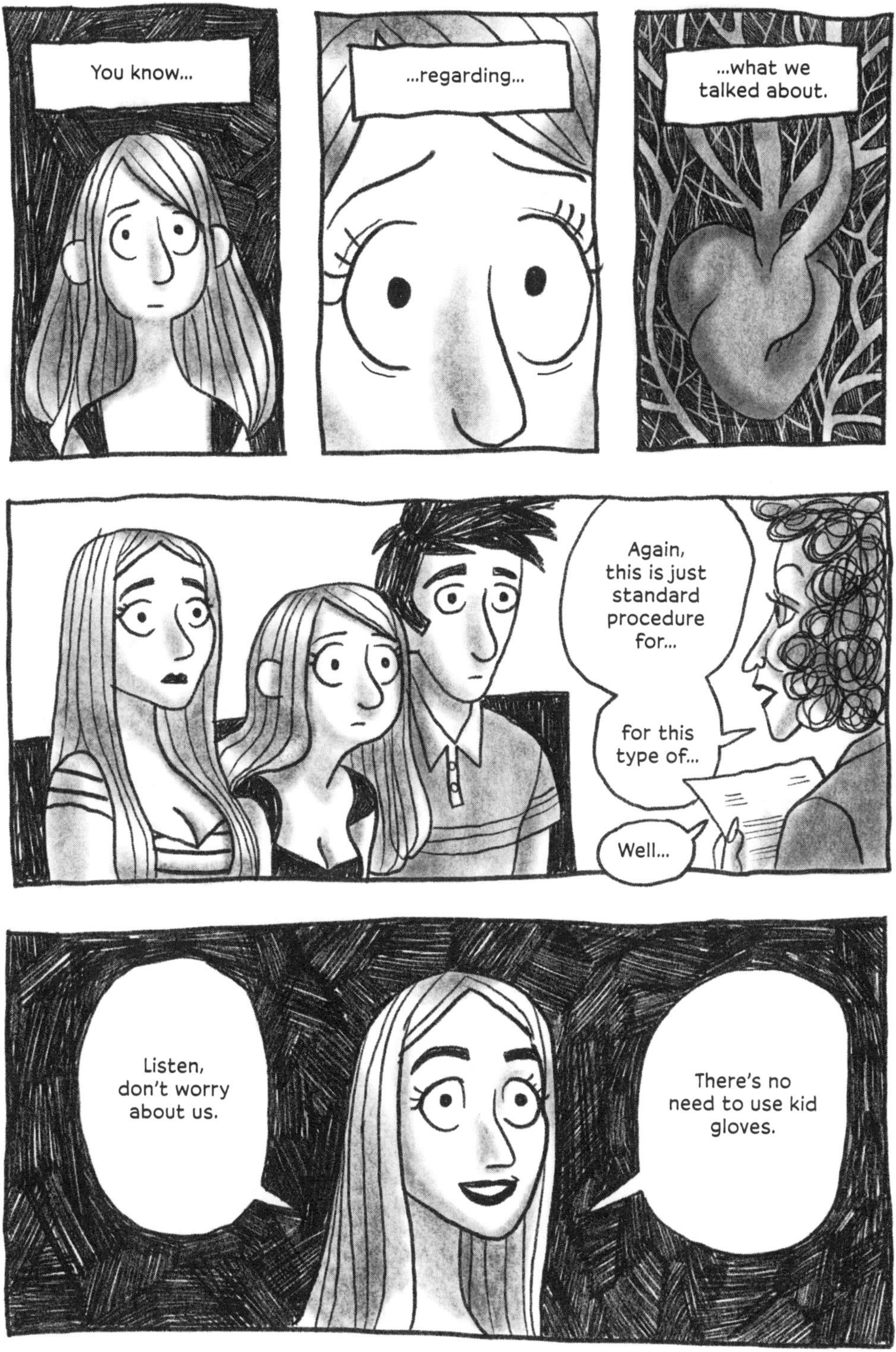

You know...
...regarding...
...what we talked about.
Again, this is just standard procedure for...
for this type of...
Well...
Listen, don't worry about us.
There's no need to use kid gloves.

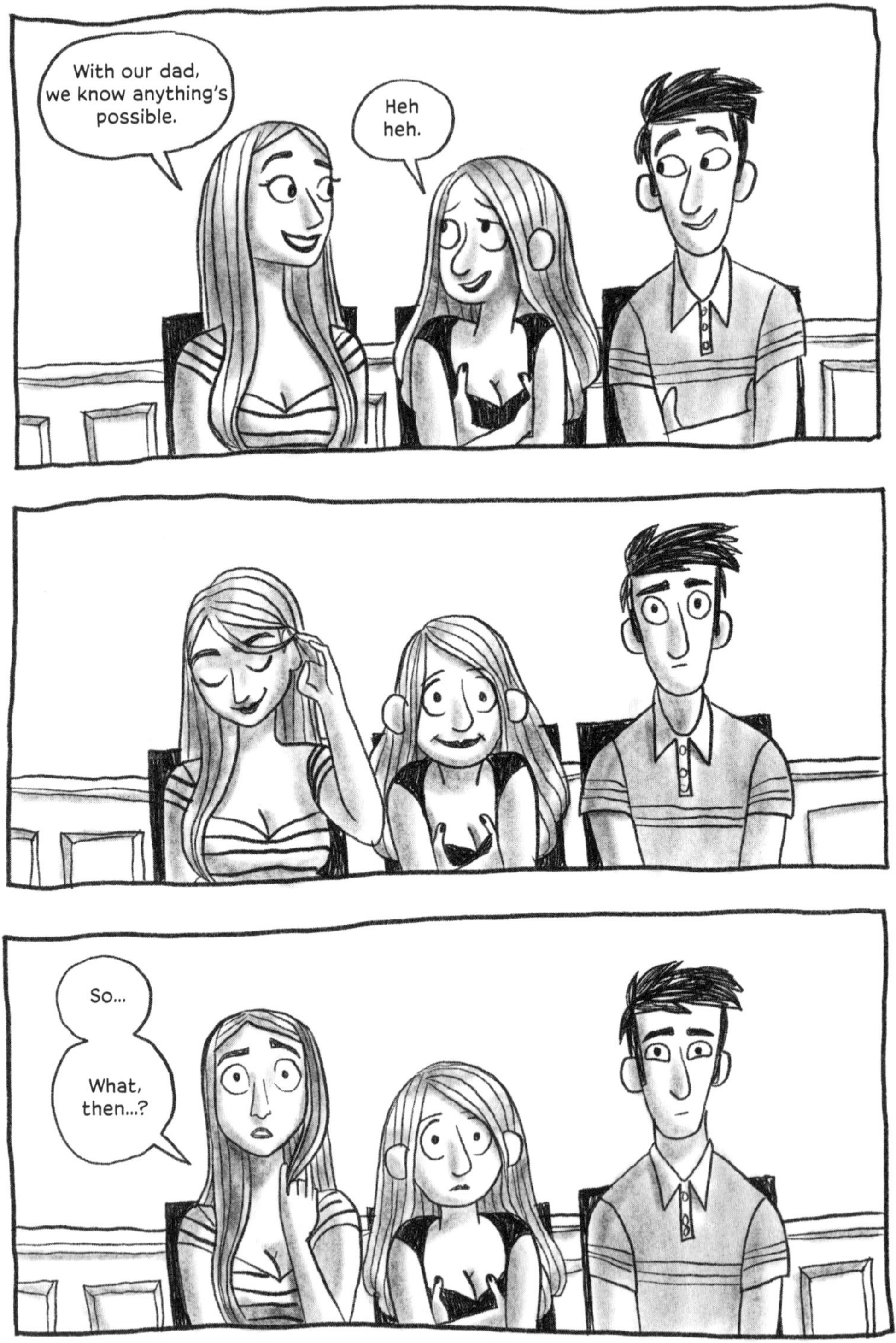
With our dad, we know anything's possible.
Heh heh.
So...
What, then...?

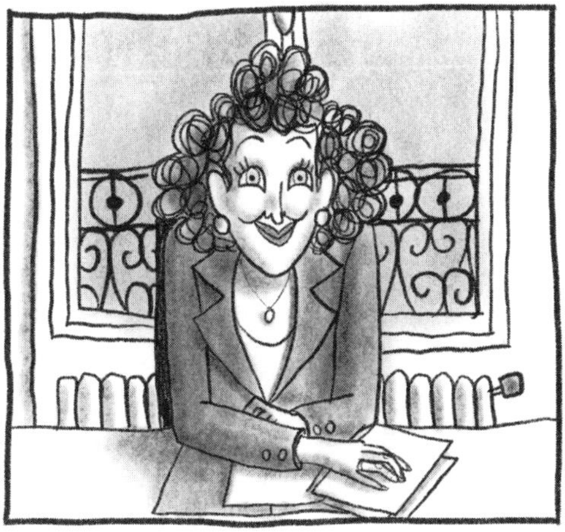

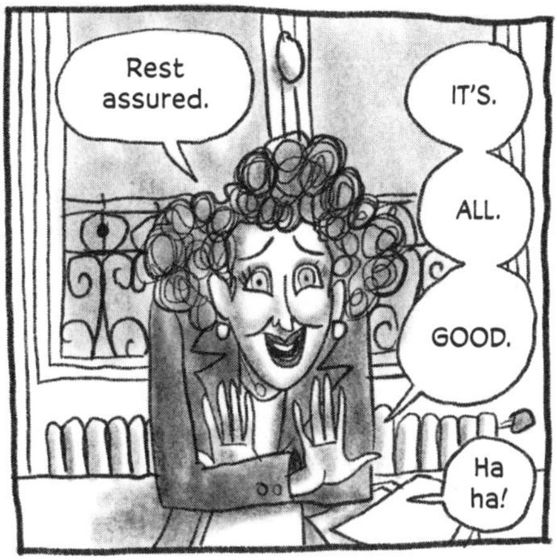
Rest assured.
IT'S.
ALL.
GOOD.
Ha ha!

It's all ***very*** good, even.

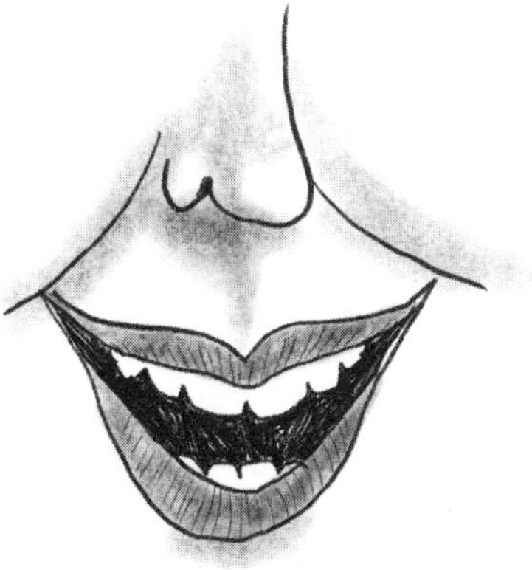

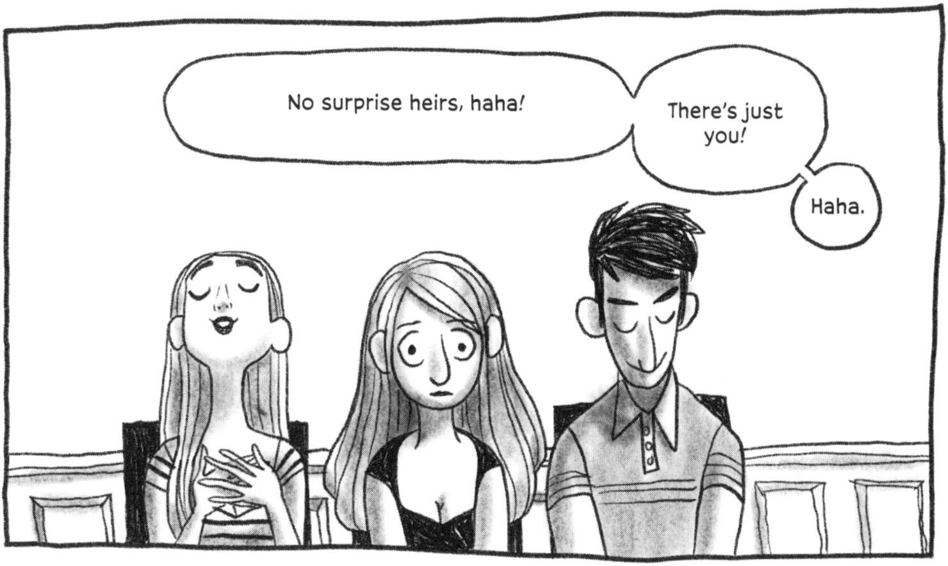
No surprise heirs, haha!
There's just you!
Haha.

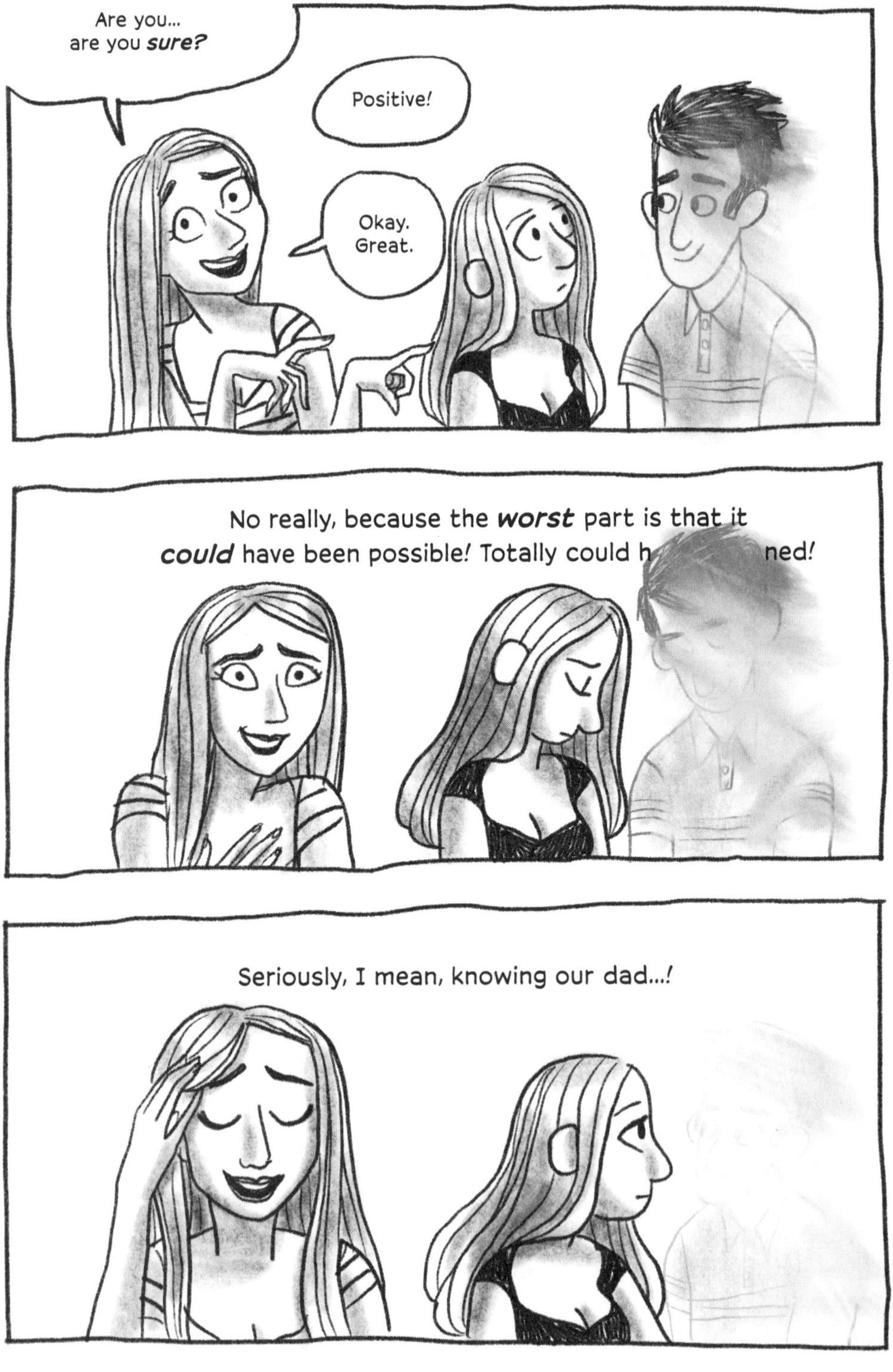
Are you... are you *sure?*
Positive!
Okay. Great.
No really, because the *worst* part is that it
could have been possible! Totally could h
ned!
Seriously, I mean, knowing our dad...!

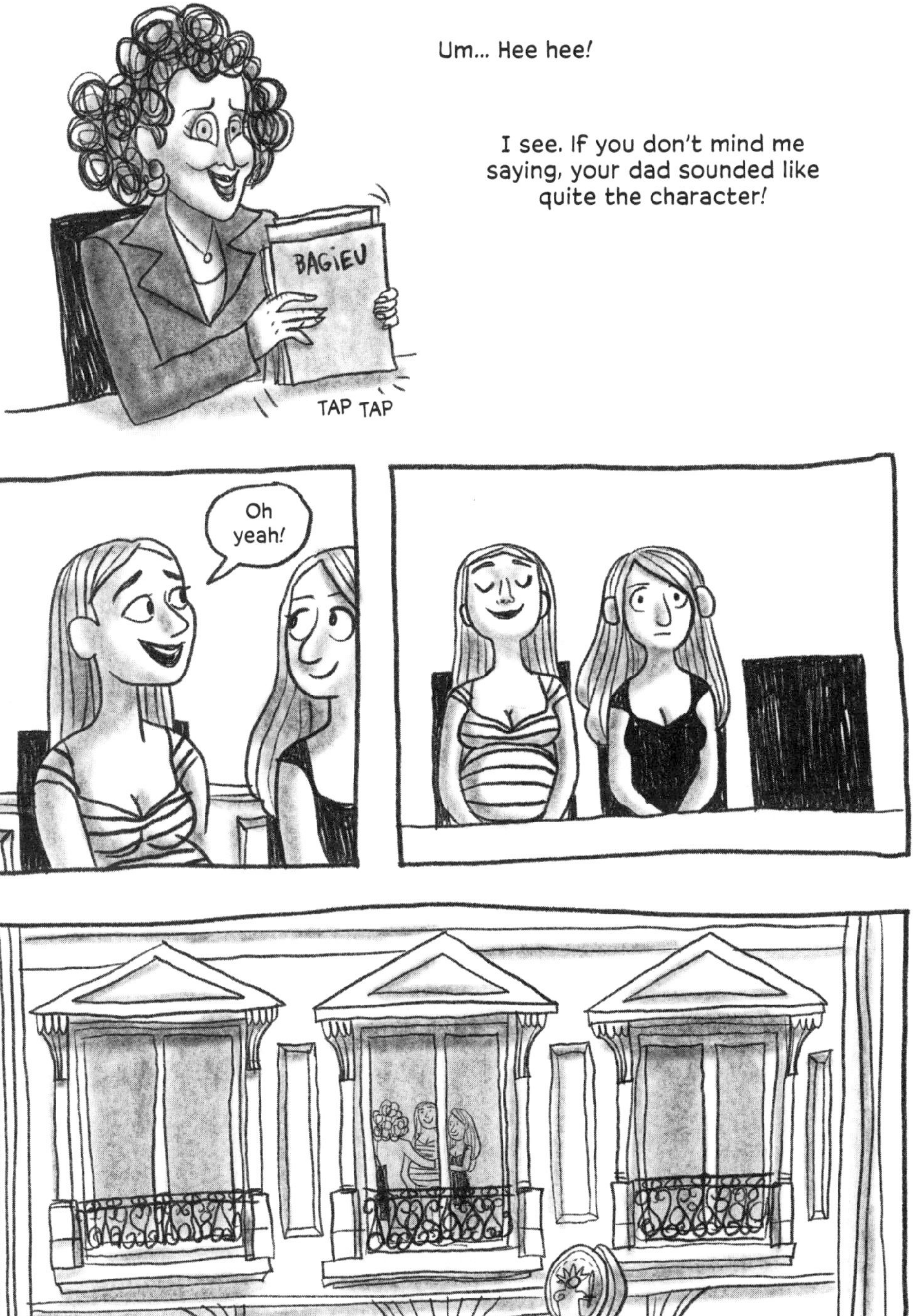
Um... Hee hee!
I see. If you don't mind me saying, your dad sounded like quite the character!
BAGIEU
TAP TAP
Oh yeah!

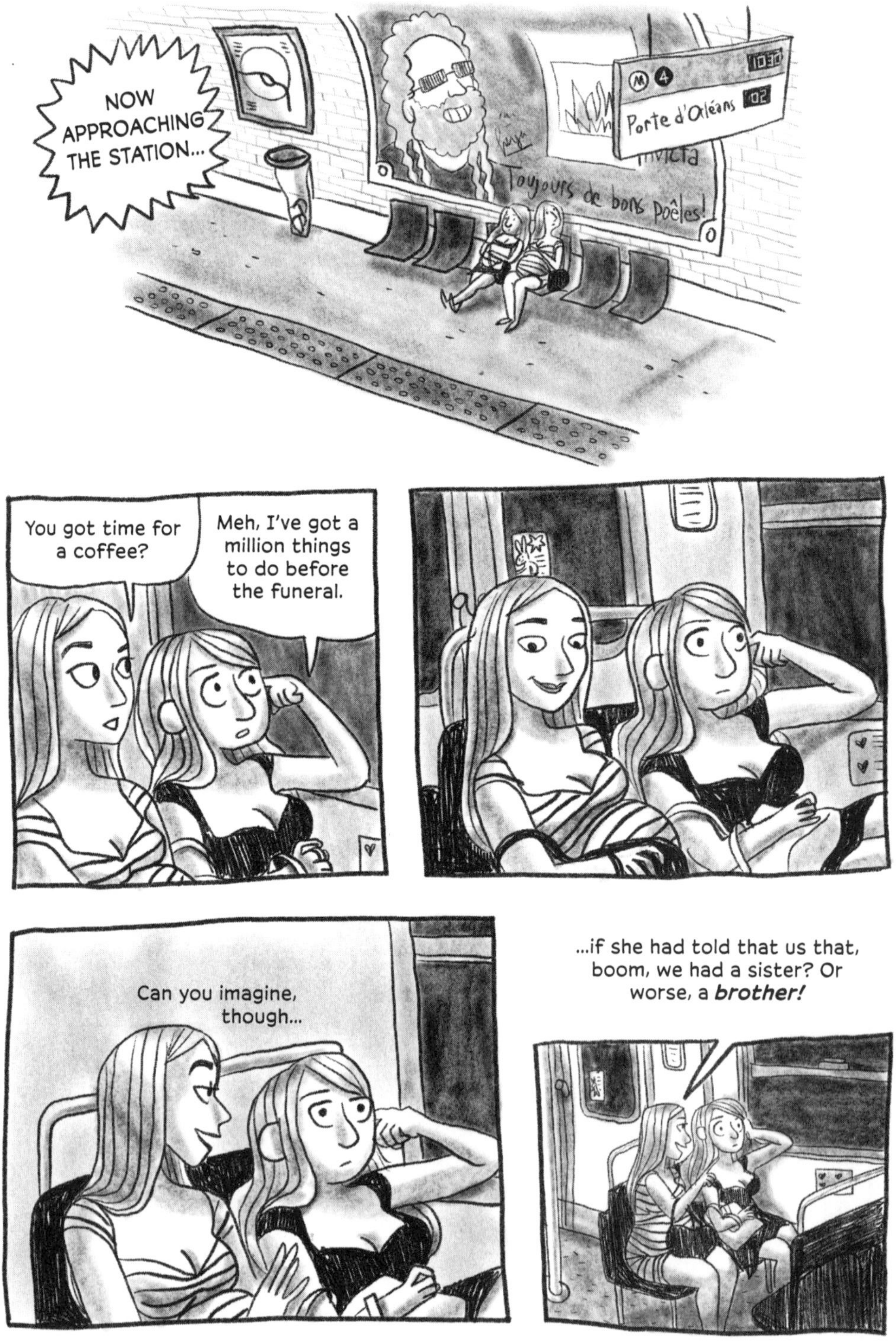
NOW APPROACHING THE STATION...
Porte d'Orléans
Toujours de bons poêles!
You got time for a coffee?
Meh, I've got a million things to do before the funeral.
Can you imagine, though...
...if she had told that us that, boom, we had a sister? Or worse, a ***brother!***

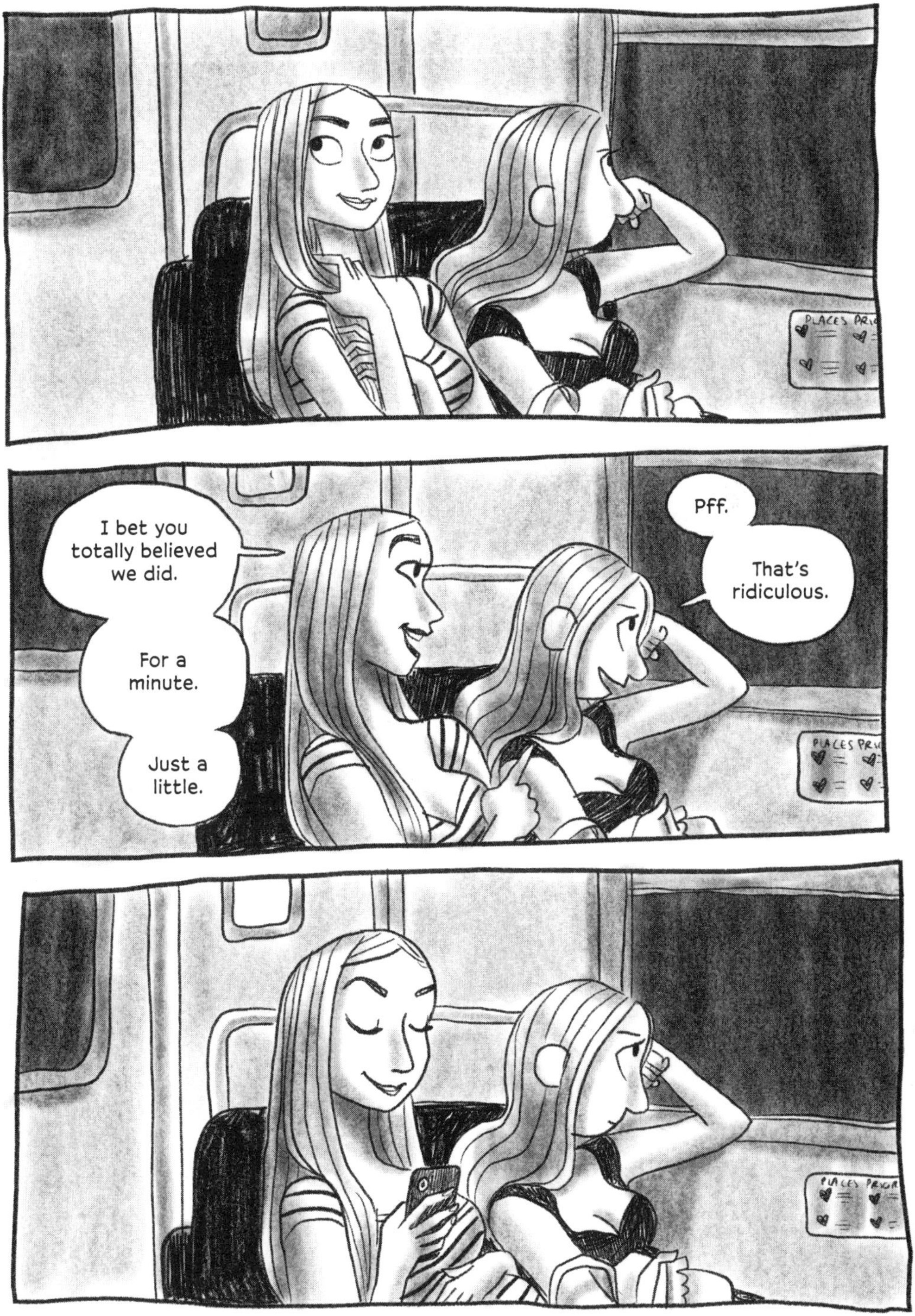

I bet you totally believed we did.
For a minute.
Just a little.
Pff.
That's ridiculous.

Once, for three days, I had a brother.

-FIN-

A STORY ABOUT MY GRAND-PARENTS

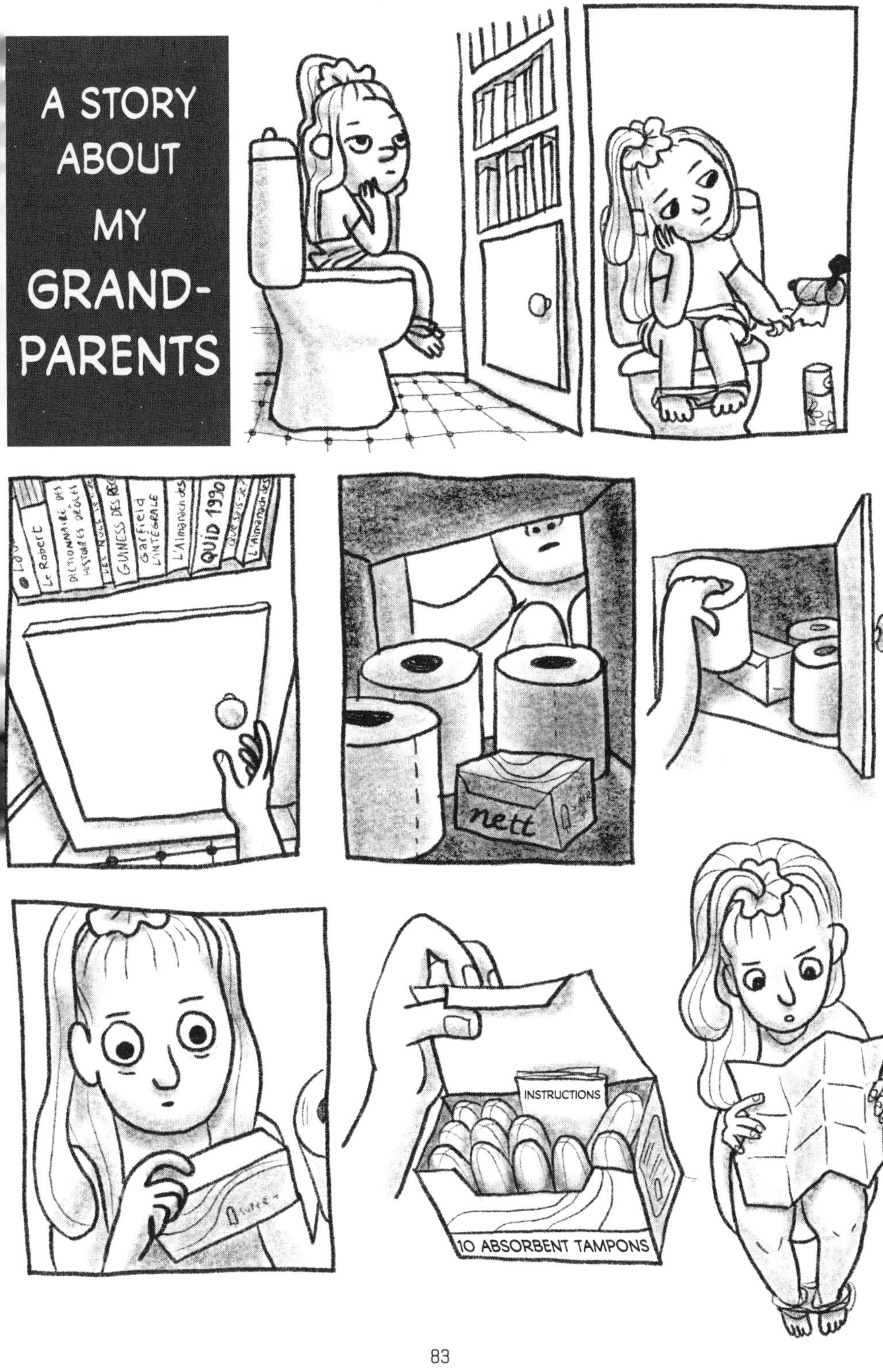
Le Robert
DICTIONNAIRE DES HISTOIRES DRÔLES
Garfield L'INTÉGRALE
L'Almanach des
QUID 1990
nett
INSTRUCTIONS
10 ABSORBENT TAMPONS

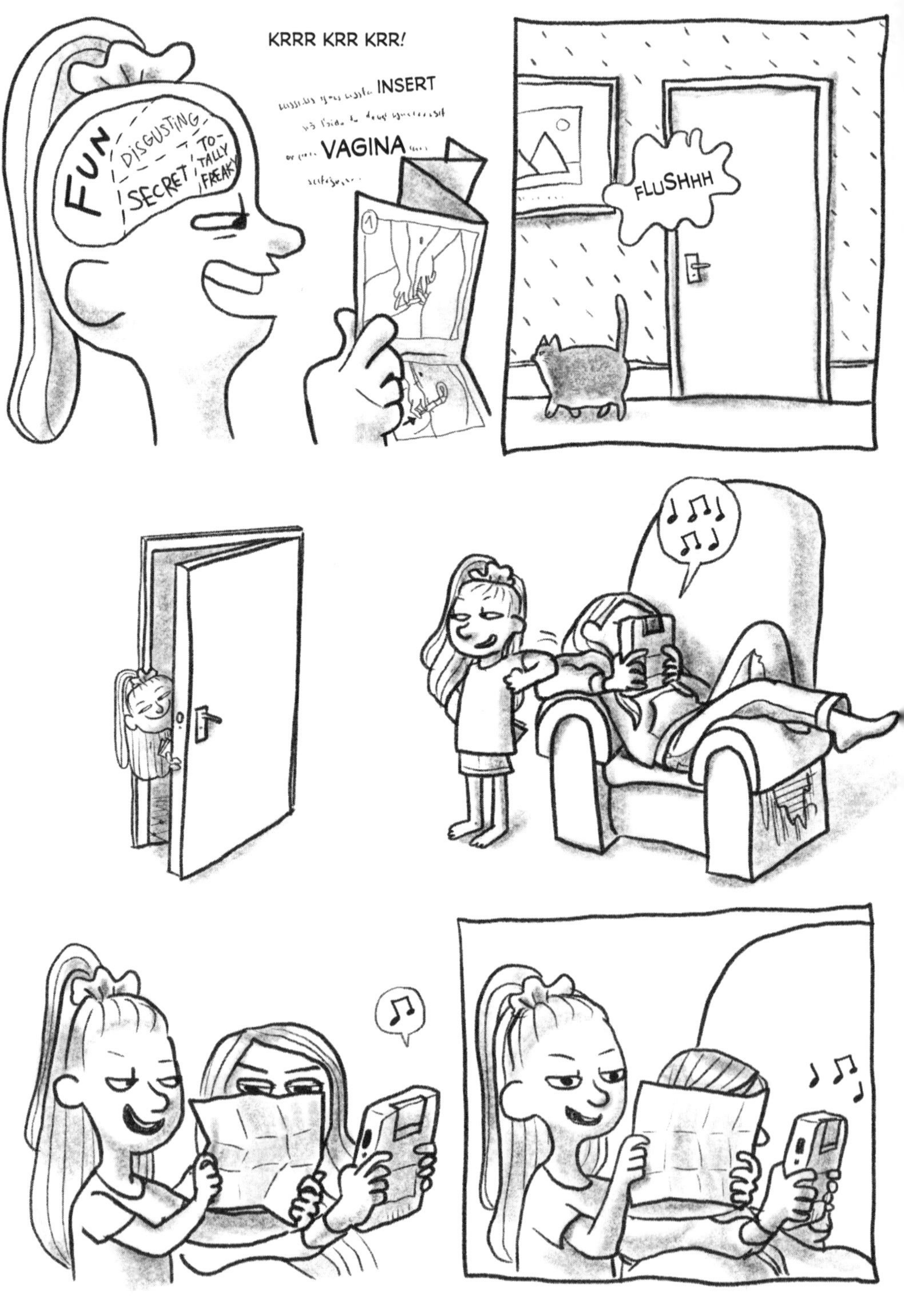
FUN
DISGUSTING
SECRET
TOTALLY FREAKY
KRRR KRR KRR!
INSERT
VAGINA
FLUSHHH

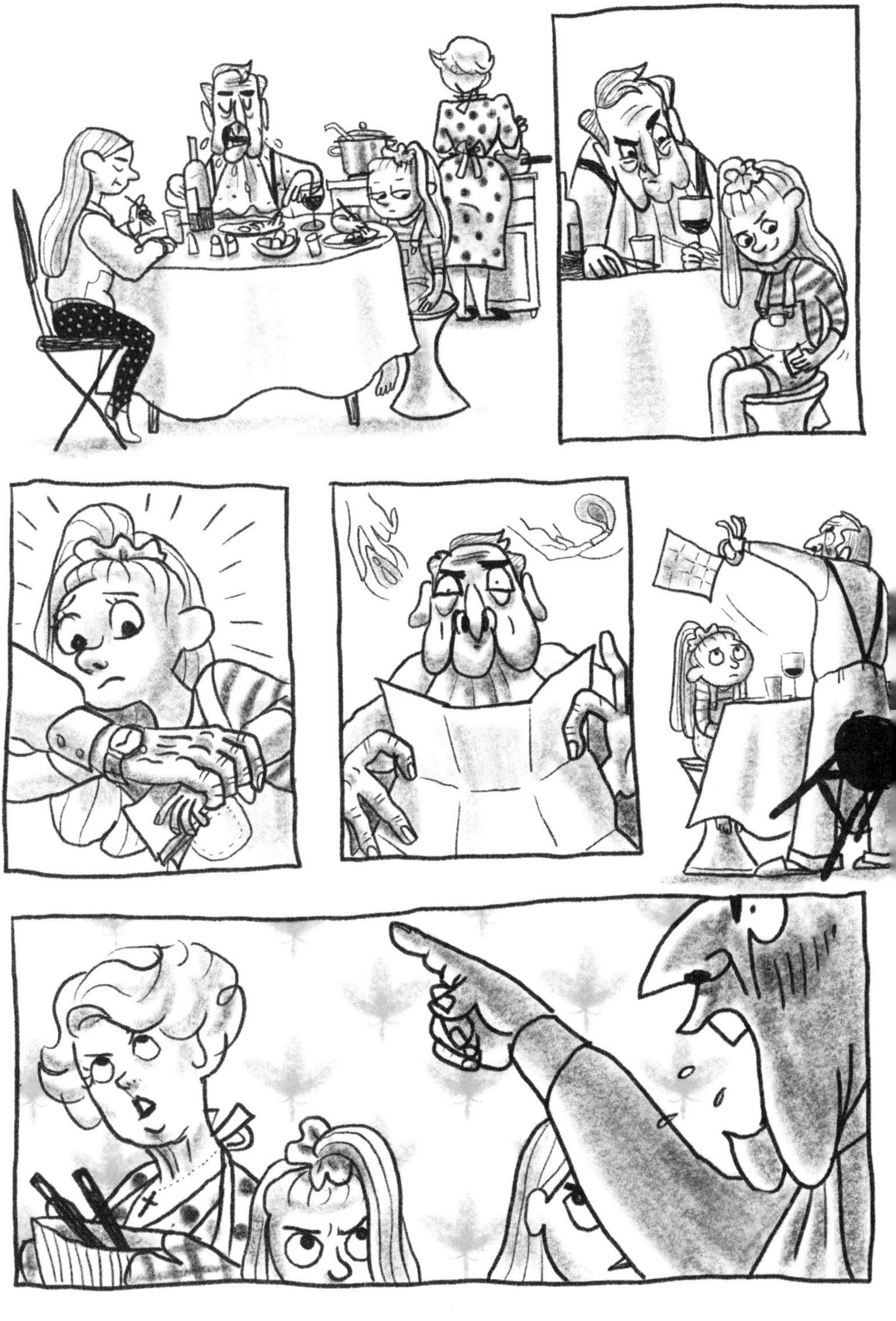

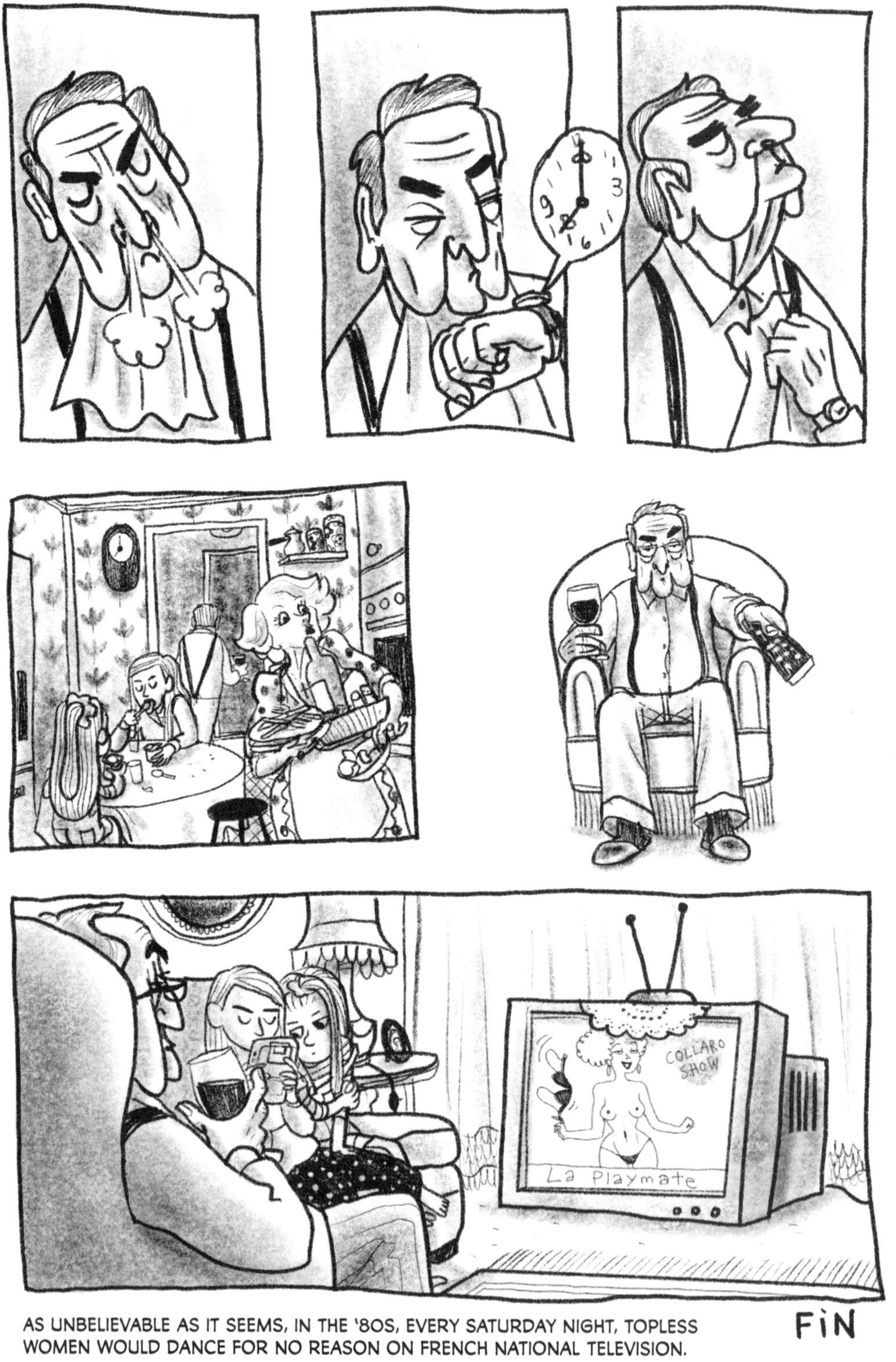
COLLARO SHOW
La Playmate

AS UNBELIEVABLE AS IT SEEMS, IN THE '80S, EVERY SATURDAY NIGHT, TOPLESS WOMEN WOULD DANCE FOR NO REASON ON FRENCH NATIONAL TELEVISION.

FIN

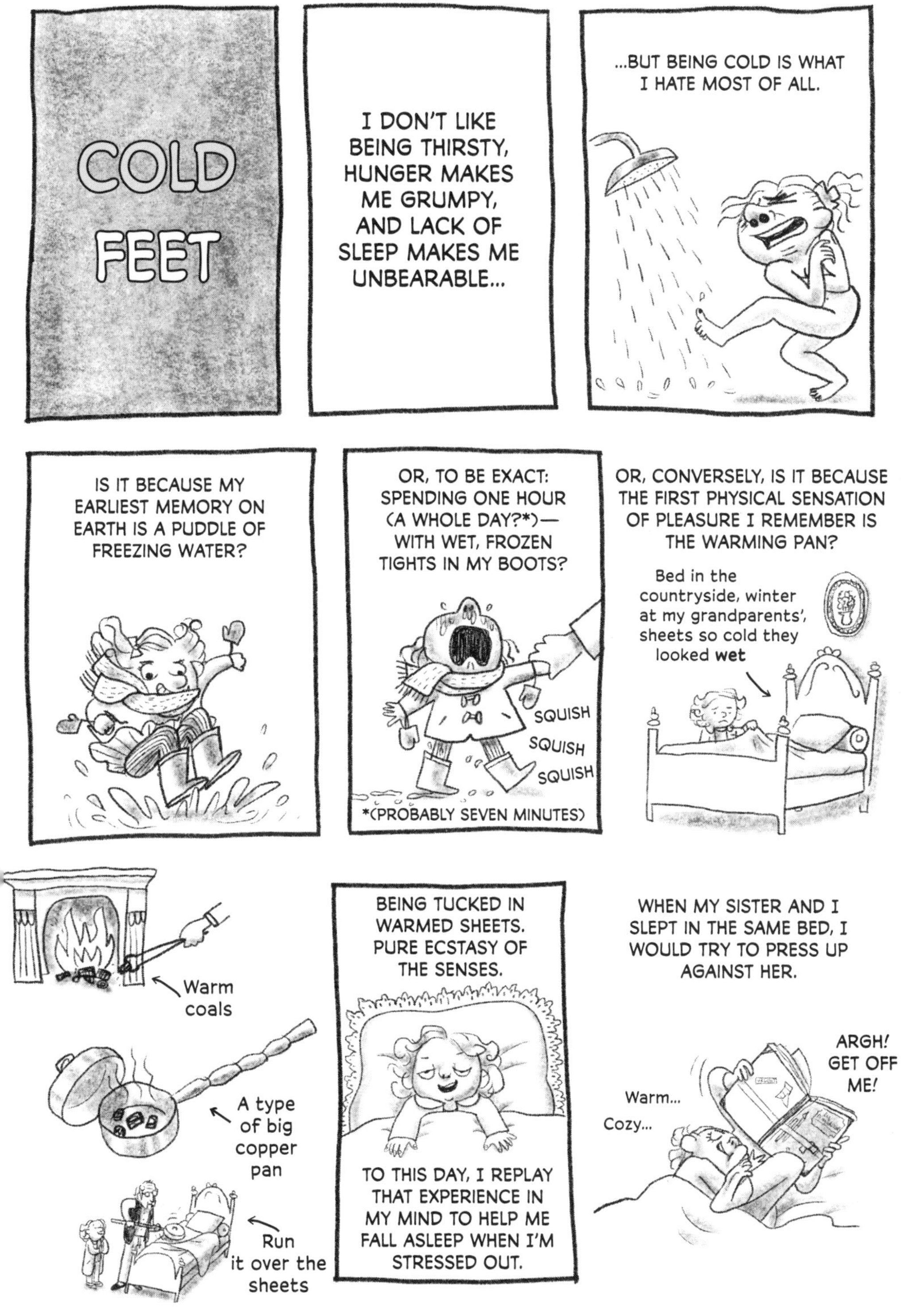
COLD FEET
I DON'T LIKE BEING THIRSTY, HUNGER MAKES ME GRUMPY, AND LACK OF SLEEP MAKES ME UNBEARABLE...
...BUT BEING COLD IS WHAT I HATE MOST OF ALL.
IS IT BECAUSE MY EARLIEST MEMORY ON EARTH IS A PUDDLE OF FREEZING WATER?
OR, TO BE EXACT: SPENDING ONE HOUR (A WHOLE DAY?*)— WITH WET, FROZEN TIGHTS IN MY BOOTS?
SQUISH
SQUISH
SQUISH
*(PROBABLY SEVEN MINUTES)
OR, CONVERSELY, IS IT BECAUSE THE FIRST PHYSICAL SENSATION OF PLEASURE I REMEMBER IS THE WARMING PAN?
Bed in the countryside, winter at my grandparents', sheets so cold they looked **wet**
Warm coals
A type of big copper pan
Run it over the sheets
BEING TUCKED IN WARMED SHEETS. PURE ECSTASY OF THE SENSES.
TO THIS DAY, I REPLAY THAT EXPERIENCE IN MY MIND TO HELP ME FALL ASLEEP WHEN I'M STRESSED OUT.
WHEN MY SISTER AND I SLEPT IN THE SAME BED, I WOULD TRY TO PRESS UP AGAINST HER.
Warm...
Cozy...
ARGH! GET OFF ME!

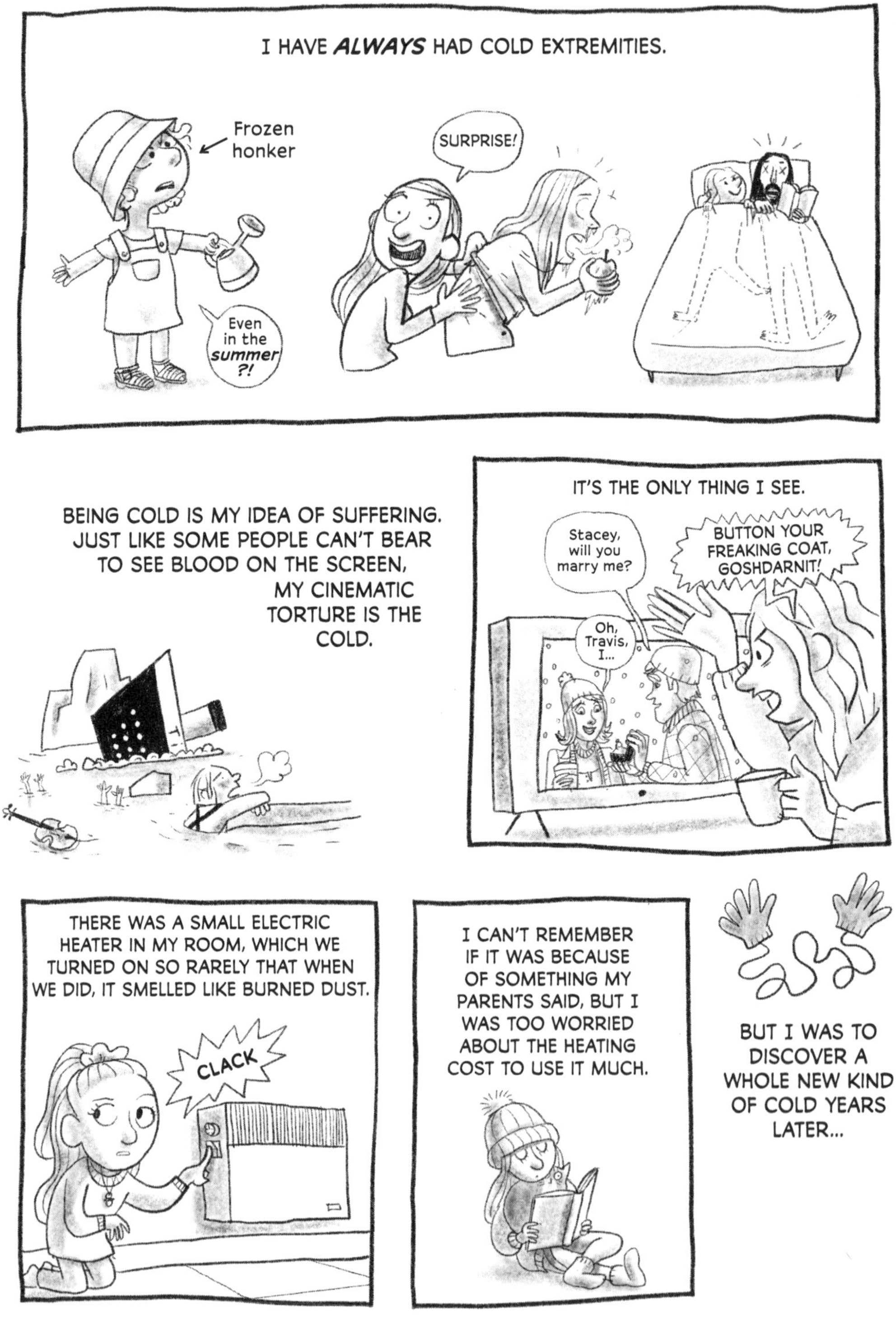
I HAVE ***ALWAYS*** HAD COLD EXTREMITIES.
Frozen honker
Even in the ***summer ?!***
SURPRISE!
BEING COLD IS MY IDEA OF SUFFERING. JUST LIKE SOME PEOPLE CAN'T BEAR TO SEE BLOOD ON THE SCREEN, MY CINEMATIC TORTURE IS THE COLD.
IT'S THE ONLY THING I SEE.
Stacey, will you marry me?
BUTTON YOUR FREAKING COAT, GOSHDARNIT!
Oh, Travis, I...
THERE WAS A SMALL ELECTRIC HEATER IN MY ROOM, WHICH WE TURNED ON SO RARELY THAT WHEN WE DID, IT SMELLED LIKE BURNED DUST.
CLACK
I CAN'T REMEMBER IF IT WAS BECAUSE OF SOMETHING MY PARENTS SAID, BUT I WAS TOO WORRIED ABOUT THE HEATING COST TO USE IT MUCH.
BUT I WAS TO DISCOVER A WHOLE NEW KIND OF COLD YEARS LATER...

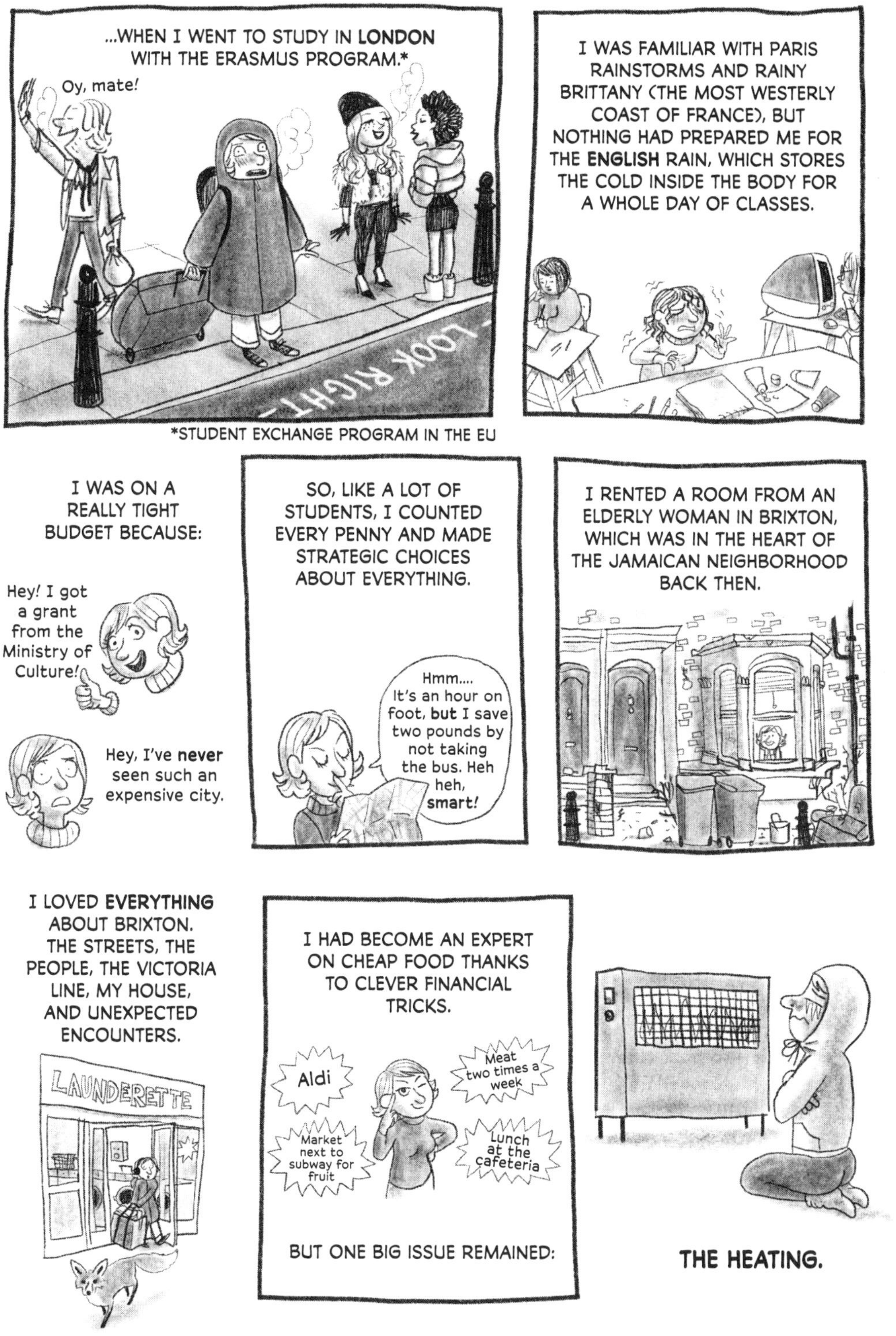
...WHEN I WENT TO STUDY IN LONDON WITH THE ERASMUS PROGRAM.*
Oy, mate!
LOOK RIGHT
*STUDENT EXCHANGE PROGRAM IN THE EU
I WAS FAMILIAR WITH PARIS RAINSTORMS AND RAINY BRITTANY (THE MOST WESTERLY COAST OF FRANCE), BUT NOTHING HAD PREPARED ME FOR THE ENGLISH RAIN, WHICH STORES THE COLD INSIDE THE BODY FOR A WHOLE DAY OF CLASSES.
I WAS ON A REALLY TIGHT BUDGET BECAUSE:
Hey! I got a grant from the Ministry of Culture!
Hey, I've never seen such an expensive city.
SO, LIKE A LOT OF STUDENTS, I COUNTED EVERY PENNY AND MADE STRATEGIC CHOICES ABOUT EVERYTHING.
Hmm.... It's an hour on foot, but I save two pounds by not taking the bus. Heh heh, smart!
I RENTED A ROOM FROM AN ELDERLY WOMAN IN BRIXTON, WHICH WAS IN THE HEART OF THE JAMAICAN NEIGHBORHOOD BACK THEN.
I LOVED EVERYTHING ABOUT BRIXTON. THE STREETS, THE PEOPLE, THE VICTORIA LINE, MY HOUSE, AND UNEXPECTED ENCOUNTERS.
LAUNDERETTE
I HAD BECOME AN EXPERT ON CHEAP FOOD THANKS TO CLEVER FINANCIAL TRICKS.
Aldi
Meat two times a week
Market next to subway for fruit
Lunch at the cafeteria
BUT ONE BIG ISSUE REMAINED:
THE HEATING.

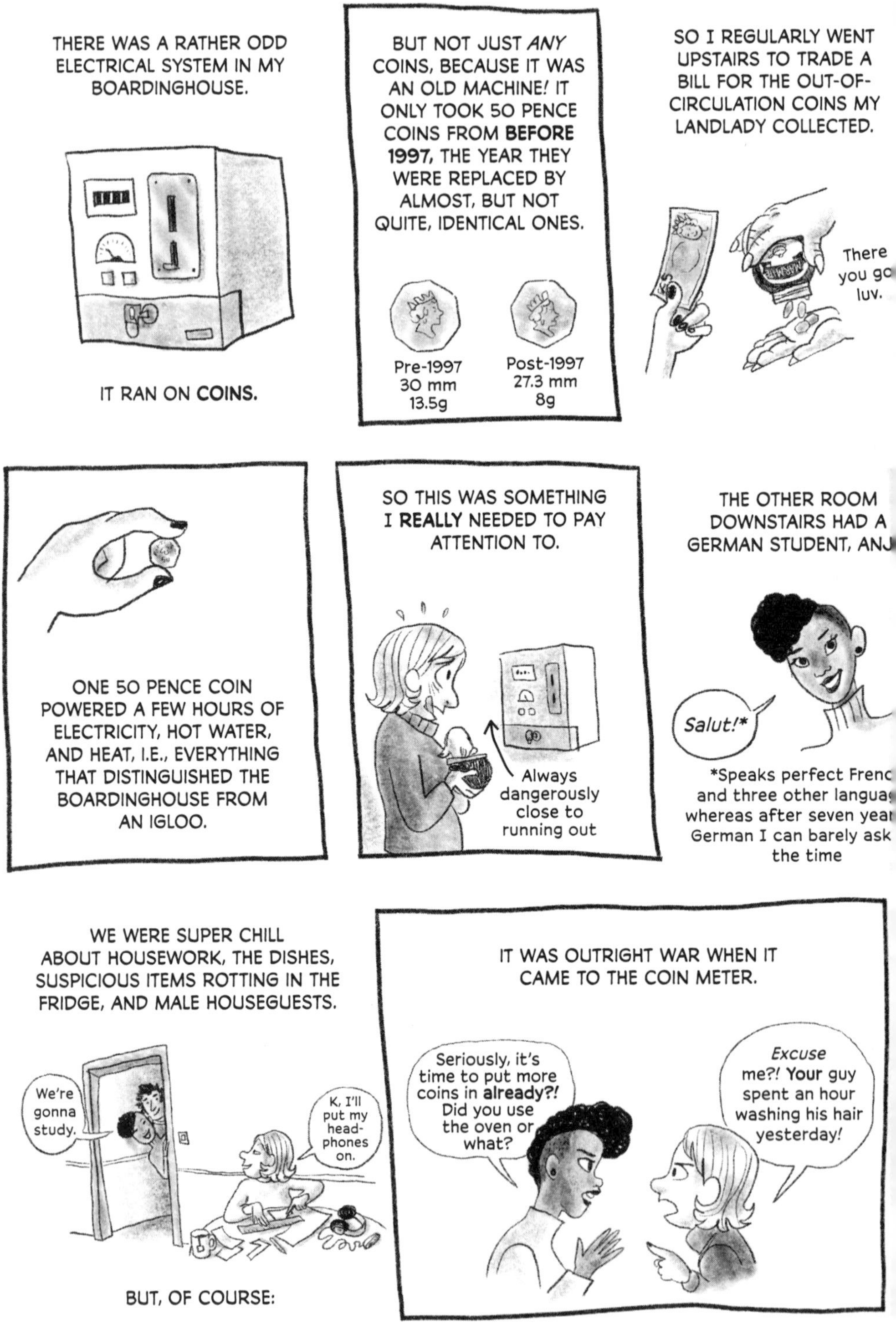
THERE WAS A RATHER ODD ELECTRICAL SYSTEM IN MY BOARDINGHOUSE.
IT RAN ON **COINS.**
BUT NOT JUST *ANY* COINS, BECAUSE IT WAS AN OLD MACHINE! IT ONLY TOOK 50 PENCE COINS FROM **BEFORE 1997,** THE YEAR THEY WERE REPLACED BY ALMOST, BUT NOT QUITE, IDENTICAL ONES.
Pre-1997 30 mm 13.5g
Post-1997 27.3 mm 8g
SO I REGULARLY WENT UPSTAIRS TO TRADE A BILL FOR THE OUT-OF-CIRCULATION COINS MY LANDLADY COLLECTED.
There you g
luv.
ONE 50 PENCE COIN POWERED A FEW HOURS OF ELECTRICITY, HOT WATER, AND HEAT, I.E., EVERYTHING THAT DISTINGUISHED THE BOARDINGHOUSE FROM AN IGLOO.
SO THIS WAS SOMETHING I **REALLY** NEEDED TO PAY ATTENTION TO.
Always dangerously close to running out
THE OTHER ROOM DOWNSTAIRS HAD A GERMAN STUDENT, ANJ
*Salut!**
*Speaks perfect Frenc and three other langua whereas after seven year German I can barely ask the time
WE WERE SUPER CHILL ABOUT HOUSEWORK, THE DISHES, SUSPICIOUS ITEMS ROTTING IN THE FRIDGE, AND MALE HOUSEGUESTS.
We're gonna study.
K, I'll put my head-phones on.
BUT, OF COURSE:
IT WAS OUTRIGHT WAR WHEN IT CAME TO THE COIN METER.
Seriously, it's time to put more coins in **already?!** Did you use the oven or what?
Excuse me?! **Your** guy spent an hour washing his hair yesterday!

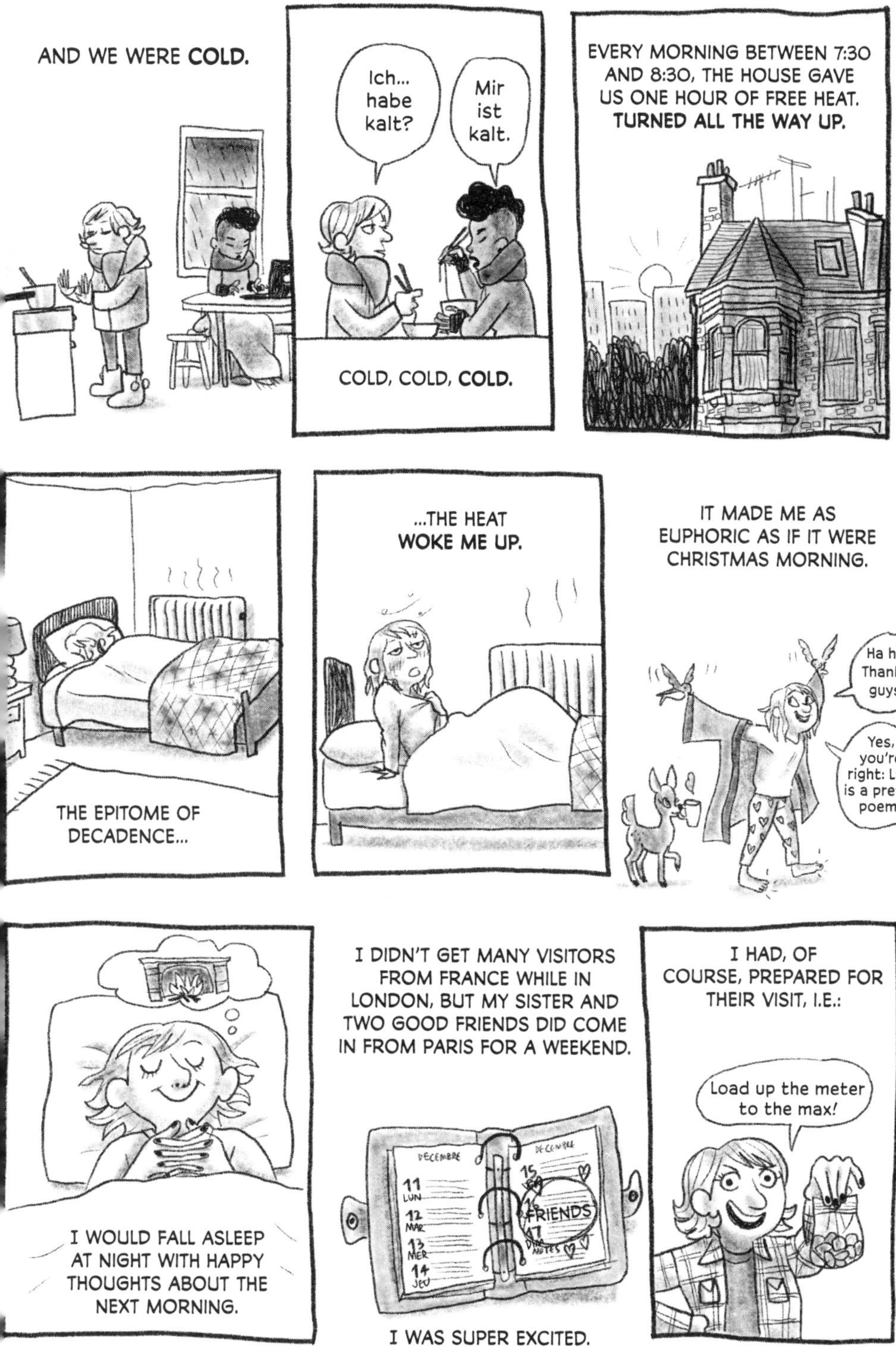
AND WE WERE **COLD.**
Ich... habe kalt?
Mir ist kalt.
COLD, COLD, **COLD.**
EVERY MORNING BETWEEN 7:30 AND 8:30, THE HOUSE GAVE US ONE HOUR OF FREE HEAT.
TURNED ALL THE WAY UP.
THE EPITOME OF DECADENCE...
...THE HEAT **WOKE ME UP.**
IT MADE ME AS EUPHORIC AS IF IT WERE CHRISTMAS MORNING.
Ha ha. Thanks, guys!
Yes, you're right: Life is a pretty poem!
I WOULD FALL ASLEEP AT NIGHT WITH HAPPY THOUGHTS ABOUT THE NEXT MORNING.
I DIDN'T GET MANY VISITORS FROM FRANCE WHILE IN LONDON, BUT MY SISTER AND TWO GOOD FRIENDS DID COME IN FROM PARIS FOR A WEEKEND.
FRIENDS
I WAS SUPER EXCITED.
I HAD, OF COURSE, PREPARED FOR THEIR VISIT, I.E.:
Load up the meter to the max!

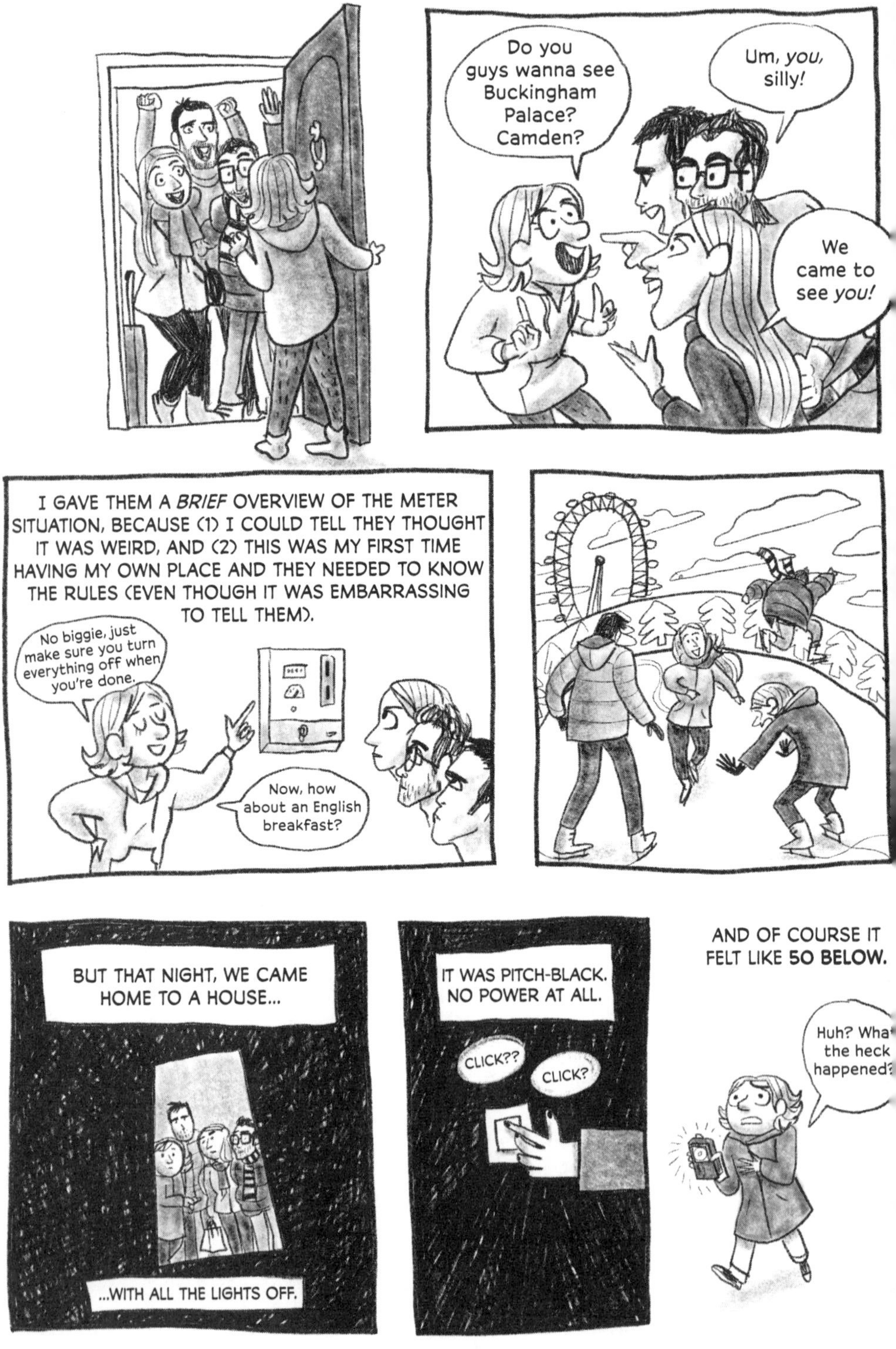

Do you guys wanna see Buckingham Palace? Camden?
Um, *you*, silly!
We came to see *you!*
I GAVE THEM A *BRIEF* OVERVIEW OF THE METER SITUATION, BECAUSE (1) I COULD TELL THEY THOUGHT IT WAS WEIRD, AND (2) THIS WAS MY FIRST TIME HAVING MY OWN PLACE AND THEY NEEDED TO KNOW THE RULES (EVEN THOUGH IT WAS EMBARRASSING TO TELL THEM).
No biggie, just make sure you turn everything off when you're done.
Now, how about an English breakfast?
BUT THAT NIGHT, WE CAME HOME TO A HOUSE...
...WITH ALL THE LIGHTS OFF.
IT WAS PITCH-BLACK. NO POWER AT ALL.
CLICK??
CLICK?
AND OF COURSE IT FELT LIKE **50 BELOW.**
Huh? Wha the heck happened?

AFTER A THOROUGH SEARCH OF THE APARTMENT, WE FOUND THE CULPRIT:

THE LITTLE HEATER IN THE BATHROOM HAD BEEN LEFT ON ALL DAY, USING UP ALL THE COINS, AFTER WHICH THE POWER WENT OUT.

I'm so sorry! I bet I was the one who...

No, wait, I think I took a shower, and then...

It's nobody's fault. It's a stupid system.

SOMETIME LATER, THE EUROSTAR BROUGHT THE LOVE OF MY LIFE* UP FOR THE WEEKEND.

Your place is so cold. This sucks!

Just hold on *two* seconds!

*AT LEAST, HE WAS AT THE TIME.

THE FIRST NIGHT, WE WENT OUT FOR A BEER WHERE WE ALWAYS DID WHEN HE CAME, NEAR COVENT GARDEN.

IN MY PURSE, I HAD AN ENVELOPE CONTAINING MY RENT MONEY IN CASH (MY LANDLADY HAD A NO-CHECK POLICY).

NATURALLY, SINCE IT WOULDN'T BE A FUNNY STORY OTHERWISE, SOMEONE STOLE THE WHOLE LOT OF IT WHEN MY BACK WAS TURNED.

Hey...wasn't my purse closed...?

MAJOR PANIC ATTACK, NATURALLY.

No... No! No!!!

That... that was all my money for the *month...!*

AND I REMEMBER CRYING OUT:

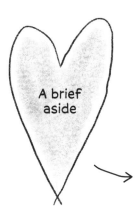

I'M GOING TO BE SO **COLD!**

A brief aside

95

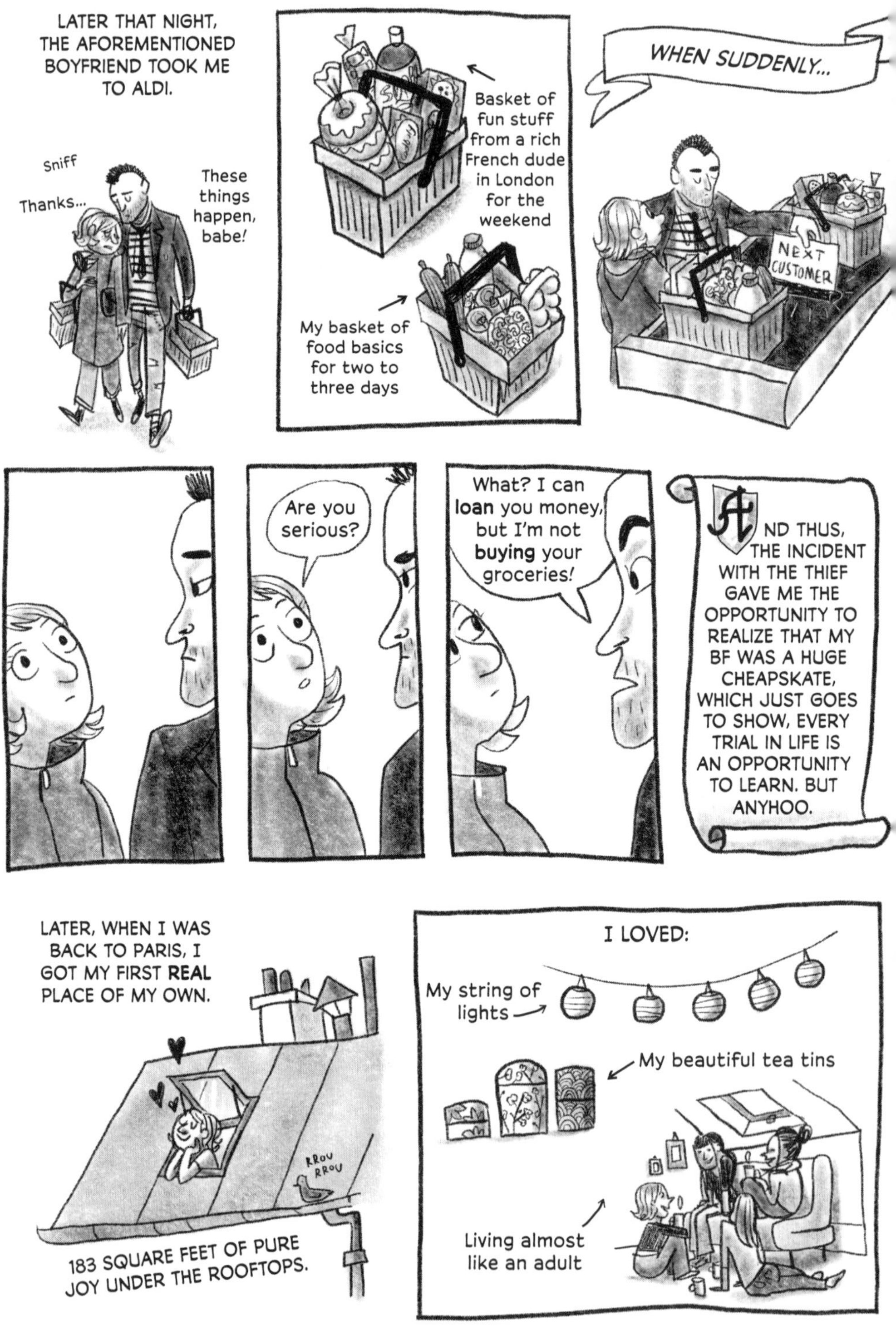
LATER THAT NIGHT, THE AFOREMENTIONED BOYFRIEND TOOK ME TO ALDI.
Sniff
Thanks...
These things happen, babe!
Basket of fun stuff from a rich French dude in London for the weekend
My basket of food basics for two to three days
WHEN SUDDENLY...
NEXT CUSTOMER
Are you serious?
What? I can **loan** you money, but I'm not **buying** your groceries!
AND THUS, THE INCIDENT WITH THE THIEF GAVE ME THE OPPORTUNITY TO REALIZE THAT MY BF WAS A HUGE CHEAPSKATE, WHICH JUST GOES TO SHOW, EVERY TRIAL IN LIFE IS AN OPPORTUNITY TO LEARN. BUT ANYHOO.
LATER, WHEN I WAS BACK TO PARIS, I GOT MY FIRST **REAL** PLACE OF MY OWN.
RROU RROU
183 SQUARE FEET OF PURE JOY UNDER THE ROOFTOPS.
I LOVED:
My string of lights
My beautiful tea tins
Living almost like an adult

I HATED WITH EVERY FIBER OF MY BEING:

Working under a comforter from October on.

Argh! When I grow up, it's going to be hot in my place!

↗ (26 years old)

I'D OCCASIONALLY GIVE IN AND TURN ON THE SPACE HEATER...

CLACK

...AND IMMEDIATELY WATCH THE LITTLE GAUGE ON THE ELECTRIC METER START TO SPIN SO FAST IT BECAME BLURRY.

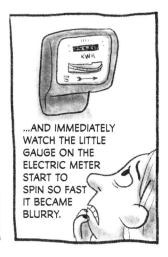

HOW IS IT THAT AFTER SUCH A PRIVILEGED UPBRINGING, WHERE I NEVER WANTED FOR ANYTHING, I DEVELOPED SUCH AN ODD OBSESSION?

Whew, it's a little hot in here, no?

Ooh, thaaaanks!

NOWADAYS, I'M LUCKY NOT TO HAVE TO WORK UNDER A COMFORTER, AND YET THIS OBSESSION PERSISTS.

Death   War   Famine   Conquest   Bare feet on cold tiles

OVER THE YEARS, I'VE ENHANCED MY LIFE BY USING NUMEROUS TRICKS. SUCH AS A SUPER-WARM YET STYLISH INDOOR SWEATER.

RECENTLY, I LEARNED THAT IN TRADITIONAL RUSSIAN WOOD HOMES, THE FIREPLACE WAS IN THE MIDDLE OF THE LIVING ROOM. THE FAMILY SLEPT AROUND (AND ON TOP OF!) THE "PETCHKA."

And this is now my life goal.

CLAP

-FIN-

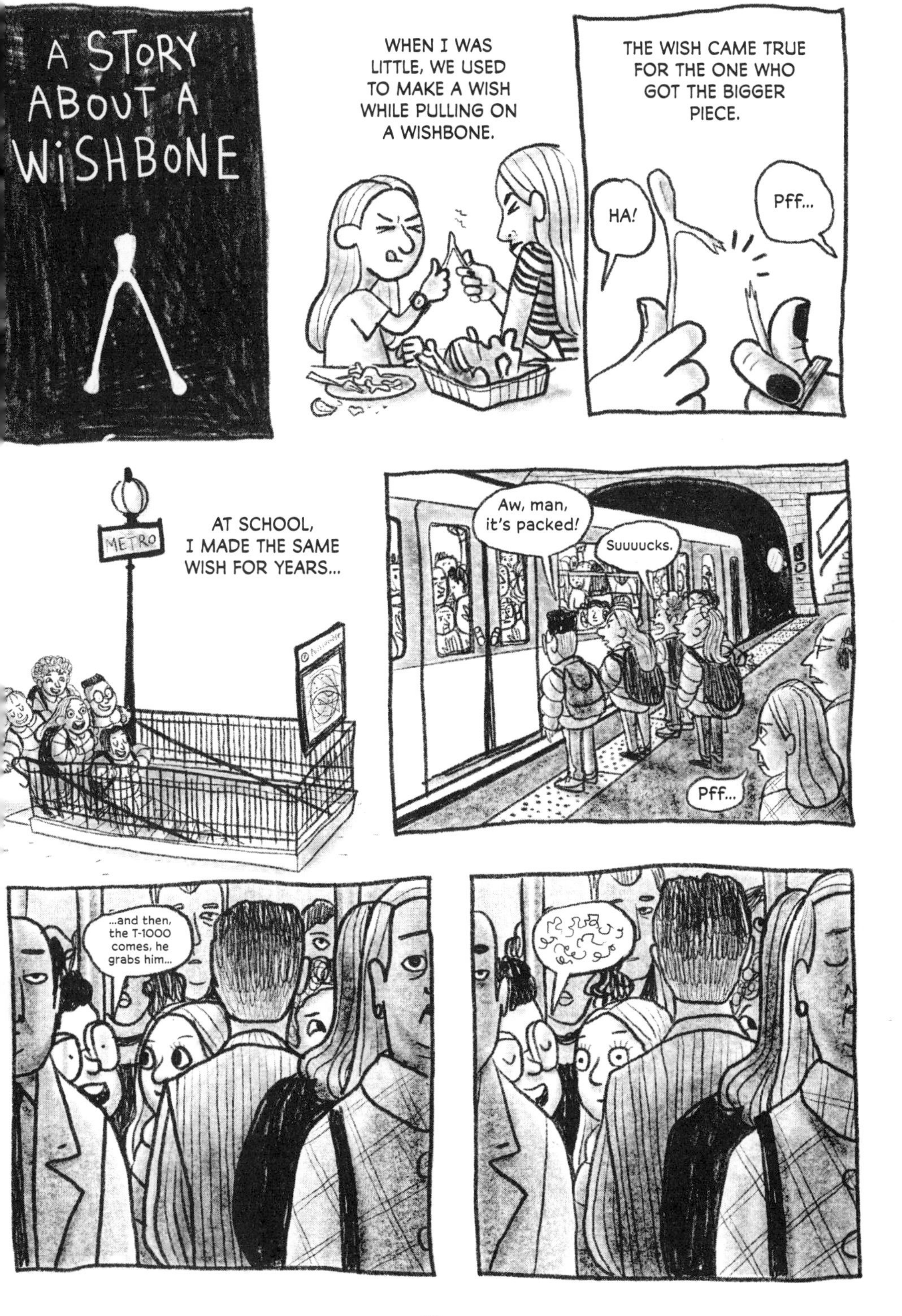
A STORY ABOUT A WISHBONE
WHEN I WAS LITTLE, WE USED TO MAKE A WISH WHILE PULLING ON A WISHBONE.
THE WISH CAME TRUE FOR THE ONE WHO GOT THE BIGGER PIECE.
HA!
Pff...
METRO
AT SCHOOL, I MADE THE SAME WISH FOR YEARS...
Aw, man, it's packed!
Suuuucks.
Pff...
...and then, the T-1000 comes, he grabs him...

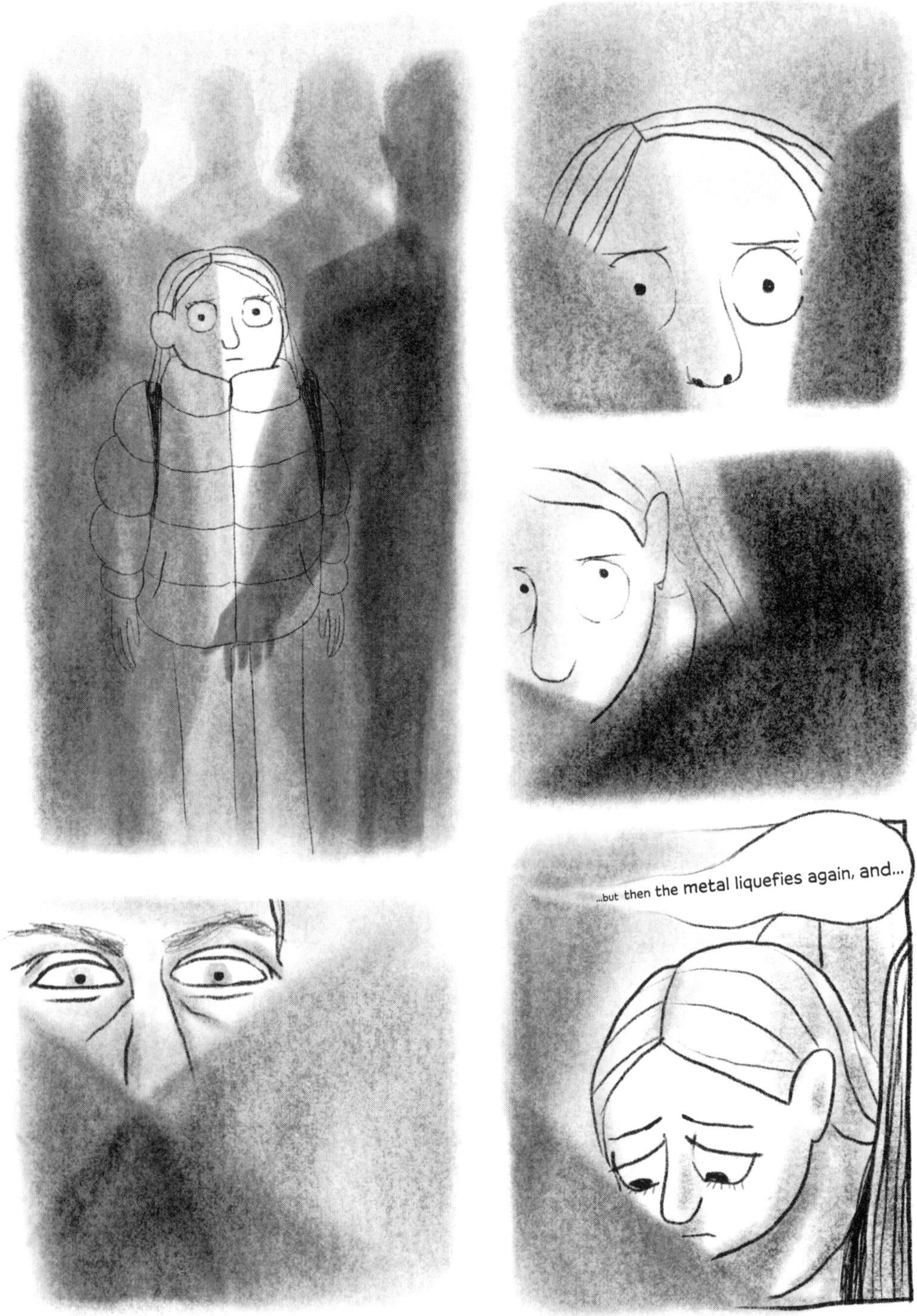
...but then the metal liquefies again, and...

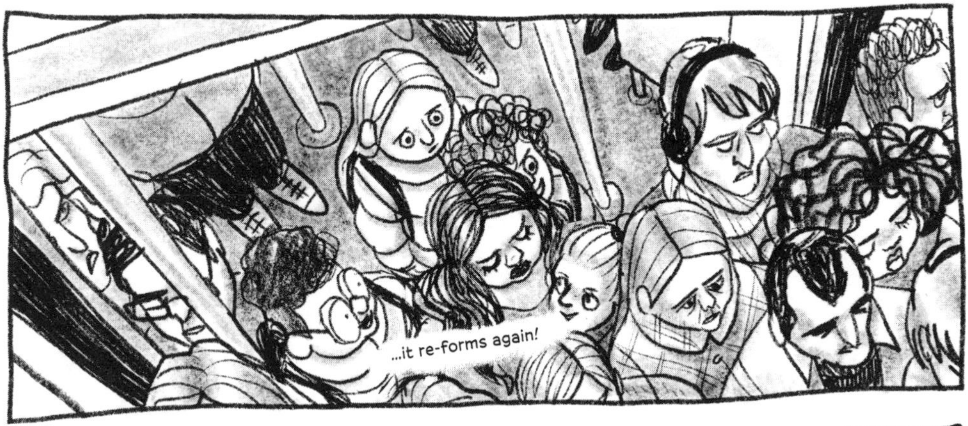
...it re-forms again!

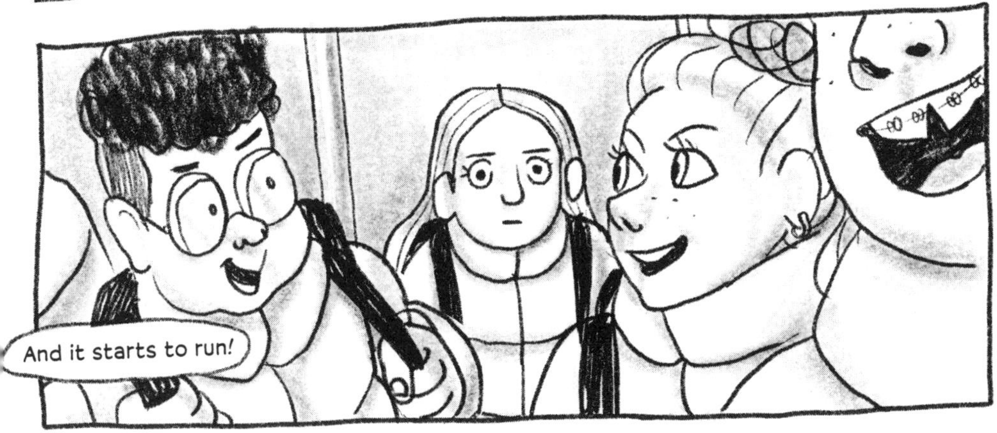
And it starts to run!

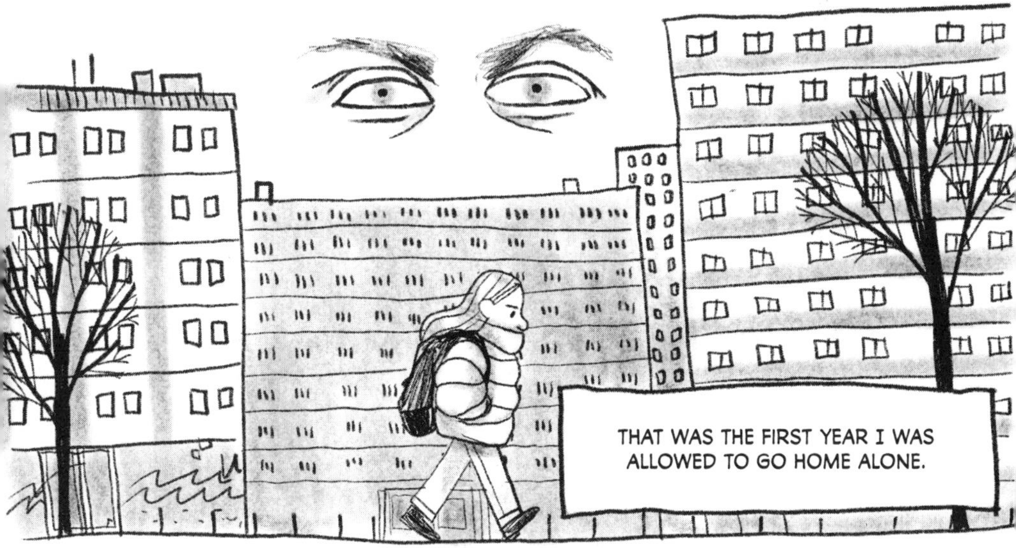
THAT WAS THE FIRST YEAR I WAS
ALLOWED TO GO HOME ALONE.

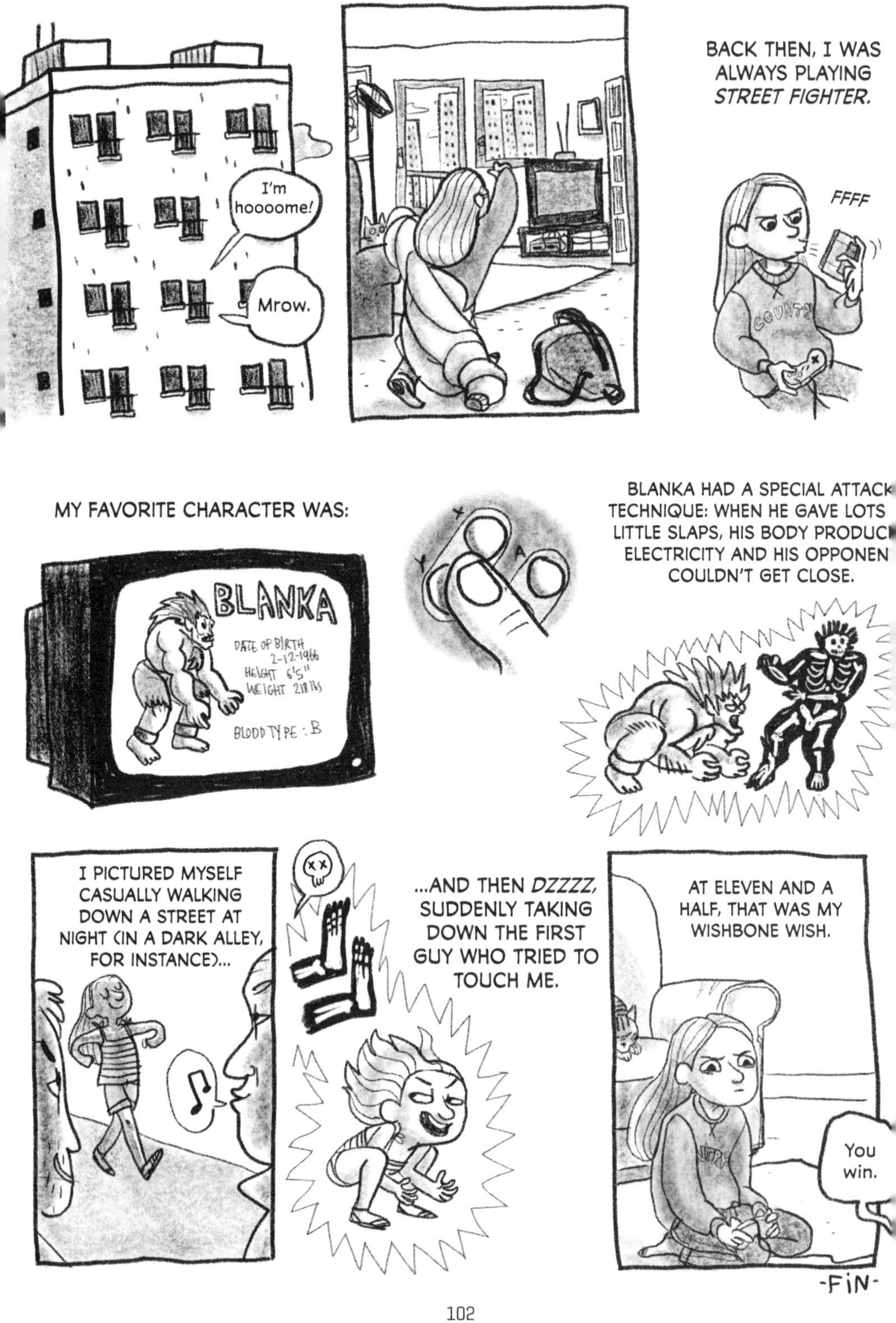
I'm hoooome!
Mrow.
BACK THEN, I WAS ALWAYS PLAYING *STREET FIGHTER.*
FFFF
COUNTRY
MY FAVORITE CHARACTER WAS:
BLANKA
DATE OF BIRTH 2-12-1966
HEIGHT 6'5"
WEIGHT 218 lbs
BLOOD TYPE : B
X
Y
A
BLANKA HAD A SPECIAL ATTACK
TECHNIQUE: WHEN HE GAVE LOTS
LITTLE SLAPS, HIS BODY PRODUC
ELECTRICITY AND HIS OPPONEN
COULDN'T GET CLOSE.
I PICTURED MYSELF CASUALLY WALKING DOWN A STREET AT NIGHT (IN A DARK ALLEY, FOR INSTANCE)...
...AND THEN *DZZZZ,* SUDDENLY TAKING DOWN THE FIRST GUY WHO TRIED TO TOUCH ME.
AT ELEVEN AND A HALF, THAT WAS MY WISHBONE WISH.
You win.
-FIN-

DÉJÀ VU 2

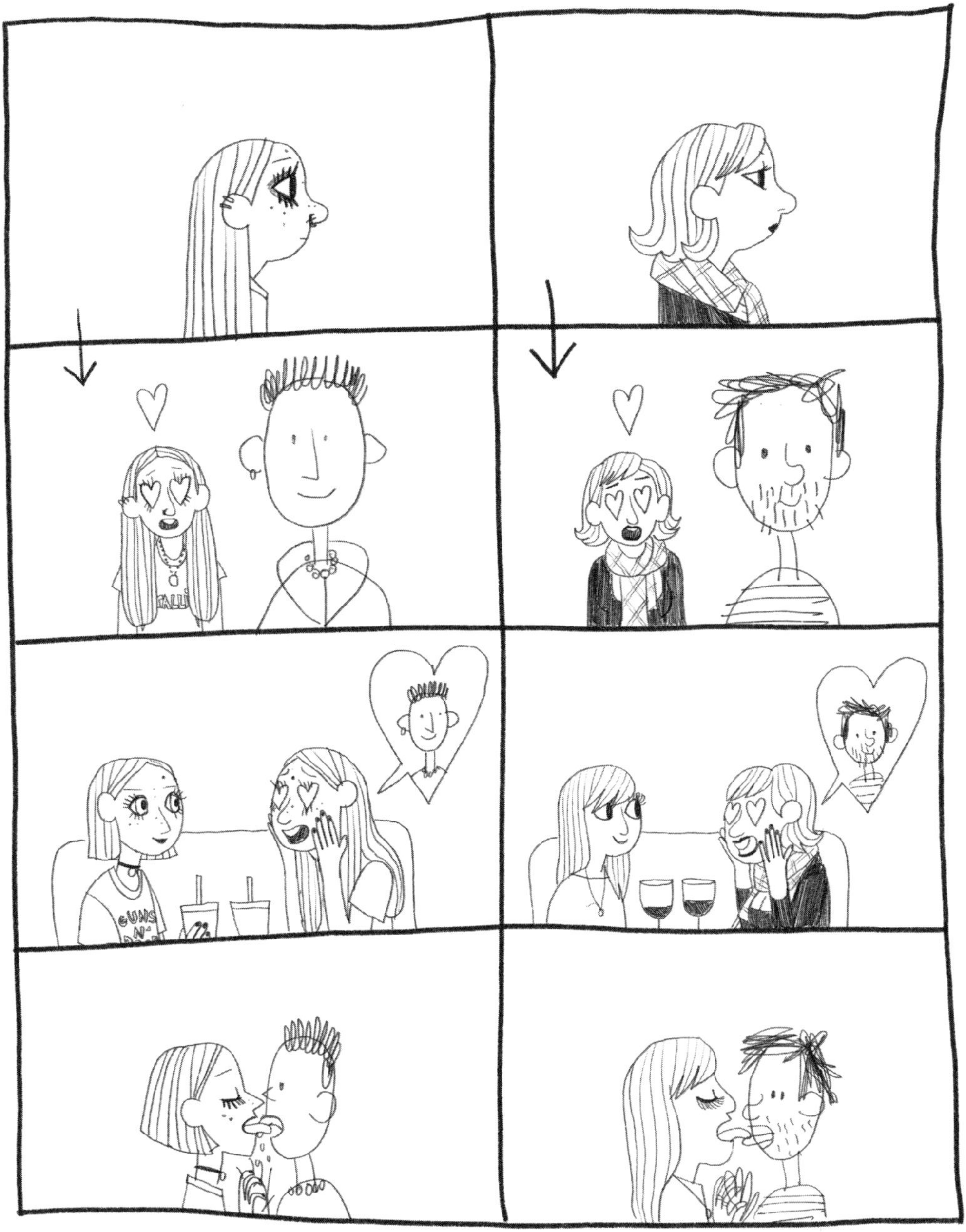

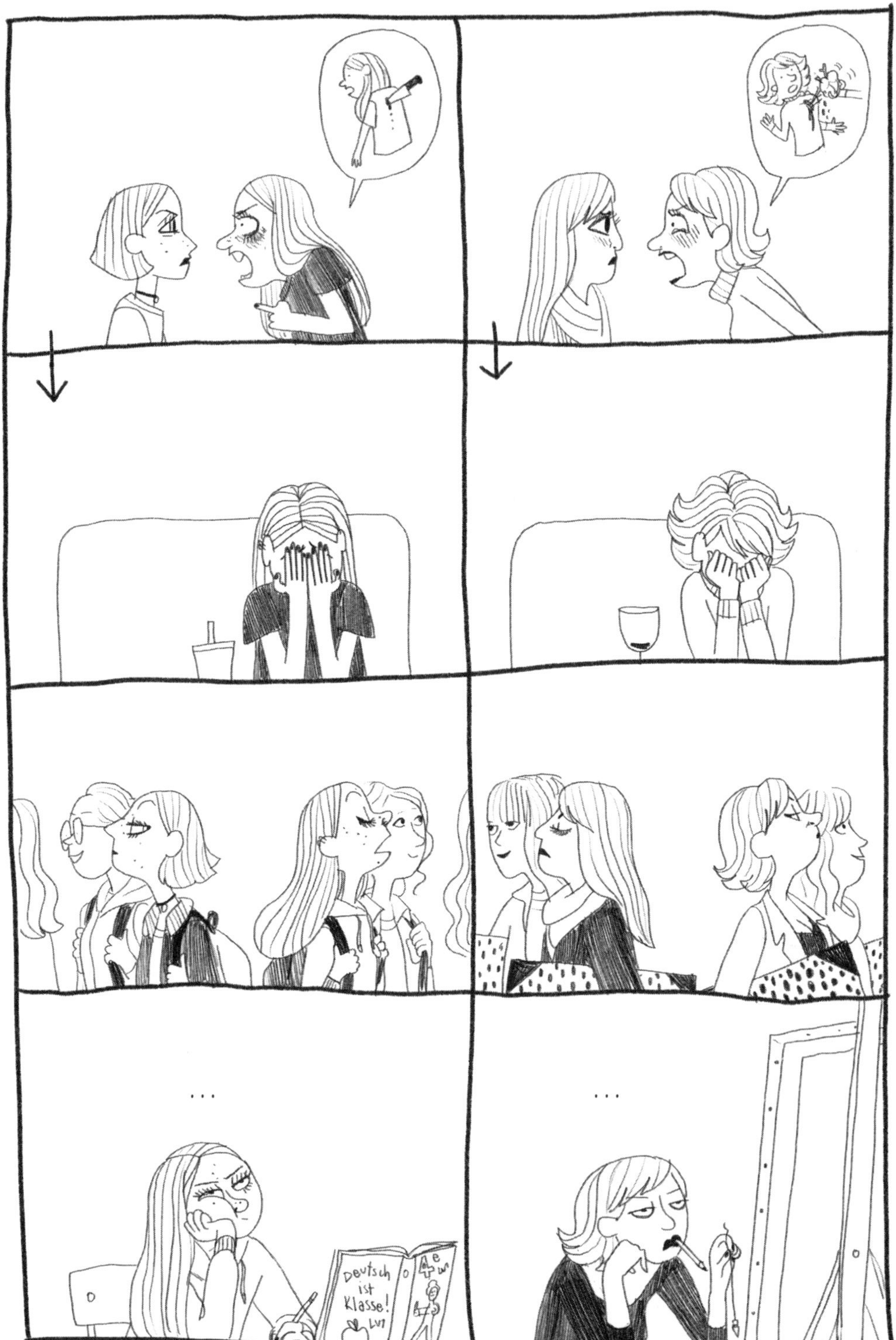
...
Deutsch ist Klasse!
...

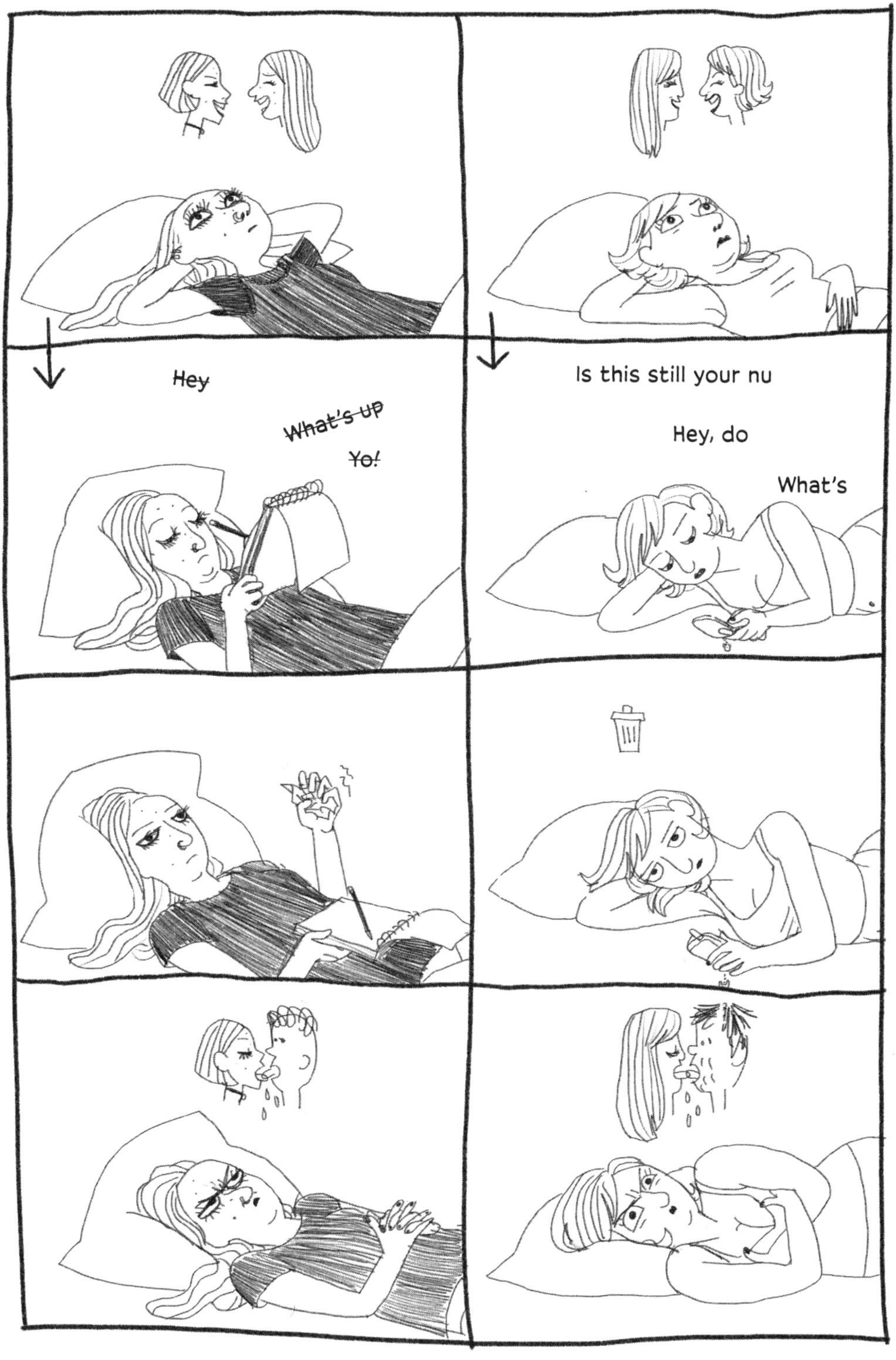

Hey
What's up
Yo!
Is this still your nu
Hey, do
What's

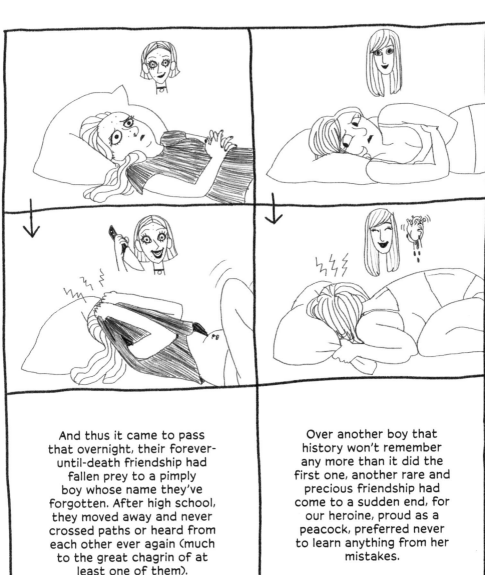

And thus it came to pass that overnight, their forever-until-death friendship had fallen prey to a pimply boy whose name they've forgotten. After high school, they moved away and never crossed paths or heard from each other ever again (much to the great chagrin of at least one of them).

THE END

Over another boy that history won't remember any more than it did the first one, another rare and precious friendship had come to a sudden end, for our heroine, proud as a peacock, preferred never to learn anything from her mistakes.

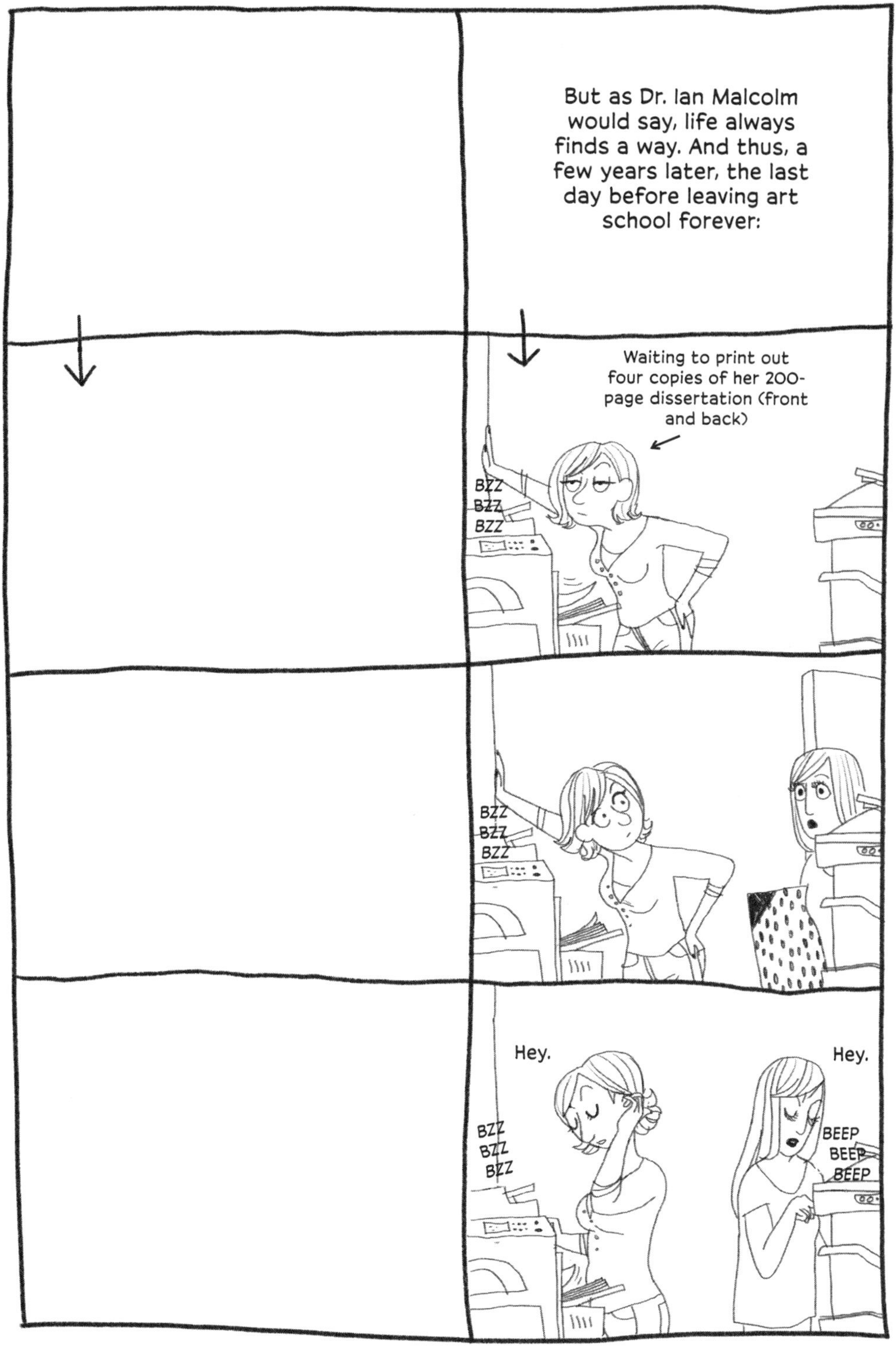
But as Dr. Ian Malcolm would say, life always finds a way. And thus, a few years later, the last day before leaving art school forever:
Waiting to print out four copies of her 200-page dissertation (front and back)
BZZ BZZ BZZ
BZZ BZZ BZZ
Hey.
Hey.
BZZ BZZ BZZ
BEEP BEEP BEEP

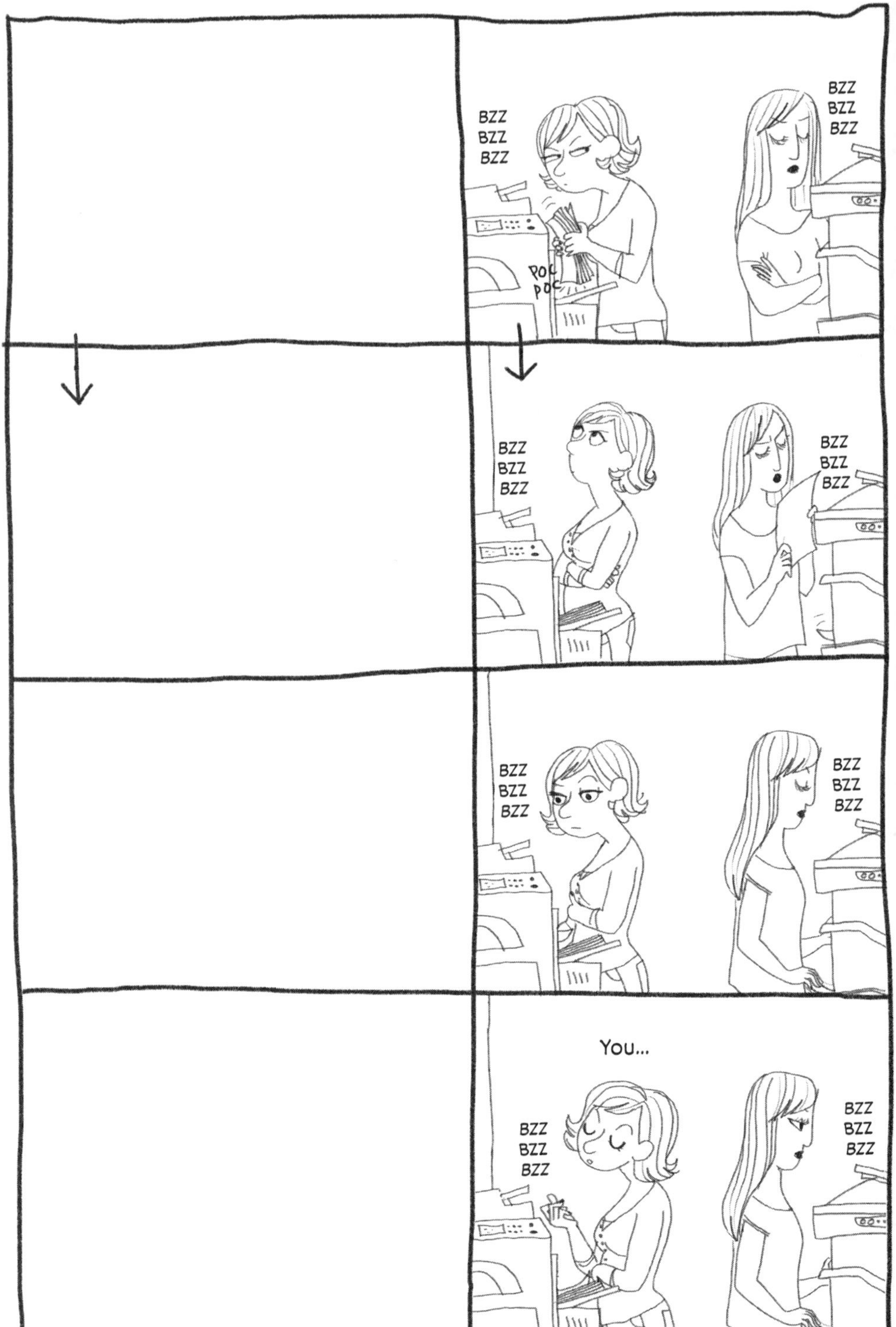
BZZ
BZZ
BZZ
POC
POC
BZZ
BZZ
BZZ
BZZ
BZZ
BZZ
BZZ
BZZ
BZZ
BZZ
BZZ
BZZ
BZZ
BZZ
BZZ
You...
BZZ
BZZ
BZZ
BZZ
BZZ
BZZ

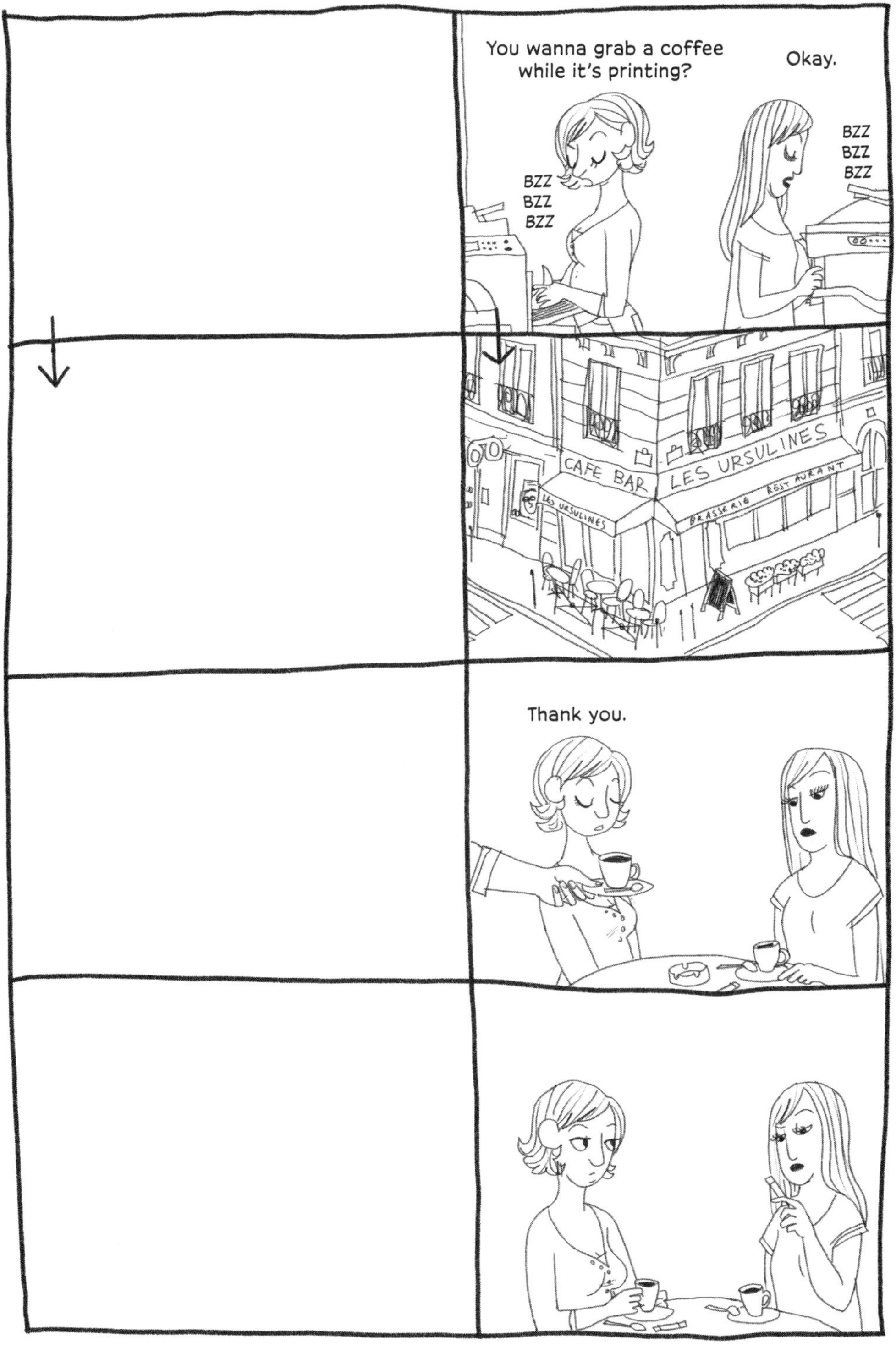
You wanna grab a coffee while it's printing?
Okay.
BZZ BZZ BZZ
BZZ BZZ BZZ
CAFE BAR
LES URSULINES
LES URSULINES
BRASSERIE RESTAURANT
Thank you.

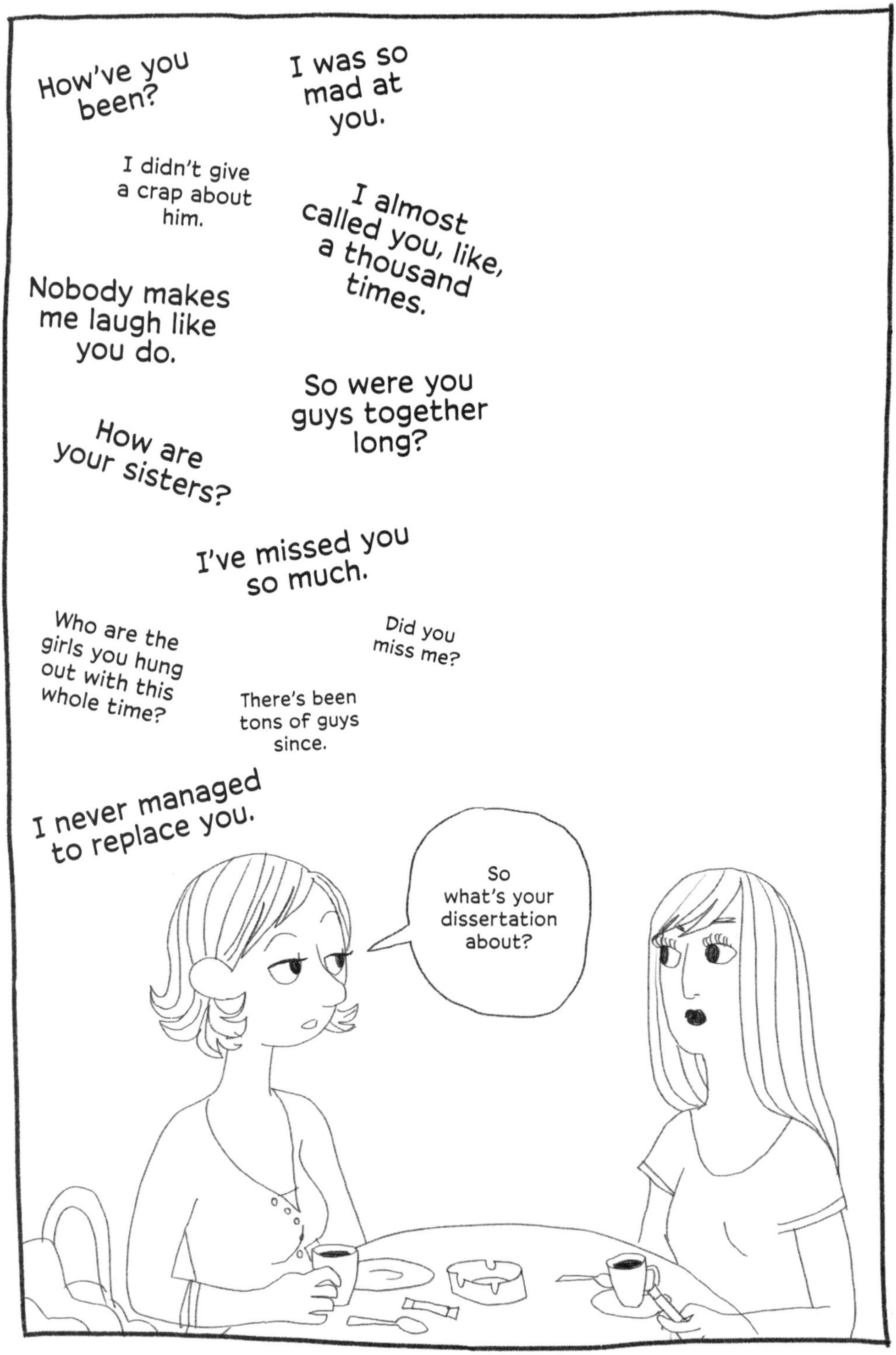
How've you been?
I was so mad at you.
I didn't give a crap about him.
I almost called you, like, a thousand times.
Nobody makes me laugh like you do.
So were you guys together long?
How are your sisters?
I've missed you so much.
Who are the girls you hung out with this whole time?
Did you miss me?
There's been tons of guys since.
I never managed to replace you.
So what's your dissertation about?

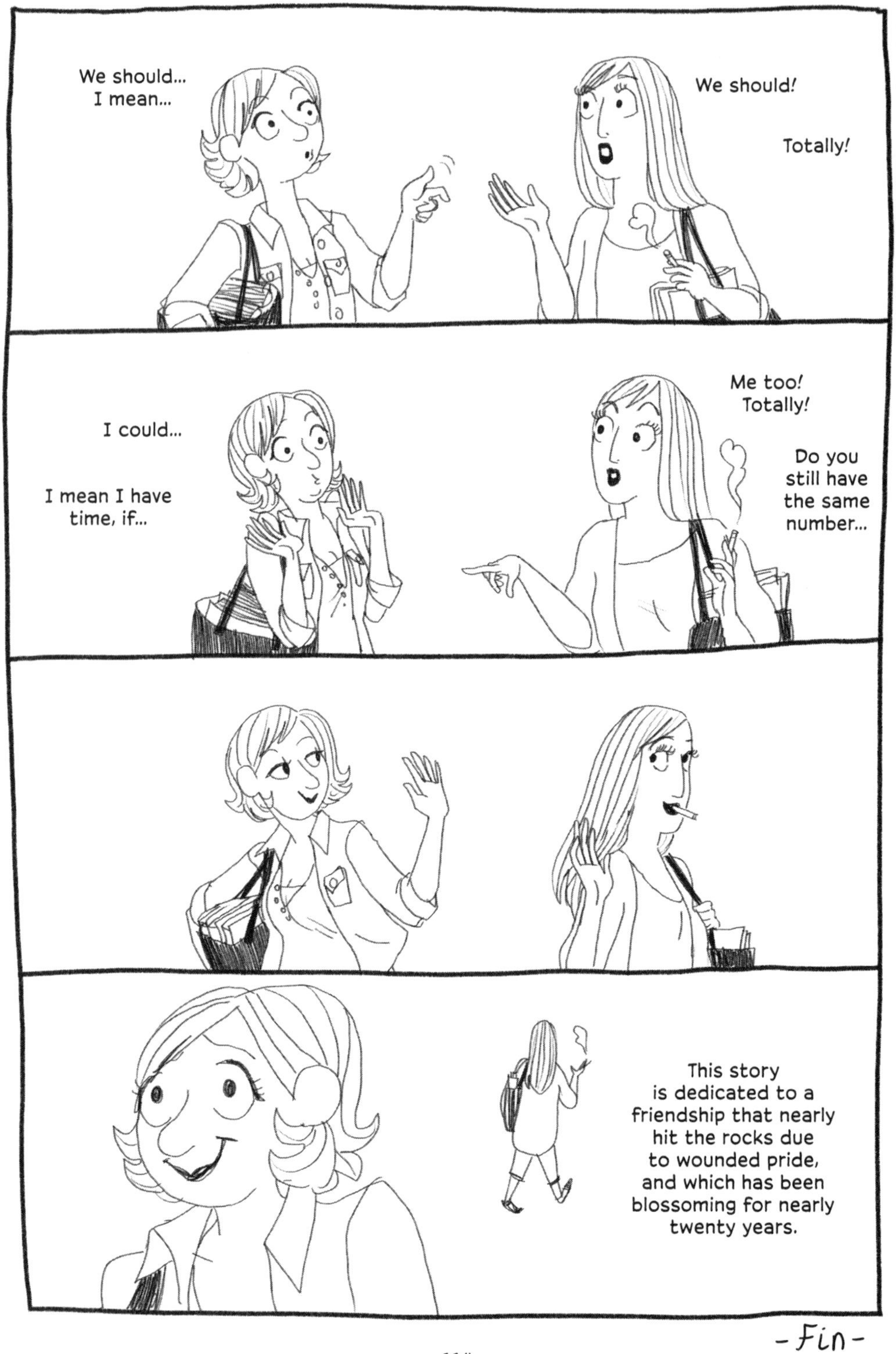
We should...
I mean...
We should!
Totally!
I could...
I mean I have
time, if...
Me too!
Totally!
Do you
still have
the same
number...
This story
is dedicated to a
friendship that nearly
hit the rocks due
to wounded pride,
and which has been
blossoming for nearly
twenty years.

-Fin-

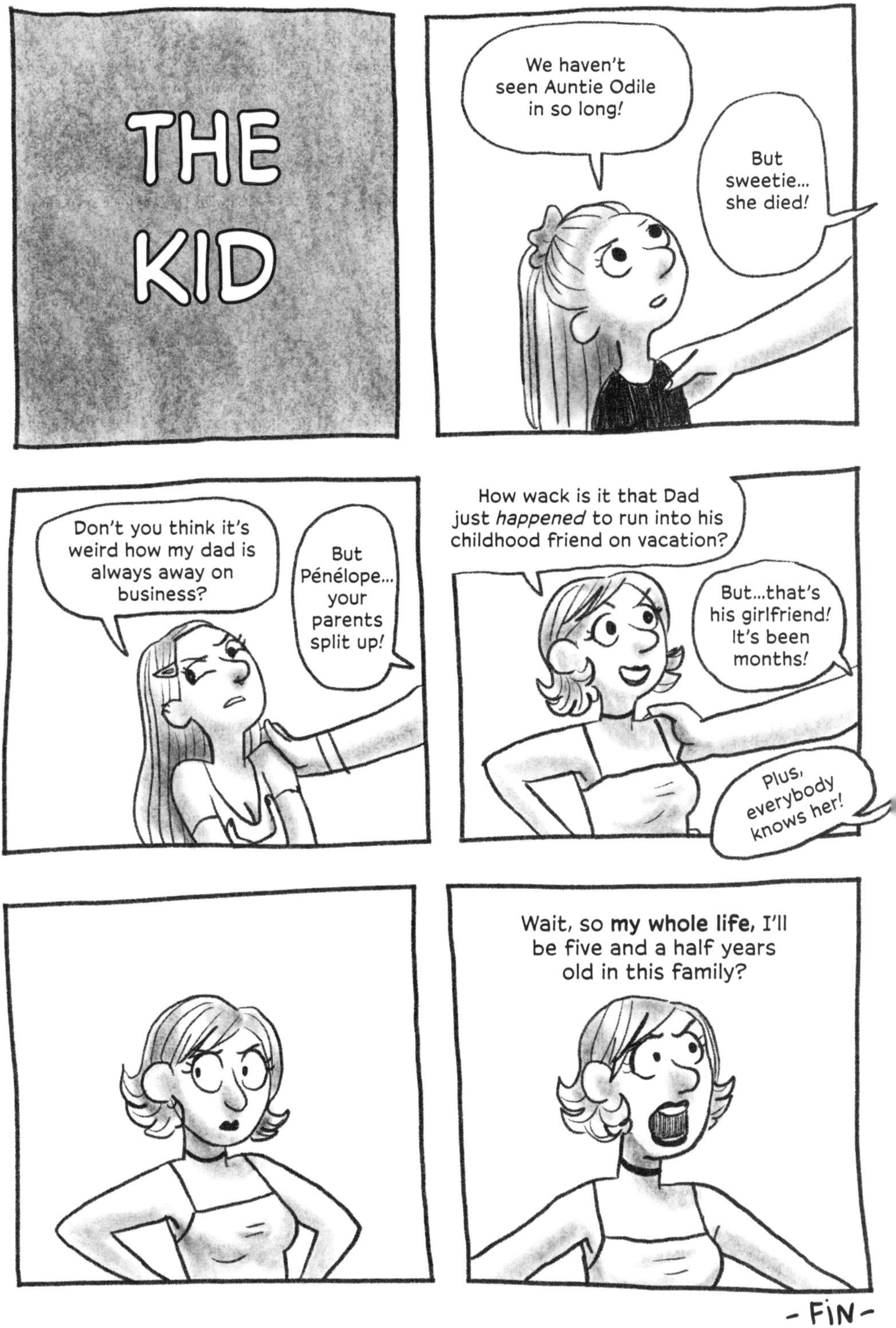
THE KID
We haven't seen Auntie Odile in so long!
But sweetie... she died!
Don't you think it's weird how my dad is always away on business?
But Pénélope... your parents split up!
How wack is it that Dad just *happened* to run into his childhood friend on vacation?
But...that's his girlfriend! It's been months!
Plus, everybody knows her!
Wait, so **my whole life,** I'll be five and a half years old in this family?
-FIN-

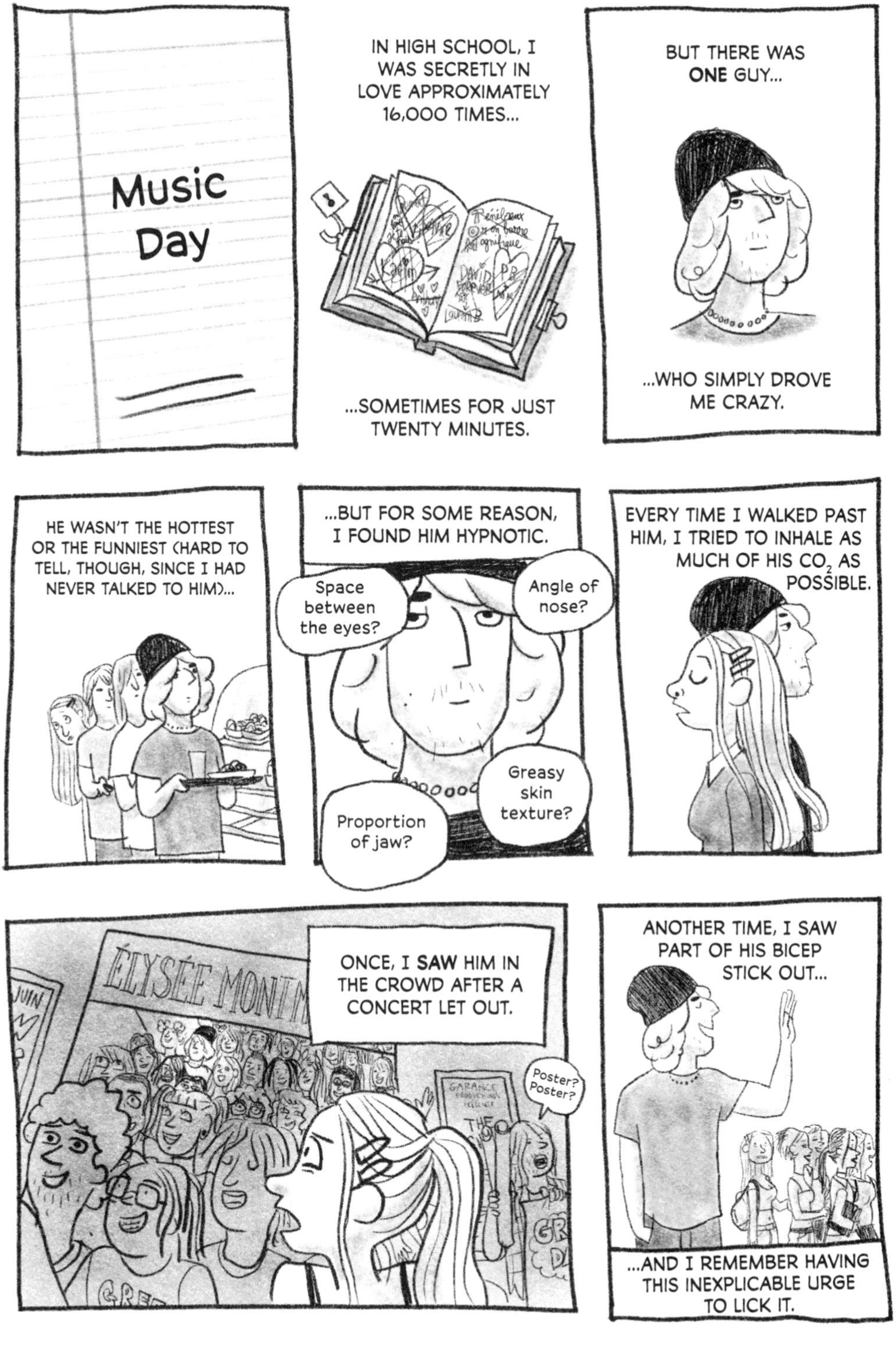
Music Day
IN HIGH SCHOOL, I WAS SECRETLY IN LOVE APPROXIMATELY 16,000 TIMES...
...SOMETIMES FOR JUST TWENTY MINUTES.
BUT THERE WAS **ONE** GUY...
...WHO SIMPLY DROVE ME CRAZY.
HE WASN'T THE HOTTEST OR THE FUNNIEST (HARD TO TELL, THOUGH, SINCE I HAD NEVER TALKED TO HIM)...
...BUT FOR SOME REASON, I FOUND HIM HYPNOTIC.
Space between the eyes?
Angle of nose?
Greasy skin texture?
Proportion of jaw?
EVERY TIME I WALKED PAST HIM, I TRIED TO INHALE AS MUCH OF HIS CO_2 AS POSSIBLE.
ÉLYSÉE
JUIN
ONCE, I **SAW** HIM IN THE CROWD AFTER A CONCERT LET OUT.
Poster? Poster?
ANOTHER TIME, I SAW PART OF HIS BICEP STICK OUT...
...AND I REMEMBER HAVING THIS INEXPLICABLE URGE TO LICK IT.

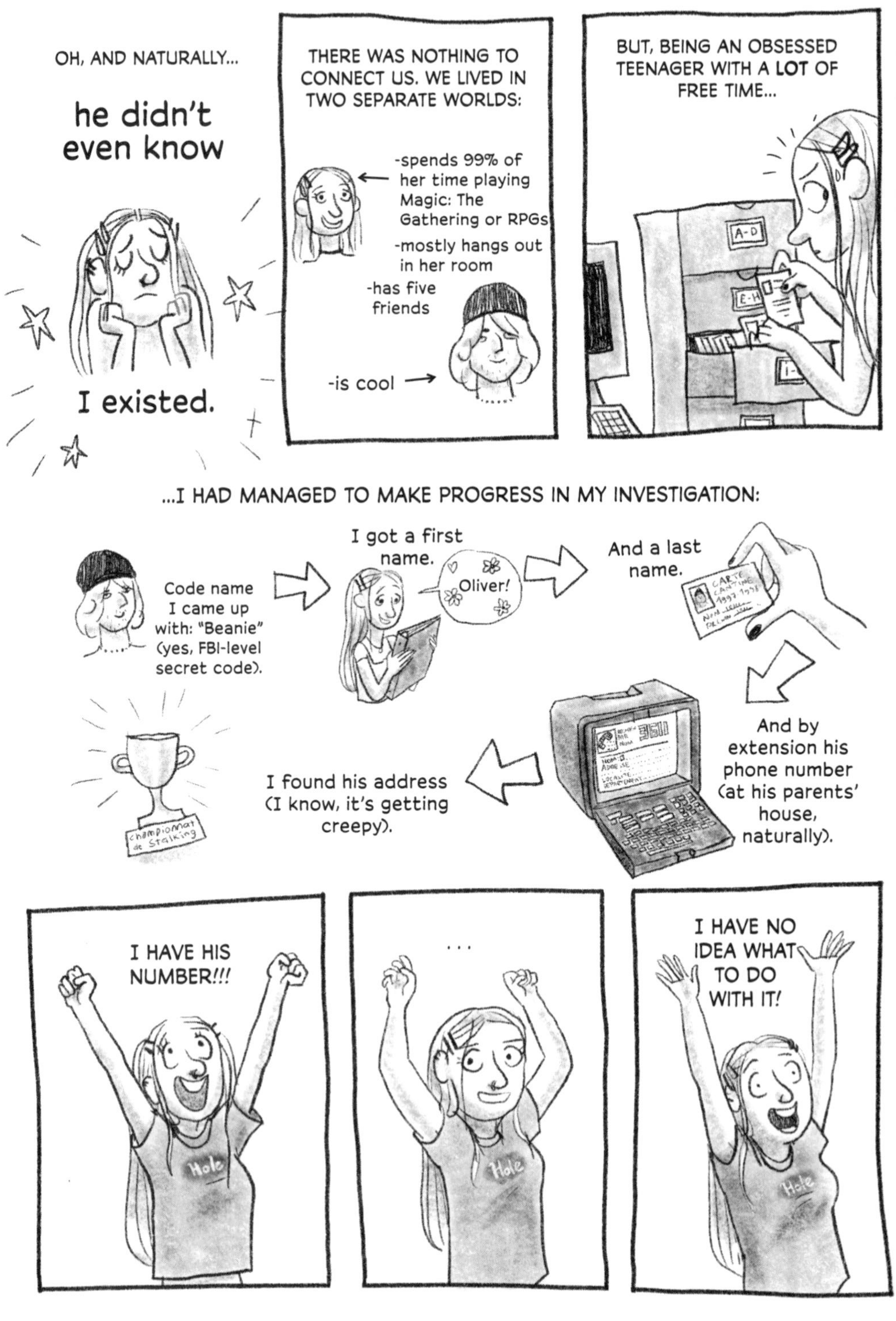

OH, AND NATURALLY...
he didn't even know
I existed.
THERE WAS NOTHING TO CONNECT US. WE LIVED IN TWO SEPARATE WORLDS:
-spends 99% of her time playing Magic: The Gathering or RPGs
-mostly hangs out in her room
-has five friends
-is cool
BUT, BEING AN OBSESSED TEENAGER WITH A **LOT** OF FREE TIME...
A-D
E-H
...I HAD MANAGED TO MAKE PROGRESS IN MY INVESTIGATION:
Code name I came up with: "Beanie" (yes, FBI-level secret code).
I got a first name.
Oliver!
And a last name.
And by extension his phone number (at his parents' house, naturally).
I found his address (I know, it's getting creepy).
championnat de stalking
I HAVE HIS NUMBER!!!
. . .
I HAVE NO IDEA WHAT TO DO WITH IT!
Hole
Hole
Hole

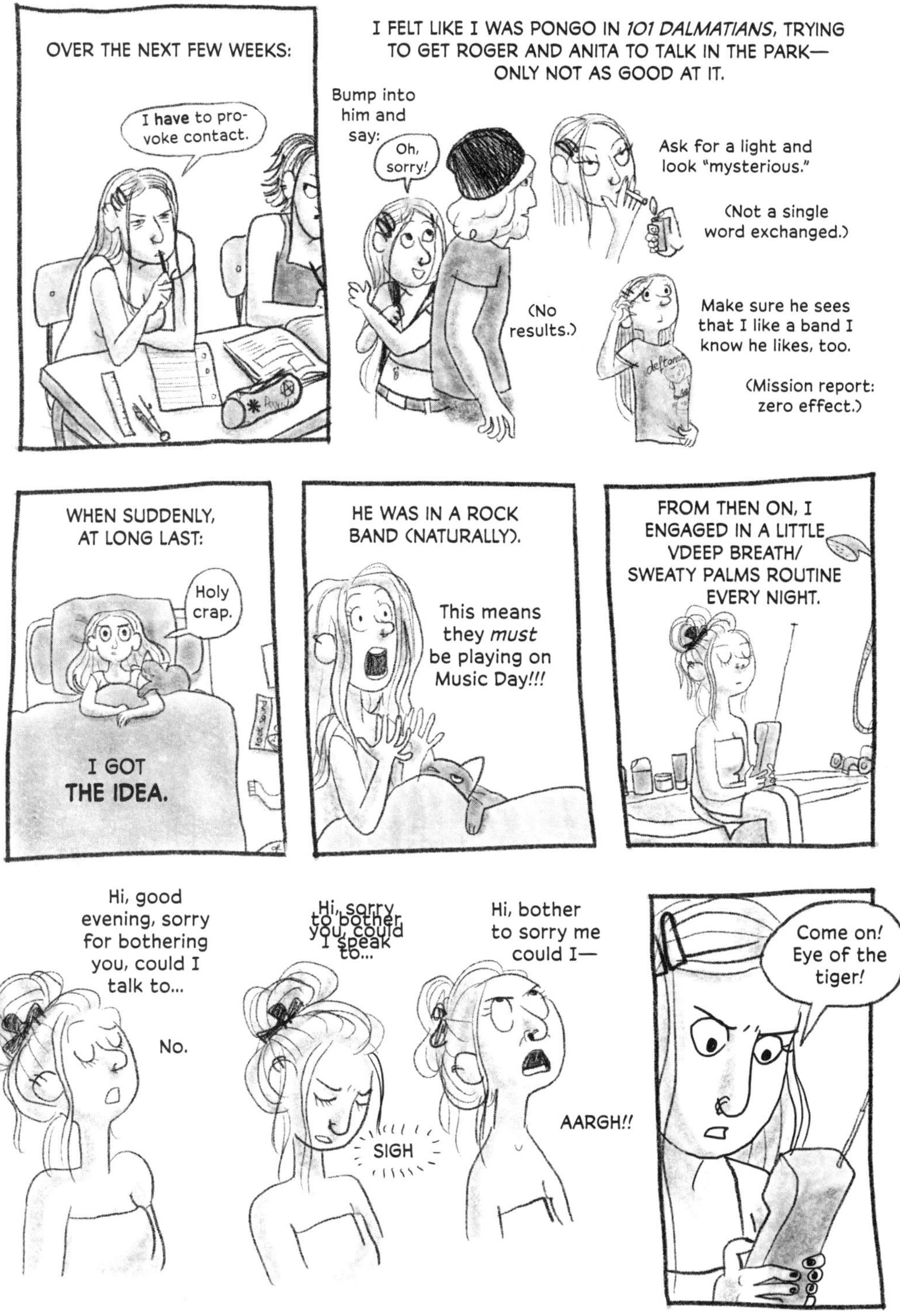
OVER THE NEXT FEW WEEKS:
I **have** to provoke contact.
I FELT LIKE I WAS PONGO IN *101 DALMATIANS*, TRYING TO GET ROGER AND ANITA TO TALK IN THE PARK—ONLY NOT AS GOOD AT IT.
Bump into him and say:
Oh, sorry!
(No results.)
Ask for a light and look "mysterious."
(Not a single word exchanged.)
Make sure he sees that I like a band I know he likes, too.
(Mission report: zero effect.)
WHEN SUDDENLY, AT LONG LAST:
Holy crap.
I GOT **THE IDEA.**
HE WAS IN A ROCK BAND (NATURALLY).
This means they *must* be playing on Music Day!!!
FROM THEN ON, I ENGAGED IN A LITTLE DEEP BREATH/SWEATY PALMS ROUTINE EVERY NIGHT.
Hi, good evening, sorry for bothering you, could I talk to...
No.
Hi, sorry to bother you, could I speak to...
SIGH
Hi, bother to sorry me could I—
AARGH!!
Come on! Eye of the tiger!

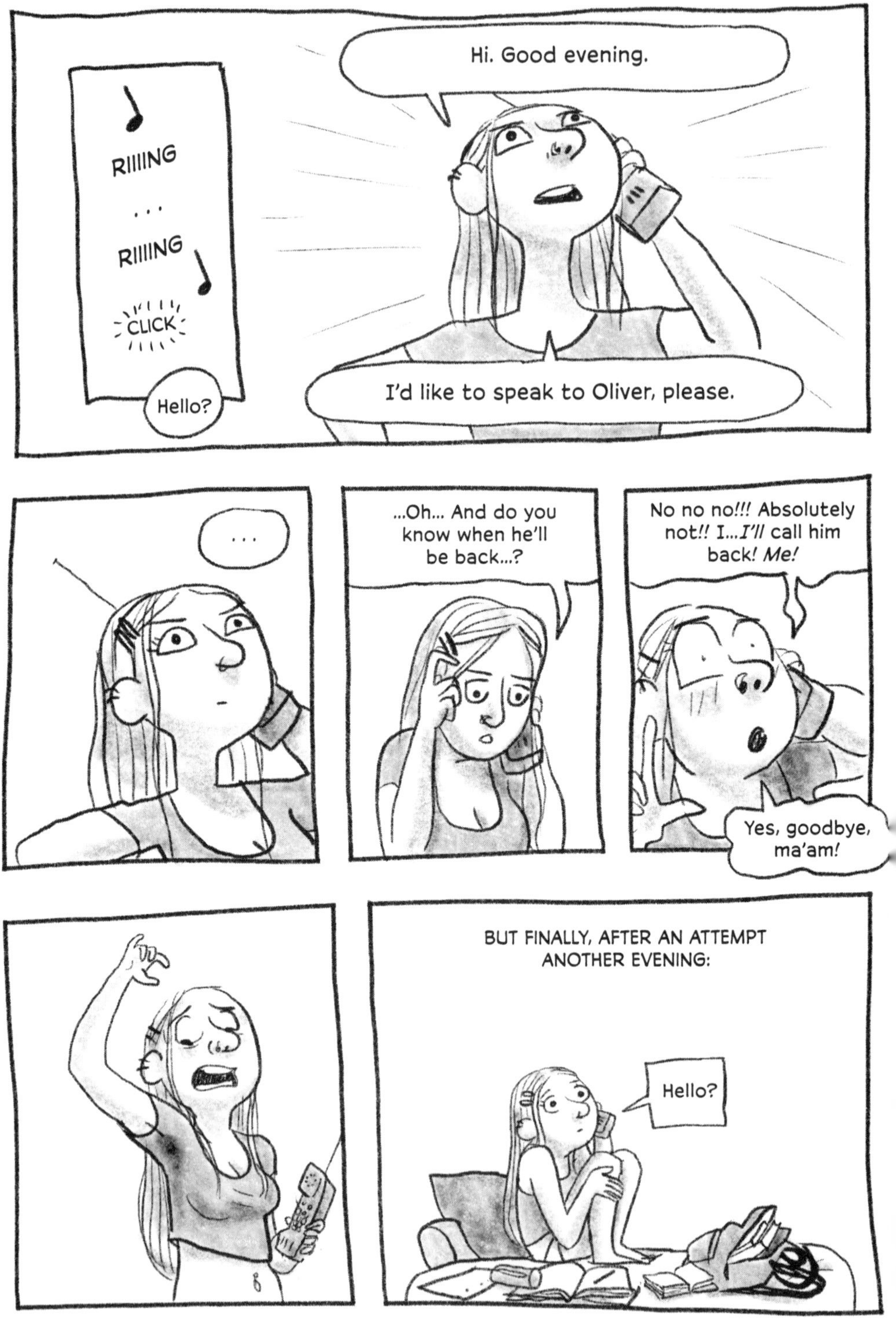
RIIIING
...
RIIIING
CLICK
Hello?
Hi. Good evening.
I'd like to speak to Oliver, please.
...
...Oh... And do you know when he'll be back...?
No no no!!! Absolutely not!! I...*I'll* call him back! *Me!*
Yes, goodbye, ma'am!
BUT FINALLY, AFTER AN ATTEMPT ANOTHER EVENING:
Hello?

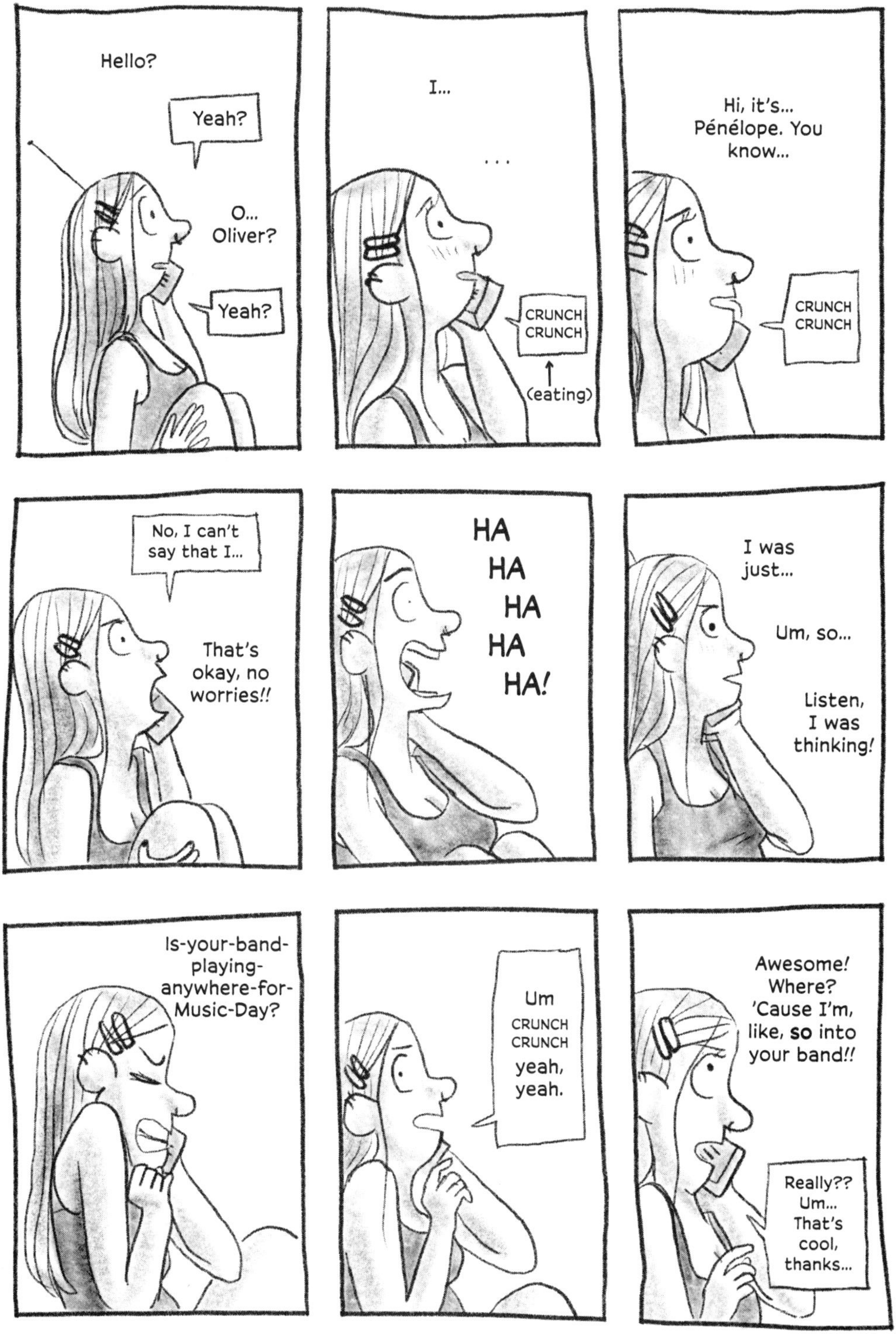

Hello?
Yeah?
O... Oliver?
Yeah?
I...
. . .
CRUNCH CRUNCH
(eating)
Hi, it's... Pénélope. You know...
CRUNCH CRUNCH
No, I can't say that I...
That's okay, no worries!!
HA HA HA HA HA!
I was just...
Um, so...
Listen, I was thinking!
Is-your-band-playing-anywhere-for-Music-Day?
Um CRUNCH CRUNCH yeah, yeah.
Awesome! Where? 'Cause I'm, like, **so** into your band!!
Really?? Um... That's cool, thanks...

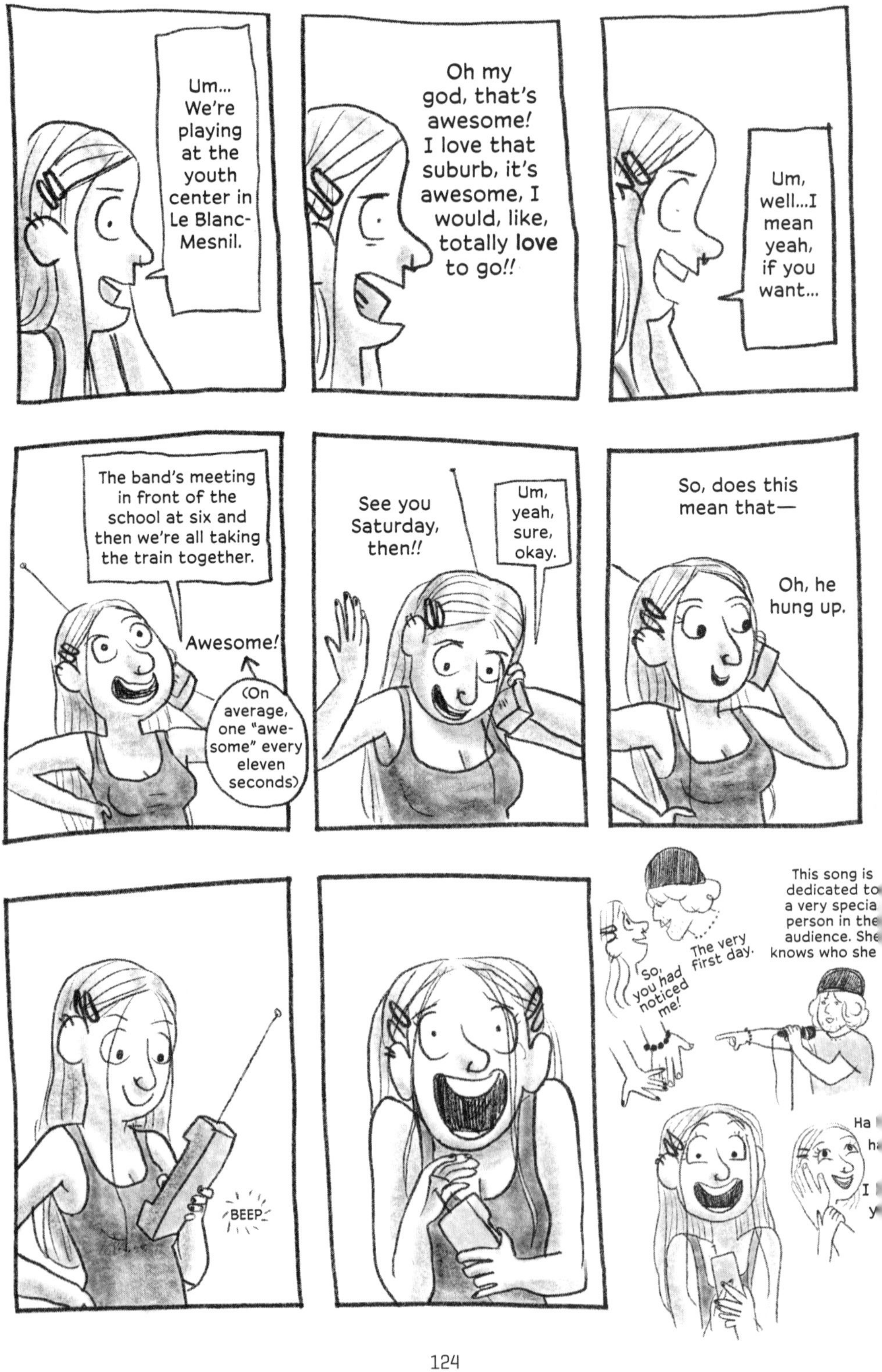

Um... We're playing at the youth center in Le Blanc-Mesnil.
Oh my god, that's awesome! I love that suburb, it's awesome, I would, like, totally **love** to go!!
Um, well...I mean yeah, if you want...
The band's meeting in front of the school at six and then we're all taking the train together.
Awesome!
(On average, one "awe-some" every eleven seconds)
See you Saturday, then!!
Um, yeah, sure, okay.
So, does this mean that—
Oh, he hung up.
BEEP
So, you had noticed me!
The very first day.
This song is dedicated to a very specia person in the audience. She knows who she
Ha

AND NOW, ONE SMALL DETAIL:

On the phone with my best friend

What do you mean, "no"?

Hey, Pen, I have to repeat this year, remember! No Music Day, no going out. I'm grounded until further notice!

But...But I can't go all by myself!!

I CALLED UP JUST ABOUT EVERYONE I HAD EVER MET.

We had dance class together in the sixth grade, remember?

Get off the phone already!

BUT I HAD TO FACE THE FACTS: NOBODY WAS DYING TO GO TO A YOUTH CENTER IN THE BURBS TO SEE SOME OBSCURE BAND.

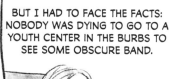

Okay! I'll just pretend I'm waiting for friends, who are running late, upon which I'll say, "Let's go, they can just meet us there!"

(Another piece-of-cake plan)

WHEN THE BIG NIGHT FINALLY CAME, I CHANGED OUTFITS EIGHT TIMES.

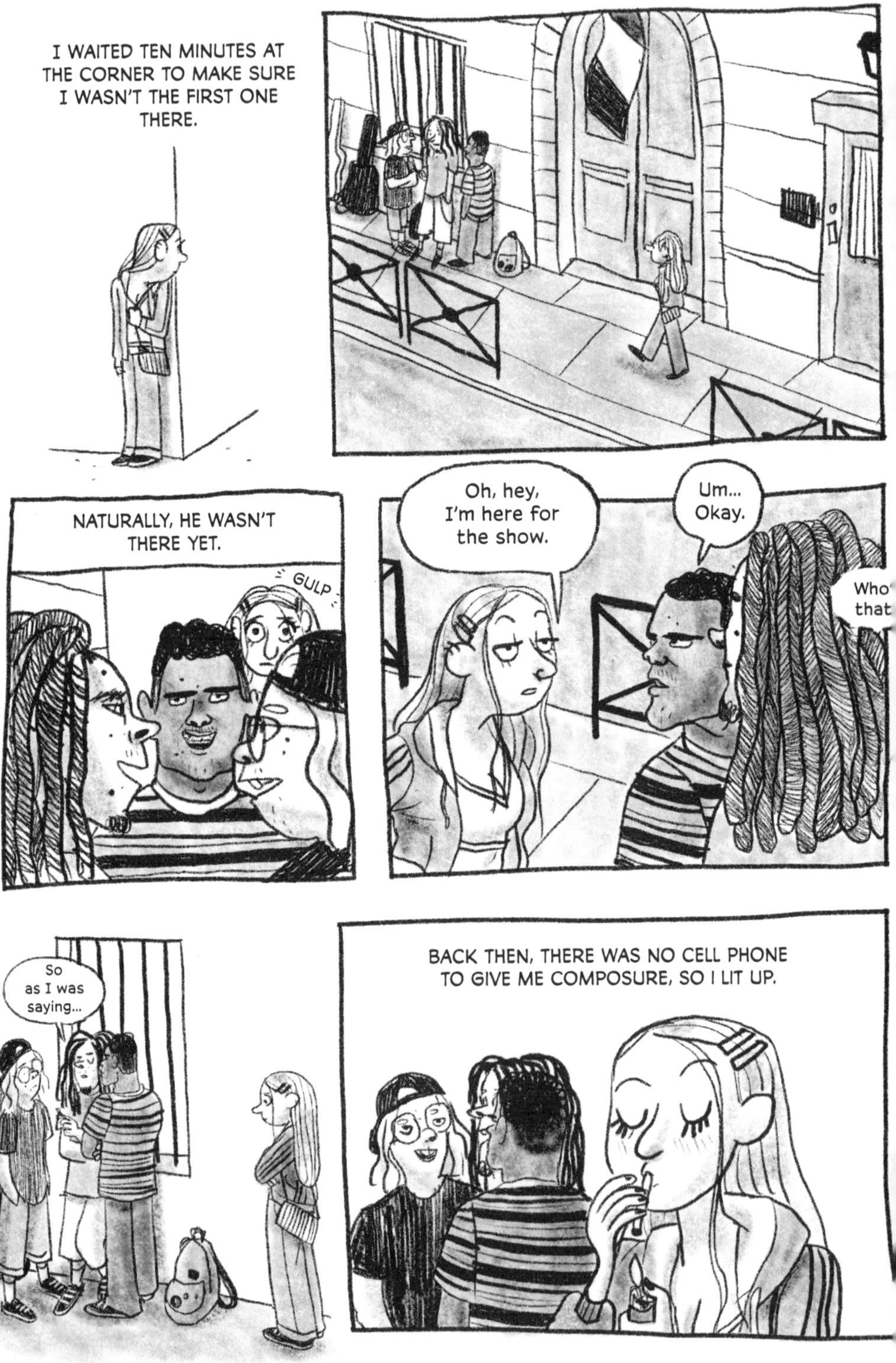

I WAITED TEN MINUTES AT THE CORNER TO MAKE SURE I WASN'T THE FIRST ONE THERE.
NATURALLY, HE WASN'T THERE YET.
GULP
Oh, hey, I'm here for the show.
Um... Okay.
So as I was saying...
BACK THEN, THERE WAS NO CELL PHONE TO GIVE ME COMPOSURE, SO I LIT UP.

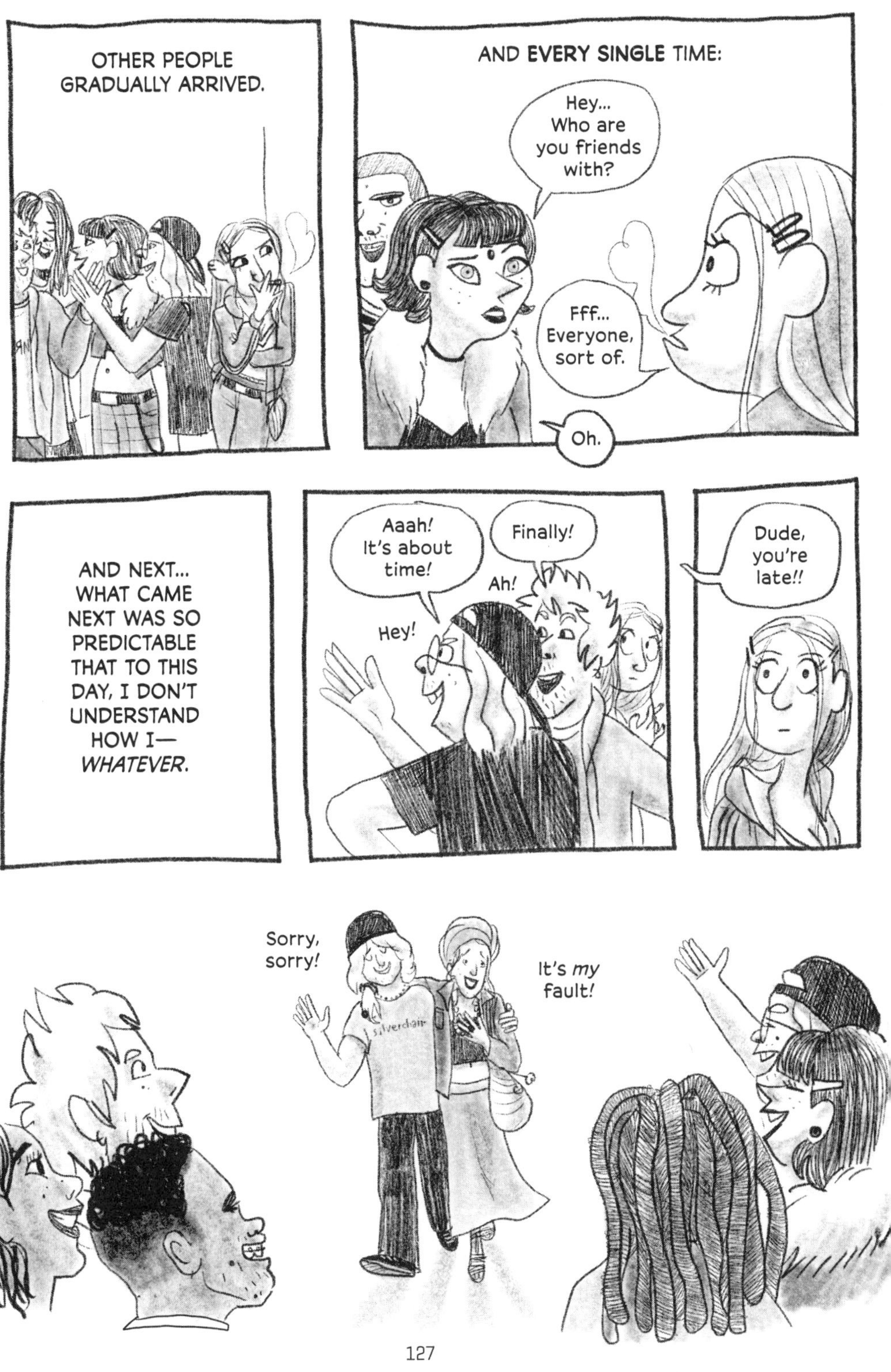
OTHER PEOPLE GRADUALLY ARRIVED.
AND **EVERY SINGLE** TIME:
Hey... Who are you friends with?
Fff... Everyone, sort of.
Oh.
AND NEXT... WHAT CAME NEXT WAS SO PREDICTABLE THAT TO THIS DAY, I DON'T UNDERSTAND HOW I— *WHATEVER*.
Aaah! It's about time!
Finally!
Ah!
Hey!
Dude, you're late!!
Sorry, sorry!
It's *my* fault!
silverchair

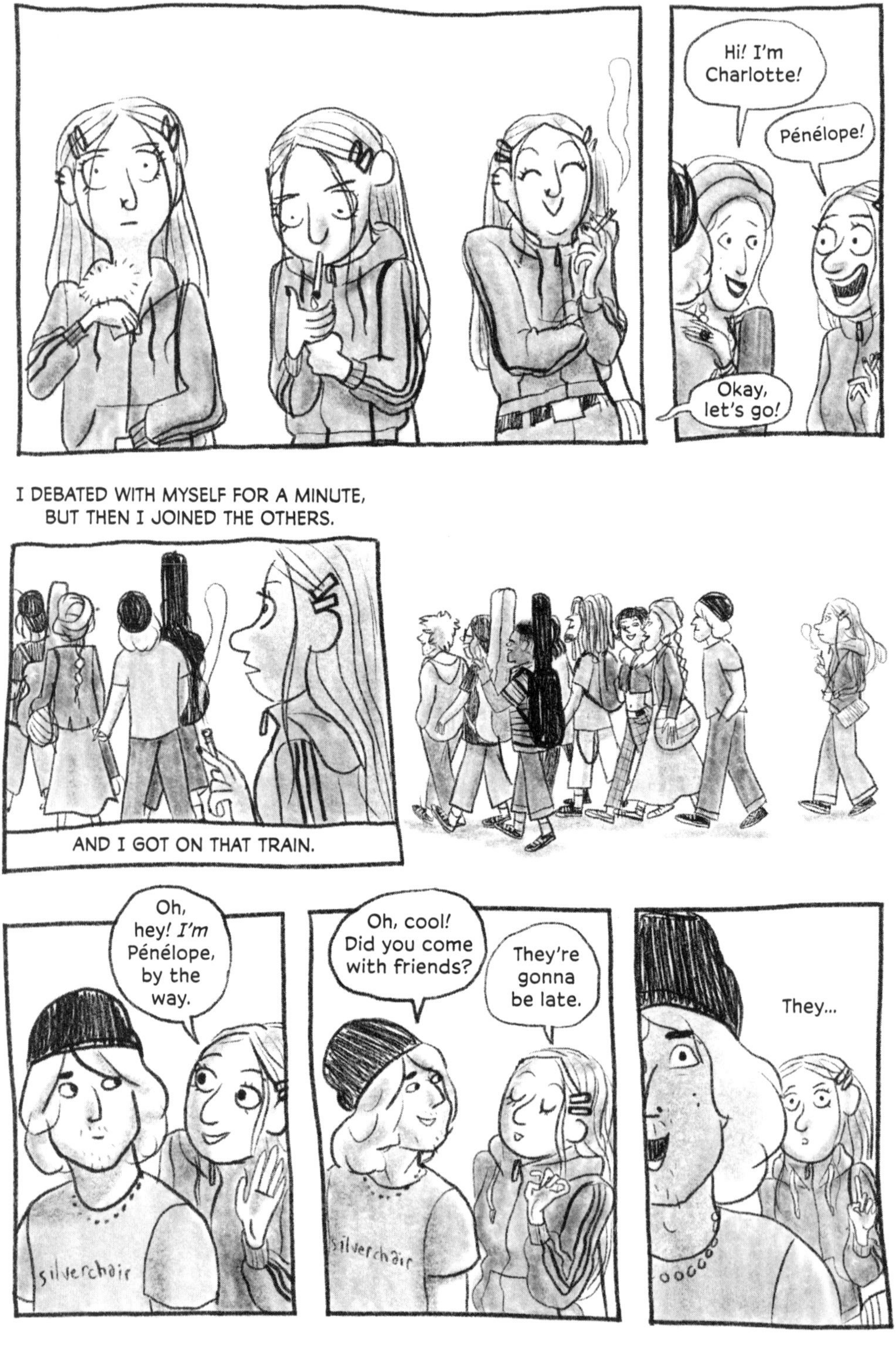
Hi! I'm Charlotte!
Pénélope!
Okay, let's go!
I DEBATED WITH MYSELF FOR A MINUTE, BUT THEN I JOINED THE OTHERS.
AND I GOT ON THAT TRAIN.
Oh, hey! *I'm* Pénélope, by the way.
silverchair
Oh, cool! Did you come with friends?
They're gonna be late.
silverchair
They...

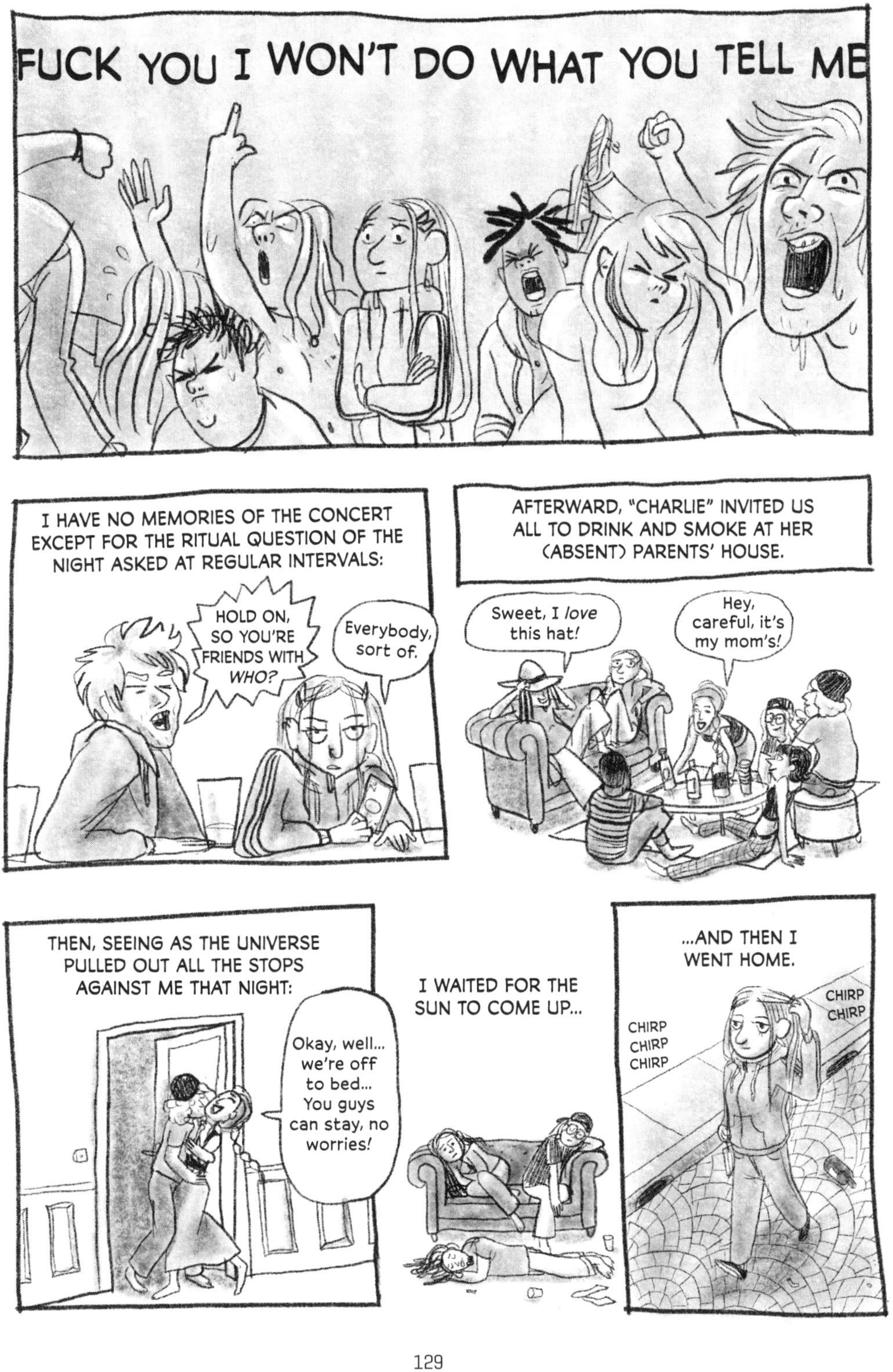
FUCK YOU I WON'T DO WHAT YOU TELL ME
I HAVE NO MEMORIES OF THE CONCERT EXCEPT FOR THE RITUAL QUESTION OF THE NIGHT ASKED AT REGULAR INTERVALS:
HOLD ON, SO YOU'RE FRIENDS WITH *WHO?*
Everybody, sort of.
AFTERWARD, "CHARLIE" INVITED US ALL TO DRINK AND SMOKE AT HER (ABSENT) PARENTS' HOUSE.
Sweet, I *love* this hat!
Hey, careful, it's my mom's!
THEN, SEEING AS THE UNIVERSE PULLED OUT ALL THE STOPS AGAINST ME THAT NIGHT:
Okay, well... we're off to bed... You guys can stay, no worries!
I WAITED FOR THE SUN TO COME UP...
...AND THEN I WENT HOME.
CHIRP CHIRP CHIRP
CHIRP CHIRP

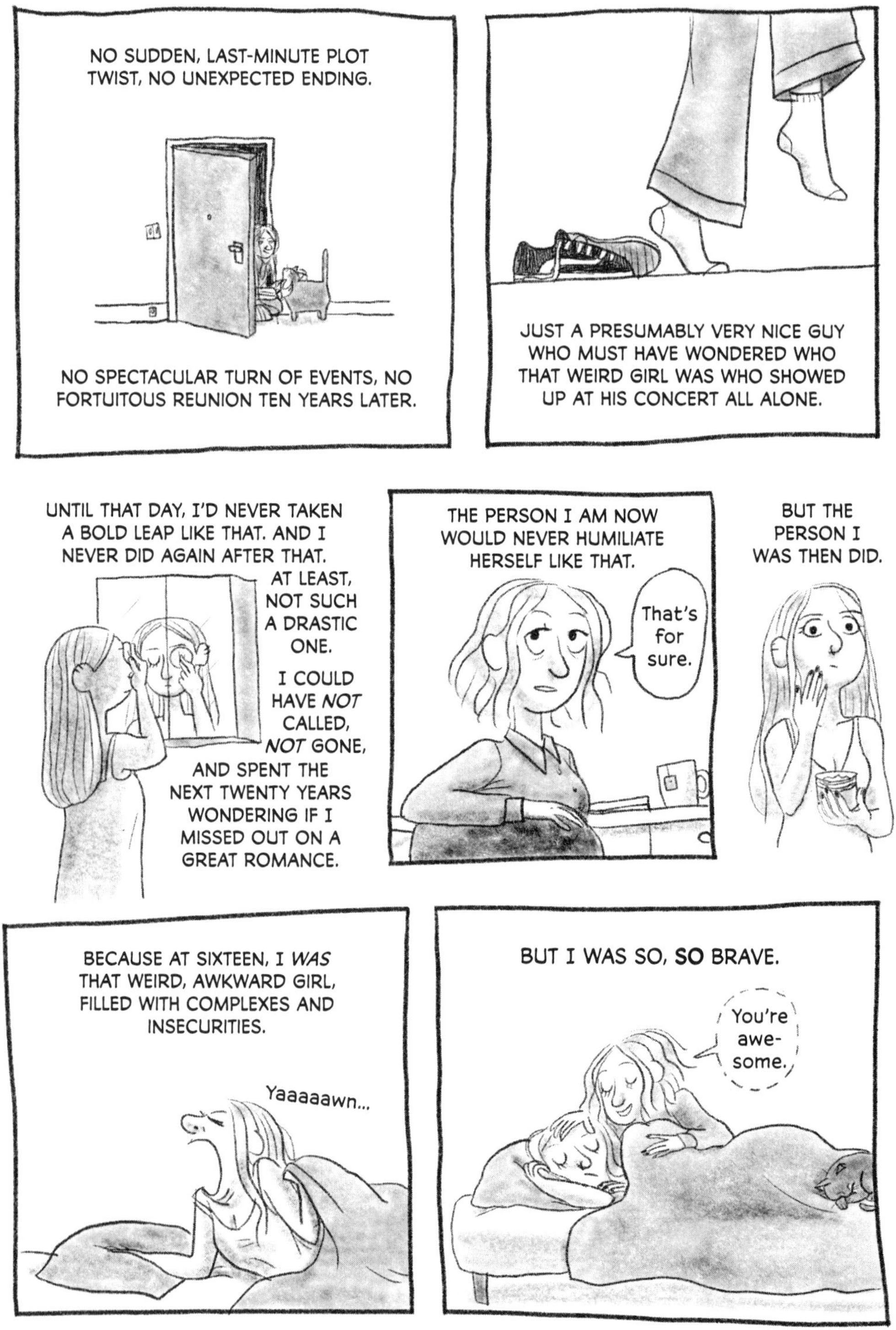
NO SUDDEN, LAST-MINUTE PLOT TWIST, NO UNEXPECTED ENDING.
NO SPECTACULAR TURN OF EVENTS, NO FORTUITOUS REUNION TEN YEARS LATER.
JUST A PRESUMABLY VERY NICE GUY WHO MUST HAVE WONDERED WHO THAT WEIRD GIRL WAS WHO SHOWED UP AT HIS CONCERT ALL ALONE.
UNTIL THAT DAY, I'D NEVER TAKEN A BOLD LEAP LIKE THAT. AND I NEVER DID AGAIN AFTER THAT.
AT LEAST, NOT SUCH A DRASTIC ONE.
I COULD HAVE *NOT* CALLED, *NOT* GONE, AND SPENT THE NEXT TWENTY YEARS WONDERING IF I MISSED OUT ON A GREAT ROMANCE.
THE PERSON I AM NOW WOULD NEVER HUMILIATE HERSELF LIKE THAT.
That's for sure.
BUT THE PERSON I WAS THEN DID.
BECAUSE AT SIXTEEN, I *WAS* THAT WEIRD, AWKWARD GIRL, FILLED WITH COMPLEXES AND INSECURITIES.
Yaaaaawn...
BUT I WAS SO, **SO** BRAVE.
You're awe-some.

-FIN-

THE COMFORT BLANKET

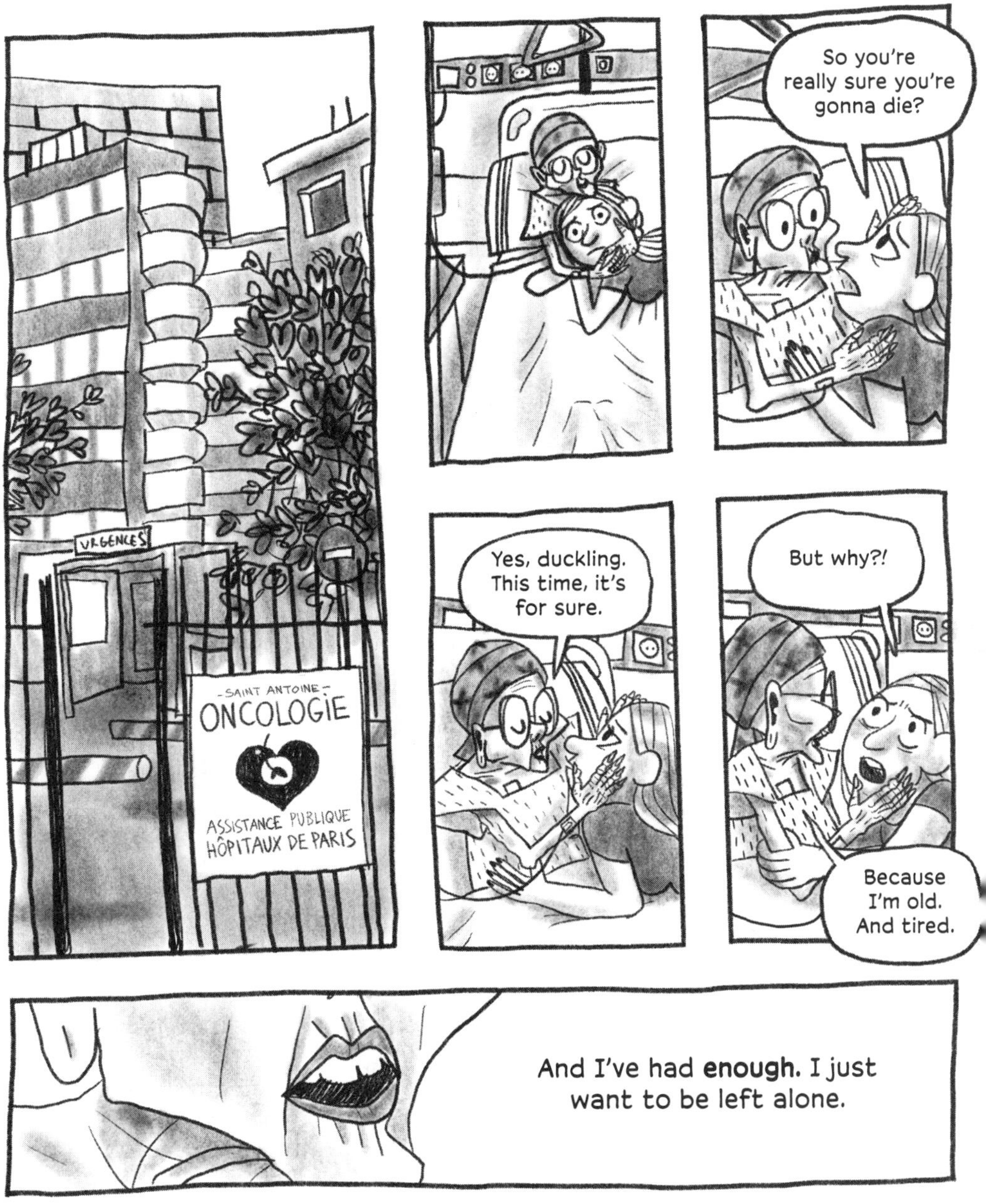
URGENCES
- SAINT ANTOINE -
ONCOLOGIE
ASSISTANCE PUBLIQUE HÔPITAUX DE PARIS
So you're really sure you're gonna die?
Yes, duckling. This time, it's for sure.
But why?!
Because I'm old. And tired.
And I've had **enough.** I just want to be left alone.

YEAH, WELL, I *DON'T* WANT TO LEAVE YOU ALONE!

Shush. No more of that.

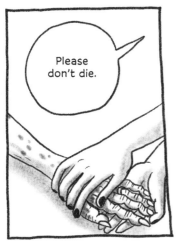

Please don't die.

Don't die don't die don't die don't die don't die don't die don't die don't die don't die don't die don't die.

We're here talking, but after, for the rest of my life, you won't be here anymore! I'll want to see you but I won't be able to ever again! What am I going to do, huh?!

What will I do when I'm sad?!

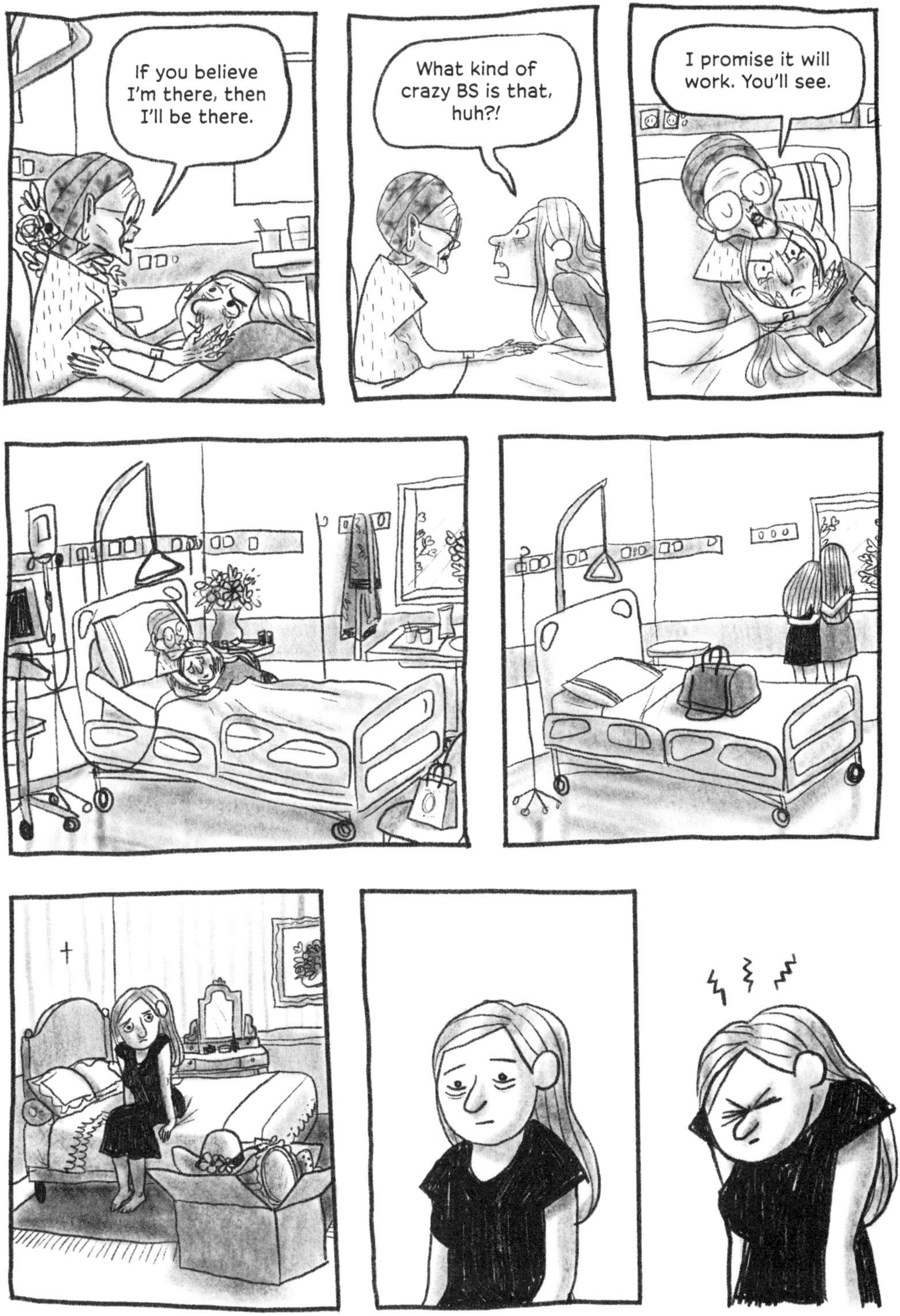
If you believe I'm there, then I'll be there.
What kind of crazy BS is that, huh?!
I promise it will work. You'll see.

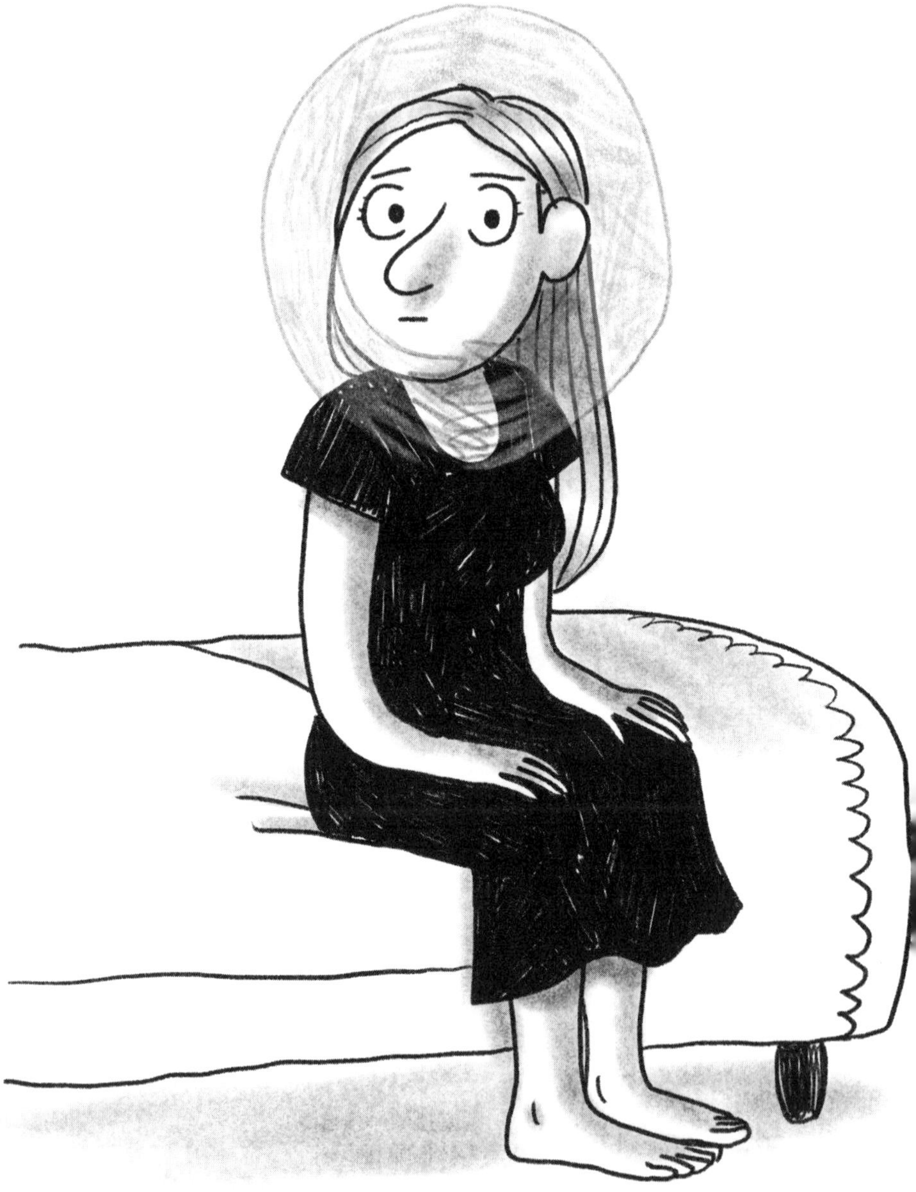

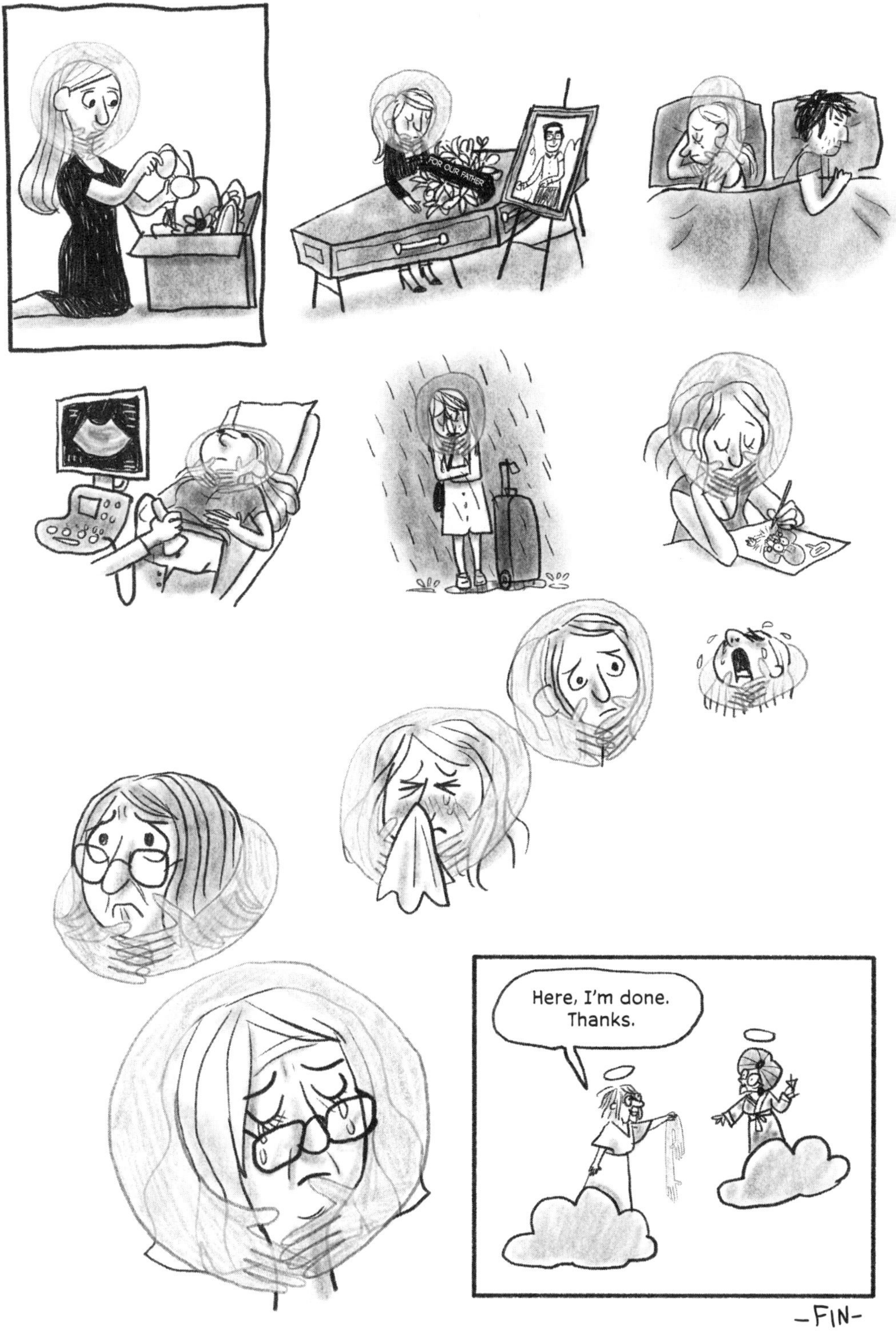
FOR OUR FATHER
Here, I'm done. Thanks.
-FIN-

I'd like to thank my mother, my big sister, and my husband, Benjamin.

Pénélope Bagieu was born in 1982, in Paris. After studying at the School of Decorative Arts in Paris and Central Saint Martins in London, she started a cartoon blog in 2007 called *Ma vie est tout à fait fascinante* (*My Life Is Absolutely Fascinating*), in which she documented the daily life of a young Parisian woman with spot-on humor and grace. When published, it became  a hit in bookstores. She dreamed up the adventures of a thirty-something woman named Joséphine, whose exploits filled three books. Pénélope worked as an illustrator in the fields of media and advertising before authoring her first full-length graphic novel in 2010, *Exquisite Corpse*, which was followed by her first graphic biography, *California Dreamin'* (2018 Harvey Award winner, Best European Book). In 2016, the feminist aspect of her work took on a new dimension in *Brazen*, a collection of stories about remarkable women throughout history. The book was trans-

lated into twenty languages, won an Eisner Award in 2019, and was adapted into an animated show for France TV. In 2020, the author set out to reach a younger audience by brilliantly revisiting Roald Dahl's novel *The Witches*.

Also by Pénélope Bagieu

REBEL
LADIES
WHO
BRAZEN
ROCKED
THE
WORLD
PÉNÉLOPE
BAGIEU

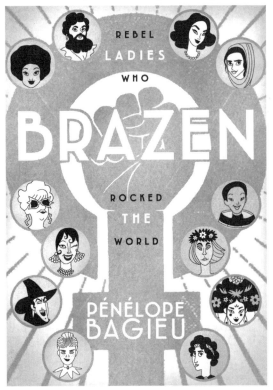

2019 Eisner Award Winner for Best U.S. Edition of International Material

"Bagieu's pen transforms these true stories into something that has the tone of a personalized fairy tale. And in the end, this turns out to be just perfect."
—***New York Times***

"The highest praise I can give *Brazen* is that it belongs in most every girl's—and boy's—hands by middle school." —***Washington Post***

"Bagieu's brand of feminism comes with frills and curlicues galore. Her voice is pert and saucy, and her cartoons are darling." —**NPR**

★★★★★★

"A pièce de résistance." —***Kirkus***, starred review

"Sly and understated." —***Publishers Weekly***, starred review

"Strikingly original." —***School Library Journal***, starred review

"Playfully expressive." —***Booklist***, starred review

"An inspiration." —***VOYA***, starred review

"Sassy." —***The Bulletin***, starred review